SEMIOTIC AND COGNITIVE STUDIES

XII
IN THE BEGINNING
Origins of Semiosis

SEMIOTIC AND COGNITIVE STUDIES

XII

SERIES EDITORS

UMBERTO ECO
and
PATRIZIA VIOLI

IN THE BEGINNING

Origins of Semiosis

EDITED BY

MORANA ALAČ and PATRIZIA VIOLI

CONTRIBUTORS:

MORANA ALAČ
PATRIZIA VIOLI
UMBERTO ECO
JÜRGEN TRABANT
HOWARD BLOCH
WINFRIED NÖTH
THOMAS SEBEOK
MAXINE SHEETS-JOHNSTONE
SHERMAN WILCOX
ALEX MARTIN
PHILIP LIEBERMAN

BREPOLS

Editing and pagination by Horizons Unlimited (Bologna, Italy).

D/2004/0095/20

ISBN 2-503-51590-8

IN THE BEGINNING: ORIGINS OF SEMIOSIS

Edited by Morana Alač and Patrizia Violi

Morana Alač

INTRODUCTION

1. Why "Origins of Semiosis"?

This volume gathers essays presented at the symposium on the *Origins of Semiosis* that took place at the University of San Marino in spring of 2000. Why "Origins of Semiosis"? What is the reason for choosing to speak about "Origins of Semiosis" rather that about "Evolution of Language", for example?

In the human realm (zoosemiotics, biosemiotics and physicosemiotics [see Nöth, this volume] apart), semiosis may be taken to cover language, but also gesture, posture, kinesics, facial expression, sign languages, writing systems, etc. Charles Sanders Peirce defines semiosis as:

> [...] an action, or influence, which is, or involves, a cooperation of *three* subjects, such as a sign, its object, and its interpretant, this tri-relative influence not being in any way resolvable into actions between pairs. Σημείωσις in Greek of Roman period, as early as Cicero's time, if I remember rightly, meant the action of almost any kind of sign; and my definition confers on anything that so acts the title of a *sign*. (CP 5.484)

Even though Peirce proposed different typologies of signs, for reasons of simplicity we can assume here that what he means by "any kind of sign" is comprised by his three broad classes of signs: *symbol*, *icon*, and *index* (for more complete definition of semiosis see Nöth, this volume). Here we take *symbol* to denote abstractness and convention, and hence to respect bifurcation of form and meaning (see Wilcox, this volume), and *icon* and *index* as reflecting bodily action in some specific environment.

Linguistic signs are usually thought of as being conventional or symbolic, while semiosis comprises action of "any kind of signs", and hence may rely on indexical and iconic signs. Thus, it can be concluded that semiosis is simply a broader term than that of language. Even though this is not entirely false, what contributors to this volume have often underlined is that language itself, inasmuch as it is an embodied and distributed system, cannot be exhaustively described in terms of abstract symbolic representations, and hence is also constituted by indexical and iconic representations.

The second term in the title is “origin”. At first glance, it seems that in order to speak about the origins of semiosis we have two options. We can speak of language and semiosis as having an abrupt origin: we can postulate an evolutionary new “language organ”; or, we can speak of them in terms of an evolutionary continuum, where we learn about the origins of a qualitatively distinct human behavior (such as language) by looking at the biology and behavior of other species. However, by choosing to speak about the origins of semiosis vs. the origins of language, we are biased in one direction. When speaking of semiosis as “action of any kind of sign”, a distinction between the origins as an abrupt or evolutionary process is not a genuine option. If we describe semiosis and language as inseparable from bodily experience (i.e., based on the use not only of symbolic, but iconic and indexical representations as well), can we speak about their origins as not being fundamentally related to biology and the evolutionary paths of other species? And what can the evolution of semiosis and language tell us about systems of communication and thought described in terms of systems that use embodied, distributed representations?

2. Language as symbolic and arbitrary human capacity

According to a prevalent view in the study of language and communication, language is the unique human ability to refer abstractly or symbolically. This position is more or less directly influenced by the Saussurian idea (Saussure 1916) of the arbitrary nature of the sign and the linear nature of the sound-image as the principles of language. Hockett’s (1960) advocacy to restrict the term “human language” to just those dimensions of communication that are vocal, syntactic, and arbitrary in relation to their referents, independent of the immediate context of utterance and learned, is emblematic of this tendency as well.

The same tendency to deny the role of iconicity in the study of language has dominated cognitive science, at least in its classical form. Early cognitive science inherited from AI, analytical philosophy, and generative linguistics the idea that the human mind is a disembodied system that formally composes static symbols, and that natural language is modeled by analogy to the operating principles of a formal information processing system. An important source for the definition of language adopted in cognitive science was Jerry Fodor’s (1983)

Modularity of Mind. Fodor defined language as a perceptual or input system that (1) applies only to a limited domain, (2) is informationally encapsulated, and (3) is associated with fixed neural architecture. It is evident that this dominant paradigm, by underlying the arbitrary and symbolic nature of human language, puts a chasm between animal communication and human language.

However, contemporary research in cognitive science and neuroscience is assembling evidence in favor of more interpenetration and interdependence of the many dimensions of human communicative acts and cognition. This type of research indicates the inadequacies of the early view (Cognitivism and Turing Machine model of Mind) according to which cognition is purely rational, abstract activity, and mind is an ahistorical, culture-free, and disembodied logical system. Instead, since the late 80s, many researchers have pointed out the importance of studying cognition in the context of the action in the world (e.g., Hutchins 1995; Zhang and Norman 1994; Suchman 1987), intention, emotion, bodily grounded experience (e.g., Freeman and Núñez 1999, Ballard et al. 1997; Fuster 1997; Carpenter et al. 2000; Jeannerod et. al. 1995), as well as everyday unconscious processes and creativity (e.g., Coulson 2000; Fauconnier and Turner 2002). In the same vein, traditional cognitive notions of internal representation and computation have been questioned, and the interest in both the bodily/biological mechanisms underlying cognition and the role of the environment has continuously been emphasized. According to the general trend, representations are not conceived as static, localized entities, but as fluid, distributed structures in brains (e.g., Barsalow 1999; Medin et al. 1993, 2000; Lakoff and Johnson 1999; Greeno and Moore 1993; Kosslyn 1999; Wexler et al. 1998), as well as spread across diverse media, social space, and time (Hutchins *ibid.*). Andy Clark's quote successfully reassumes the general idea of mind as a complex system, inseparable from its cultural and social dimensions:

> Mindfulness arises at the productive collision points of multiple factors and forces – some bodily, some neural, some technological, and some social and cultural. As a result, the project of understanding what is distinctive about human thought and reason may depend on a much broader focus than that to which cognitive science has been most accustomed, one that includes not just body, brain and natural world, but the props and aides in which our biological brains learn, mature and operate. (Clark 2001: 141)

Thus, the new trend in cognitive science is moving toward a definition of language which sees language as an embodied system deeply connected with cognition and action. In order to refer to this view of language, we speak here about "semiosis", inasmuch as semiosis means "the action of almost any kind of sign" (Peirce *ibid.*).

Hence, Peircian semiotics and contemporary cognitive neuroscience converge on their view of language as an embodied system, dependent on the external environment. What makes this volume quite unique is its positioning between the two domains: semiotics and cognitive science. Each essay, by constructing itself under the sign of semiosis, more or less explicitly presents an orientation toward a bridging of the two disciplines, and hence promotes the interdependence of multiple faces of communication and cognition.

3. A road map of the book

This brief introduction is followed by Patrizia Violi's original introduction to the conference. Violi defines some general questions, which were used as guidelines in designing the conference. The opening essays of the volume, Umberto Eco's, Jürgen Trabant's and R. Howard Bloch's, are oriented towards historical aspects of the debate centered around the origins of semiosis. Eco, in his opening note to the symposium, illustrates a whole array of different proposals running parallel to the concept of origins of language. He traces through the history of western though such ideas as the search for *perfect language,* or the proposal of *universal grammar* in order to show the generality of interest for be it historical or biological origins of language. The essay highlights the complexities of research that "has no testable object". Eco points out that a discipline that studies origins of semiosis focuses on an object that is definitely palpable, i.e., people communicate linguistically and there must have been a point in the evolution when this capacity first took place, but at the same time cannot be scientifically tested.

Trabant opens his essay "From semiogenesis to glottogenesis in the 18th century debate" by pointing out the divide that exists in today's discussion about the origin of language. He individualizes in Thomas Sebeok a representative of the Chomskian tradition according to which language should be treated as an innate mental mechanism clearly separated from semiosis and speech. On the other hand, he takes Philip Lieberman's approach as an example of research showing that language cannot be understood without taking speech and vocalization into consideration. Trabant demonstrates that these oppositions have certain structural similarities with the 18th century discussion about the origin of language. The idea is that the knowledge about the 18th century "stories" can help us in better understanding the contemporary debate.

While Trabant is interested in the 18th century debate about the origin of language, "Etymologies and genealogies: History, words, and the world" explores more closely the philosophical enterprises in Middle Ages. In order to discuss the idea of origins of semiosis, Bloch describes the medievals' undertakings in search for the founding linguistic moment. He points out that the search for the origins of primeval language and the sources of words is intrinsically connected with the acquisition of knowledge about the reality and the retracing of the history of humanity. This search through the history of languages resurfaces in the 18th century philosophy, and is not as distant from today's pleasure of philological enterprise.

Winfried Nöth's and Thomas Sebeok's essays deal directly with central questions in semotics. Nöth is interested in the primal relationship between the sign and its producer: what existed first, a sign or its producer. This is the problem of the semiotic threshold. In other words, we can account for the origin of semiosis once we place a border, be it abrupt or gradual, between a lower level devoid of semiosis, and a higher level where semiosis occurs. Nöth investigates how modern semiotics has localized this threshold and points out that in Peirceian theory of *synechism* mind and semiosis precede the existence of matter.

One of the four major paradigms of twentieth century semiotics that Nöth illustrates in his intervention is *biosemiotics*. In his essay "Origins: Semiosis the domain vs. Semiotics the field" Sebeok points out that the dominant type of semiotic inquiry is *anthropocentric* or *logocentric*. However, Jacob von Uexkull's biosemiotics presents a significant challenge to this dominant paradigm. Sebeok gives an account, at times clearly autobiographical, of the development of the field of biosemiotics through the 20th century.

While the previous essays are more or less explicitly grounded in semiotics, Maxine Sheets-Johnstone adopts an epistemological perspective. She points out how questions about origins of semiosis or evolutionary semantics have to be rooted in the study of the ways in which living organisms create meaning. It is underlined that an account of meaning has to be based in experience: the sense-making is based in bodily gesture and action. From this perspective, an account of how sense-making has evolved in the course of evolution cannot be adequately given if we adopt a perspective of Peircian semiotics. Sheets-Johnstone claims that the creation of meaning should not be based on sign as triadic function, but on the subject of experience, as Husserlian phenomenology proposes.

The last three essays in this volume, Sherman Wilcox', Alex Martin's, and Philip Lieberman's, present more directly the perspective of contemporary cognitive science and neuroscience. Wilcox's intervention is centered around the nature of signed languages and how they can provide knowledge about origins of semiosis. It points out the inadequacy of the Cartesian view, adopted by Chomskian-style linguistics, where sign languages are associated with body, movement and iconicity, and hence separated from reason and pure knowledge. Wilcox shows, on the contrary, that body-based abilities provide grounding for meaning production. Taking this perspective portrays semiosis as an emergent property of embodied cognition.

Martin investigates how information about object concepts is represented in the brain. Of particular interest is the evidence provided by the functional brain imaging studies that suggests that object knowledge may be represented, in part, by distributed networks of cortical regions that parallel the organization of sensory as well as motor systems. These data are consistent with the idea that information about object-specific features may be stored within the same neural systems that are active during perception and motor action. Hence, the evidence from neuroscience points out that an adequate account of meaning production should be grounded in embodied cognition.

Lieberman bases his account of origins of semiosis in evolutionary biology and cognitive neuro-science. His proposal is that the neural basis of semiosis may derive from the evolution of basal ganglia activity. By grounding the understanding of language in the relationship with the neural structures involved in the control of speech sequencing, Lieberman links motor aspects (i.e., non arbitrary or conventional but rather iconic aspects) with language and thought. By grounding the language capacity in the distributed network that implicates cortical as well as subcortical brain structures, he shows the inevitability of the evolutionary origins of semiosis.

References

BALLARD, D.H., HAYHOE, M.M., POOK, P.K. & R.P.N. RAO
1997 "Deictic codes for the embodiment of cognition", *Behavioral and Brain Sciences*, 20: 723-767.

BARSALOU, L.W.
1999 "Perceptual symbol systems", *Behavioral and Brain Sciences*, 22: 577-660.
1986 "Concepts: Static definitions or context-dependent representations", *Cahiers de Psychologie Cognitive*, 6 (2): 187-202.

CARPENTER, P., JUST, M.A. & E.D. REICHLE
2000 "Working memory and executive function: Evidence from neuroimaging", *Current Opinion in Neurobiology* 10: 195-199.

CLARK, A.
2001 *Mindware: An Introduction to the Philosophy of Cognitive Science*, Oxford: Oxford UP.

COULSON, S.
2000 *Semantic Leaps: Frame-Shifting and Conceptual Blending in Meaning Construction*, Cambridge: Cambridge UP.

FAUCONNIER, G. & M. TURNER
2002 *The Way We Think: Conceptual Blending and the Mind's Hidden Complexities*, New York: Basic Books.

FODOR, J.
1983 *Modularity of Mind*, Cambridge, MA: MIT Press.

FUSTER, J.M.
1997 "Network memory", *Trends in Neuroscience*, 20: 451-459.

GREENO, J. & K. MOORE
1993 "Situativity and symbols: Response to Vera & Simon", *Cognitive Science*, 17 (1): 49-59.

HOCKETT, C.F.
1960 "The origin of speech", *Scientific American* (also published in: W.S-Y. Wang (ed.), *Human communication: Language and its Psychobiological Bases*, Scientific American, 1982).

HUTCHINS, E.
1995 *Cognition in the Wild*. Cambridge, MA: MIT Press.

JEANNEROD, M., ARBIB, M.A., RIZZOLATTI, G. & H. SAKATA
1995 "Grasping objects: The cortical mechanisms of visuomotor transformation", *Trends in Neurosciences*, 18 (5): 314-320.

KOSSLYN, S.M. *ET AL.*
1999 "The role of Area 17 in visual imagery: Convergent evidence from fMRI and rTMS", *Science*, 284 (5411): 167.

LAKOFF, G. & M. JOHNSON
1999 *Philosophy in the Flesh: The Embodied Mind and Its Challenge to Western Thought*, New York: Basic Books.

MEDIN, D.L., GOLDSTONE, R.L. & D. GENTNER
1993 "Respects for similarity", *Psychological Review*, 100(2): 254-278.

MEDIN, D.L., LYNCH, E.B. & K.O. SOLOMON
2000 "Are there kinds of concepts?", *Annual Review of Psychology*, 51: 121-147.

NUNEZ, R. & W. FREEMAN (EDS.)
1999 *Reclaiming Cognition: The Primacy of Action, Intention and Emotion, Journal of Consciousness Studies*, Vol. 6, November/Dicember.

PEIRCE, C.S.
1934-1948 *Collected Papers* (4. voll.), Cambridge, MA: Harvard UP.

SAUSSURE, F. DE
1916 *Cours de linguistique générale,* Lausanne-Paris: Payot.

SUCHMAN, L.
1987 *Plans and Situated Actions*, Cambridge: Cambridge UP.

WEXLER, M., KOSSLYN, S.M. & A. BERTHOZ
1998 "Motor processes in mental rotation", *Cognition*, 68: 77-94.

ZHANG, J. & D.A. NORMAN
1994 "Representations in distributed cognitive tasks", *Cognitive Science*, 18: 87-122.

Patrizia Violi

IN THE BEGINNING: THE VOICE OF GOD AND THE VOICE OF THE WORLD. TWO STORIES ABOUT ORIGINS

First of all I would like to start with a brief reflection upon the very title of our conference.

Why should I have chosen to have us speak here of the "origins of semiosis" instead of the "origins of language", although it is of course language which will be at the center of our inquiry during the present conference? My choice of title is not only due to the fact that, being a semiotician, I wanted to provide as broad a scope as possible for our discussions of the more general question of origins. There are other reasons too, and I'd like to mention a few of these now.

Often, in looking at the contemporary debate on the origins of language, we notice that the very word *language* comes to acquire a quite restricted meaning: one which basically coincides with nothing more than syntactic structure (or "grammar"). The "language instinct", if we are to speak of such a thing, seems to be a very grammatical kind of instinct. Now, whether we actually are in possession of such an instinct or not, this particular understanding of language leaves out a great deal of what I would certainly like to include in any kind of broader definition of language, and indeed, that which seems to me first and foremost the *main* issue regarding how language and any other kind of symbolic system "works": namely meaning and sense.

If the very content of the structure being investigated is that which is left outside, this is not by chance. It is because "instinctual" theories of language presuppose an "autonomist" view of language – where linguistic structure is seen as autonomous in relation to meaning systems, and the language organ of the brain is seen as autonomous in relation to other kinds of faculties or capacities found in the brain.

Leaving meaning out of the picture also implies the exclusion of several other important dimensions of our human linguistic and semiotic functioning: the connection between meaning and experience, our interpersonal relationships and the interactive, communicational aspects of language. Briefly, it leaves out human subjectivity and intersubjectivity. These kinds of issues all appear to be relegated to the prelinguistic realm. This in itself would be a good enough reason for me to want to broaden our perspective on language in order to include these sorts of issues too, since, as a semiotician, I would consider these some of the most important questions that we can imagine in relation to language (and its origins).

The shift I propose, then, from an inquiry into the origins of language over to an inquiry into the origins of semiosis, presupposes taking an implicit standpoint in relation to the more general issue of origins, namely that we want to look at language not as the product of a completely separate and autonomous acquisition module in the brain, cut off from all other components of our cognitive and semiotic functioning, but as a highly integrated element, and indeed, probably the most complex and sophisticated such element, of our overall symbolic functioning.

Such a very general perspective on origins seems to me to be consistent with many of the lines of research currently being pursued on this topic. I am thinking, for instance, of Terrence Deacon's idea of language as an adaptive system which has evolved in order to facilitate and accommodate human cognitive capacities and, within such an evolution, the emergence of a broader mental ability to represent complex and abstract systems of meaning (Deacon 1997). Then there is Philip Lieberman's idea of language as a learned skill, distributed over many parts of the human brain (Lieberman 1991). Within such a perspective some important questions arise.

1. The question of boundaries

The question of boundaries has always been a central semiotic concern. As Winfred Noth (1994) reminds us, Peirce took a very broad view on this issue: in his physico-semiotics he claimed there is a general form of continuity between nature and culture, postulating that semiosis occurs even in the physical world, and indeed, lies at the very roots of the evolution of the universe.

This particular view of things doesn't come without its own problems, however.

In 1975 in his *Theory of Semiotics* Umberto Eco depicted a much more strict lower threshold for the semiotic realm, a limit which excluded all forms of natural phenomena. Since then however, much has happened in the field of semiotics, and fruitful discussions have taken place with scientists from many different fields. I shall only recall here an interesting confrontation we had with the immunologists some time ago, as well as the many exchanges with people working in the field of zoosemiotics, starting with our friend Tom Sebeok.[1] If, in a broader perspective, we begin by saying that semiosis began with the emergence of life on Earth, and that the biological world is already endowed with semiosis, then we will certainly be in need of many further, much finer-grained distinctions as far as understanding human semiosis is concerned. In particular we would want to distinguish between the development of a more general semiotic functioning – one that we may well share with many other species – and language development. In this particular vein for example, Walter Koch (1986, 1991) suggested a distinction between *semiogenesis*, which is the origin of human culture and *glottogenesis*, the origins of language.

But what might be the nature of the relationship between these two developmental stages, one of continuity or of discontinuity?

2. Preconditions

This brings us to another related issue: the evolutionary antecedents of language and the preconditions for its appearance.

Here the whole issue of the symbolic and communicative functioning of gestures is of a central interest, not so much in order to repropose the old 'gesture theory' of origins, but in order to investigate in more depth the integration of distributed, multimodal components of our linguistic behaviour. Here I am obviously thinking of work in this area by David McNeill (1992), Sherman Wilcox (1990, 1992) and Armstrong, Stokoe and Wilcox (1995).

Recent work in neurophysiology, such as the discovery of the mirror neurons – could also be very interesting in this particular respect. The present data would suggest that the same areas of human brains (the premotor cortex) that are involved in language use, are also involved in gesture recognition, and that the same type of functioning is also present in equivalent areas of primate brains. Broca's area then would be active not only during language-based activities, but also during the execution of movements by arms and hands, during the formation of mental images of those movements, as well as during mental operations related to the subsequent or ongoing rotation of arms. All these data would suggest a continuity between language skills and prelinguistic manual behaviour. In this perspective the specialisation for language of Broca's area in humans would derive from an ancient mechanism (the mirror system) originally developed to facilitate the interpretation and understanding of complex actions.

This would suggest a way of looking at the relationship between the linguistic and pre-linguistic spheres which is quite different from the one suggested within the tradition of structural linguistics, where meaning only appears from within a fully organized system of linguistic structure. Instead, the prelinguistic sphere itself would become endowed with meaning, and the same patterns and schema that underlie actions and perceptions of these actions, would be common to language, a position supported today in most of the research being carried out in cognitive semantics – as in recent. work by George Lakoff, Len Talmy, Ron Langacker and many others.[2]

3. Innateness and brain localization

Of course all these issues open up for a further, third level of questions, connected with the issue of brain localization and innateness.

Certainly it seems as if language is something which is unique to our species and we need to explain this fact in a satisfactory way, but this still leaves room for a variety of different positions. It seems to me that the whole issue of innateness can be seen as varying in a continuum from a *most specific* form of innateness to a *least specific* form of innateness. At the one extreme of the continuum we find the positions of those who claim there exist specific forms of brain circuitry, "designed" through natural selection, and each dedicated to a particular family of computational problems. At the opposite end of the continuum, at the least specific pole of innateness, the uniqueness of language would emerge not from a separable domain-specific module, but out of interactions involving differences in non domain-specific behaviours. These two polarities go together with two quite different ideas of language, on the one hand with language per se considered as basically coinciding with grammatical structure, and seen as an autonomous brain module; and on the other side, language understood primarily as a functional system for conveying meaning and for communication, a system which is non autonomous and intimately connected to all other types of (human) functions.

If we feel sympathetic with this second position, then some other interesting issues also become relevant. I would like in particular to briefly address two of these. The first is related to emotions.

4. Emotions

I notice that in the literature regarding the origins of both language and semiosis, very little is said about the role which emotions might play in this wider picture.

This is, however, most certainly *not* the case if we look more closely at some of the theories regarding symbol formation and child language development. Though it is not at all obvious that ontogenesis and phylogenesis should mirror one another, I nonetheless believe that some very useful suggestions could come from looking at the way in which symbolic functioning emerges in human ontogenesis.

It is generally recognized that in order to develop symbolic functioning, infants need to go through a process of gradual distancing from their initial state of symbiotic fusion with the world, and with the mother in particular. Crucial in this process is the creation of an intermediate space, which Winnicott (1951) called the space of *the transitional object*, where a given object can at the same time be both itself and something else. The possibility of moving forward to such an intermediate position represents the very beginning of the symbolic capacity. From a semiotic perspective such an account parallels in quite an interesting way Peirce's system of phenomenological categories: from the fusional state of Firstness, to the forceful recognition of something else as quite distinct from ourselves (Secondness) to the stage of mediation, Thirdness — the symbolic realm.

What is essential for such a process to occur, however, is not an abstract cognitive capacity, but the crucial role played by the special kind of emotional fulfilment which the mother gives to her baby. Without this fulfilment, the developmental process can be altered in quite dramatic ways, as vast amounts of clinical data clearly show. Therefore, in children's development, affect and emotions are from the very beginning intimately connected with the subsequent emergence of symbolic forms of behaviour.

Perhaps this insight might be extendable to the phylogenetic dimension as well?

5. Narrativity and narrative structure

The last point I would like to call your attention to, is the role narrativity and narration might have played in the evolution of the semiotic system in general, and language in particular. It is my conviction – although I have no empirical evidence with which to back up this hypothesis – that narrativity is a crucial factor for human evolution. A similar claim has been put forward by Jerome Bruner, who in a series of lectures given in Bologna in 2000 and now collected in Bruner (2002), pointed out how the ability to tell stories is unique to the evolution of the human species. From a different perspective we could also suggest that the fundamental predicate-argument structure of linguistic sentences parallels a basic form of narrative schema, and that development of a complex syntactic structure would probably be impossible without the development of an equivalent level of complexity in the conceptualization of a system of relationships between actants, and the various transformations of their reciprocal actions and states, which is what lies precisely at the core of all kinds of storytelling.

In the spirit of this last point, I would like to conclude my introduction by telling you two stories about origins.

Over the last few years I have begun collecting myths about the origins of language in different cultures. It has not been that easy to do this, because, while there are many explicit myths in all cultures about the origins of the universe and of humankind, explicit myths on the origins of language are much more rare.

More often than not, however, an *implicit* story about language origins can be detected and, from what I have been seeing so far, there seem to exist two different main paradigms behind these implicit stories, representing what we could call the *innatness* and *emergence* models of language origins.

The prototypical case of the first of these two models is represented by the story of Genesis in the Old Testament. Here, Adam is created already endowed with language: he is able to give a name to all animals and creatures in the world without any problem. Since at that point Eve had not yet been created, Adam's language was certainly not motivated by any kind of communicative goal. So, where did it come from? Obviously, Adam's language came directly from God; it was a replication of the language of God, who of course, being God, already had language. Remember that the whole creation starts from a speech act by God ("and then God said: let there be light").

What better example of a pure innate mentalese, a perfect and innate language organ, "downloaded" directly by (and from) the mind of God into the one mind of Man?

We all know the continuing story of what then happened after that: at least the story the boys have always told us. Eve comes along, and then the troubles begin. And these troubles culminate in the linguistic punishment of Babel and the multiplicity of the many different, real, historical languages of men and women, which are clearly seen, in this particular story, as a base corruption and degradation of the first divine and innate purity. There are however other stories in the world.

In the *Fudoki* for example, an ancient Japanese text of the 8th century which collates a large number of local gazetteers containing information about local traditions and the origins of place names, a quite different story is told. According to the *Fudoki*, at the beginning of the universe, in the primordial stage before the appearance of human beings, there was a time, "when rocks and trees and plants could speak, where daytime was as noisy as a swarm of flies and night-time was as bright as fire".[3] The Gods were violent, and order was not yet established. Order will be established indeed, by men, and in particular by a man called Matachi who, irritated with the violent and chaotic gods which prevented man from cultivating the land, set up a staff to mark the boundaries between the domain of the gods and the land of the human beings. He then went on to build a shrine and initiated the cult of the violent gods.

Certainly this story depicts a quite different relationship between gods and men, and between order and chaos in the universe than the story of Genesis. But it also tells us of a world where language emerges from nature, from rocks, and trees, and plants...

The voice of the world in this story is not the voice of man, and this voice is present even before the appearance of the first human being. Neither is it the voice of the gods, which undoubtedly, in this cosmogenesis, are not very nice guys at all. Language appears to be an autonomous characteristic of the very cosmos itself, independent in its origins and existence of any kind of external force, either of man or of god. Language is inherent in the natural world itself, a world which is endowed with its own expressive capacity.

Now, a perspective of this kind dramatically changes the common form of opposition that we, the sons and daughters of Adam, are used to establishing between matter and logos. For us, before logos, before linguistic form, matter (and the universe) do not have a form, they cannot express themselves – as Genesis and structural linguistics have always told us. Quite the opposite, the world as portrayed in the Fudoki *has* a voice – rocks, plants and trees *can* speak. But their language is a very different one from the logos of the Adamitic language, it does not impose order in the universe through the naming of things; the voice of the world seems to emerge from the deepest, most basic, levels of the universe itself, even from the inorganic level of rocks.

Now I don't know which of these two stories might be the best metaphor for what really did happen to our own ancestors all those millions and millions of years ago.

But it can be good to remember that there is more than one myth, and more than one story that can be told about it. And indeed, in some of these stories, the main role is not played by Man and his powerful and divine Logos, but by something else, something more diffuse, pervasive and humble; the secret voice of the world that emerges through all natural entities – the secret voice of life itself.

Notes

[1] The result of the discussion between immunologists and semioticians can be found in Sercarz et al. (eds.) 1988. The work of Thomas Sebeok in the field of zoosemiotics is immense. We need only recall central works such as Sebeok 1977, Sebeok (ed.) 1968, Sebeok & Sebeok (eds.) 1992.

[2] To cite only a few pertinent references, Lakoff & Johnson 1999, Talmy 1983, 1985; Langacker 1990, 1991.

[3] For the text of the Fudoki see Higo 1942. I am using here the translation by Yamaguchi 1999.

References

ARMSTRONG, D., STOKOE, W. & S. WILCOX
1995 *Gesture and the Nature of Language*, Cambridge: Cambridge UP.

BRUNER, J.
2002 *La fabbrica delle storie. Diritto, letteratura, vita*, Rome-Bari: Laterza.

DEACON, T.
1997 *The Symbolic Species. The Co-evolution of Language and the Brain*, New York: Norton and Company.

ECO, U.
1975 *Theory of Semiotics*, Indiana: Indiana UP.

HIGO, K.
1942 *Fudokisho*, Kobundo.

KOCH, W.A.
1986 *Evolutionary Cultural Semiotics*, Bochum: Brockmeyer
1991 "Worlds and signs: Explicate and implicate order", in M. Anderson and F. Merrel (eds.), *On Semiotic Modeling*, Berlin: Mouton de Gruyter.

LAKOFF, G. & M. JOHNSON
1999 *Philosopy in the Flesh*, New York: Basic Book.

LANGACKER, R.
1990 *Concept, Image, and Symbol: The Cognitive Basis of Grammar,* Berlin: Mouton de Gruyter.
1991 *Foundations of Cognitive Grammar*, vol. 2, Stanford: Stanford University Press.

LIEBERMAN, P.
1991 *Uniquely Human: The Evolution of Speech, Thought and Selfless Behaviour*, Cambridge, MA: Harvard UP.

MCNEILL, D.
1992 *Hand and Mind: What Gestures Reveal about Thought*, Chicago: University of Chicago Press.

NOTH, W.
1994 "Opposition at the roots of semiosis", in W. Noth (ed.), *Origins of Semiosis*, Berlin: Mouton de Gruyter.

SEBEOK, T.
1977 "Zoosemiotic components of human communication", in T. Sebeok (ed.), *How Animals Communicate*, Bloomington: Indiana UP.

SEBEOK, T. (ED.)
1968 *Animal Communication*, Bloomington: Indiana UP.

SEBEOK, T. & J. SEBEOK (EDS.)
1992 *Biosemiotics*, Berlin: Mouton de Gruyter.

SERCARZ, E.E. *ET AL.* (EDS.)
1988 *The Semiotics of Cellular Communication in the Immune System*, NATO ASI Series, vol. H23, Berlin, Heidelberg: Springer.

TALMY, L.
1983 "How language structures space", in H. Pick & L. Acredolo (eds.), *Spatial Orientation: Theory, Research, and Application*, New York: Plenum Press.
1985 "Force dynamics in language and thought", *Papers from the Parasession on Causatives and Agentivity*, Chicago: Chicago Linguistic Society.

WILCOX, S.
1990 "The structure of signed and spoken language", *Sign Language Studies*, 67: 141-151.
1992 *The Phonetics of Fingerspelling*, Amsterdam: John Benjamins.

WINNICOTT, D.W.
1951 "Transitional objects and transitional phenomena", paper presented at the British Psycho-Analytical Society and published in *International Journal of Psycho-Analysis*, XXXIV, 1953.

YAMAGUCHI, M.
1999 "Nature and Culture in the *Fudoki*", *VS*, 83-84: 133-143.

Umberto Eco

ORIGINS OF SEMIOSIS

We know little about the origins of language, but we do know that this precise leap of time marks the origins of our symposium – that this is a baptismal event.

And let me start with two famous quotations. The first is from Herodotus.

> Psammetichus took two common children and gave them over to a herdsman to bring up among his flocks. He strictly charged the herdsman to let no one utter a word in the children's presence. The object herein was to know which would be the first word that the children would articulate. The herdsman obeyed this order for two years and at the end of that time period, upon one day opening the door and entering their room, both children ran up to him with outstretched arms and distinctly cried "Bekos!" Psammetichus learned that "bekos" was the Phrygian name for bread. In consideration of this circumstance, the Egyptians admitted the greater antiquity of the Phrygians. (Herodotus, *History* II 1)

The second quotation comes from Salimbene da Parma.

> Frederick II wanted to discover which language and idiom children would use upon reaching adolescence if they had grown up never having had the opportunity to speak to anyone. So he gave orders to the wet nurses and the feeders to give the infants milk but prohibited them from speaking with the children. He wanted to determine whether the children would speak Hebrew, which was the children's first language, or if they would speak Greek, Latin or Arabic, the intent being to determine whether or not the children would always speak the language of their natural parents. However, the experiment failed because all the children died.

Although these stories are frequently associated, they refer to different phenomena, namely, the origins of language and the rediscovery of a Mother Tongue. Salimbene deals with the origins of language. And the failure of Frederick II's experiment convinced the *Société de Linguistique de Pari*s in the 19th century, some centuries later, to doubt the possibility of decisive scientific agreement on phenomena whose evidence had been lost in the mists of time and for which nothing but conjecture might be offered, – so to state that "the Parisian Society would no longer accept scientific communications not only on the origins of language, but also on universal languages."

The second problem is the one considered in the Herodotus story – and we can understand why the Parisian Society considered it unscientific. The search for the Mother Tongue, be it the perfect Adamic language, the original Hebrew, or any other less acceptable candidate, lasted for centuries, and, only 50 years before the congress in Paris, had produced whimsical researches such as the *La Langue Hébraïque Restituée* by Antoine Fabre d'Olivet. While from the 17th century to the times of the Enlightenment, the European learned community was obsessed by the utopia of a philosophical universal language and the discovery of the real character. I told this story in my book *The Search for the Perfect Language*, where I explicitly avoided any exploration of the old theories about the origin of language and focused my attention on the search for the perfect language.

Since in this secular crossroad of contrasting proposals there was much confusion, the distinction between the perfect language and the universal language was not sufficiently understood. It is one thing if you search for a language that mirrors the true nature of objects, but it is quite another to search for a language that everyone might or ought to speak. There is nothing that rules out the possibility that a really perfect language might be accessible to only a few, or that a language which is spoken by everybody might be imperfect.

Moreover, the Platonic distinction between a language based upon a natural relationship between words and things and a language due to convention was not kept separate from the general problem of the origins of language. It is possible to imagine a language that expresses the nature of things but which nevertheless is not original. It is also possible to discuss whether a language originated as an imitation of nature (the so called mimological hypothesis) or as the result of convention, without necessarily posing the question of whether the former is more perfect than the latter. Consequently, claims to linguistic superiority based on an allegedly direct affiliation with an ancient language were often confused with those of mimological grounds. While the presence of onomatopoeic word in a language can be viewed as a sign of perfection, it is not proof of the direct ascent of that language from a primordial one.

Finally, there was no clear-cut distinction between primordial language and universal grammar. It is possible to search for a set of universals of language without wishing to return to a primitive tongue.

In any case the staunch refusal of the *Société de Linguistique de Paris* did not arrest further research, even in our times.

Among the most interesting contemporary returns to this theme, I would like to remember the book of Giorgio Fano, *Saggio sulle origi-*

ni del linguaggio, first published in 1962. The revised version of 1973 has the title *Origini della natura del linguaggio*. In 1992 Tom Sebeok translated it to English and it was published by Indiana UP with the title *The Origins of the Nature of Language*. Fano was not a glottologist but rather a classicist, and his book did not draw a particular audience in the academic milieu.

The search for the mother tongue has been revived in this century by Vitalij ˇevorπkin. He re-proposed the "Nostratics hypothesis" that was originally advanced in Soviet scientific circles in the 60s. According to this hypothesis, there was a Proto Indo-European language, one of many branches of the larger linguistic family deriving from Nostratics, which in turn derived from Proto-Nostratics spoken approximately 10,000 years ago. But Proto-Nostratics itself, which derived from a more ancient mother tongue spoken perhaps 50,000 years ago in Africa, spread from there throughout the entire globe. According to this so called Eve hypothesis, one can imagine a human couple born in Africa who later emigrated to the Near East, and whose descendants spread through Asia and possibly America and Australia as well.

To reconstruct an original language for which we lack any written evidence, we must proceed, says Vjaèeslav Ivanov, like molecular biologists in their quest to understand the evolution of life. The biochemist seeks to identify molecular elements that perform similar functions in widely divergent species to infer the characteristics of the primordial cells from which they are presumed to have descended. So does the linguist seek correspondences in grammar, syntax, vocabulary, and vocalization among known languages in order to reconstruct the immediate forbearers and ultimately the original tongue.

Luca Cavalli-Sforza, in his work on genetics, tries to show that linguistic affinities reflect genetic affinities. This supports the hypothesis of a single origin of all languages, reflecting the common evolutionary origin of all human groups. Just as humanity diffused across the whole planet, so did language: biological monogenesis and linguistic monogenesis thus go hand in hand and may be reconstructed differentially on the basis of mutual and comparable data.

In a different conceptual framework, the assumption that both a genetic and an immunological code can in some sense be analyzed semiotically seems to constitute the new scientific attempt to find a language that can be defined as a primitive par excellence, though not in historical, but rather in biological terms. This language would rest in the roots of evolution itself, stretching back to before the dawn of humanity. This was the thesis of our friend Giorgio Prodi, published by Tom Sebeok even in English. Just one remark, that in this last case Prodi was not looking for the historical origins language, but rather for the biological roots of semiosis, which is a different approach. And I find from the titles of some of the papers presented in this symposium, some interesting hints based not on the archeological evidence, but on the structure of the human brain.

I want also to remember that in the course of the first congress of the International Association for Semitotic Studies, held in Milano in 1974, Gordon Hewes presented a challenging paper "Implications of the Gestural Model of Language Origin for Human Scientific Behavior". Hewes, on the grounds of the study of primate behavior, held that the primordial form of language was gestural and visual rather than vocal and auditory. And that if it is impossible to find evidence for the vocal phenomena and if the structure of human language has radically evolved during the course of millennia, it is still, however, possible to investigate remaining archaic gestural systems both in other animals and human beings.

Once again, by reading some of the titles of the papers presented here, I have the impression that many speakers will not focus on any historical evidence of the original event, but rather on our physiological structure, in order to explain how our semiosic ability could have developed, and they will investigate through the analysis of gestural languages more than vocal ones.

As far as the historical origins of language are concerned, the current objection is the following: we could one day reconstruct Nostratics or any other alleged mother tongue, but this would not tell us how such a tongue originated. The problem of historical or prehistorical origins of language seems to require the existence of a scientific discipline that has no testable object. It is true that something similar seems to happen in cosmology, when scientists discuss the origins of our universe, but at least they can detect certain waves that represent for us a present witness of a very remote event. We detect these waves now, but they are supposed to have been emitted, let's say, at the very moment of the Big Bang. No such evidence exists for the first phonation emitted by one of our ancestors.

A second objection is that a research on the origins of language, science without object, resembles research on the telepathy of premonition. It is possible that there exist telepathic waves, as the supporters of this hypothesis state. However, no one has ever detected any corresponding physical phenomena, and most of the so-called telepathic behavior has proved to be explicable in more reasonable ways.

But, if we do not know if there are telepathic waves, we know for sure that human beings speak, and that in the course of evolution there must have been a moment, irrespective of whether it lasted for a second or a millennium, in which some of our ancestors started producing some sort of signs understood by their companions. Even if we take for granted biblical narration, there was a moment in which Adam didn't yet speak, and a following moment in which he started naming things and animals.

As for the problem of the analogy between origins of language and origins of the universe, the researches on language have an advantage over the search on the origin of the universe, since it can be held that the universe is eternal and never had a starting moment (I am personally, even though amateurishly, of this opinion). On the contrary, with language it happens differently. Palentological evidences tell us that neither our primate ancestors nor the first men had sufficiently developed phonatory organs, and in any case the story of evolution started a long time before the apparition of the fist proto-human beings. Thus language was certainly non eternal. The certainty that a primeval linguistic moment existed can encourage scholars to explore and test new hypotheses.

References

CAVALLI-SFORZA, L.L.

1991 "Genes, peoples and languages", *Scientific American*, 265: 194-10.

CAVALLI-SFORZA, L.L. *ET AL.*

1988 "Reconstruction of human evolution: bridging together genetics, archeological, and linguistic data", *Proceedings of the National Academy of Sciences of the USA*, 85: 6002-6.

ECO, U.

1993 *Ricerca della lingua perfetta nella cultura europea*, Rome-Bari: Laterza (English tr.: *The Search for the Perfect Language*, Oxford: Blackwell, 1995).

FANO, G.

1962 *Saggio sulle origini del linguaggio*, Turin: Einaudi, (2nd revised ed., *Origini e natura del linguaggio*, Turin: Einaudi, 1973) (English tr.: *The Origins and Nature of Language*, Bloomington: Indiana UP, 1992).

HEWES, G.
1974 "Implications of the gestural model of language origin for human scientific behavior", paper presented at *International Association for Semiotic Studies*, Milan.

IVANOV, V.
1992 "Reconstructing the past", *Intercom*, 15(1): 1-4.

PRODI, G.
1977 *Le basi materiali della significazione*, Milan: Bompiani.

ˇEVORπKIN, V.
1989 "Reconstructing languages and cultures", *Abstracts and materials from the First International Interdisciplinary Symposium on Language and Prehistory*, Ann Arbor, Michigan.

Jürgen Trabant

FROM SEMIOGENESIS TO GLOTTOGENESIS IN THE 18TH CENTURY DEBATE

1

The general background of today's discussion about the origin of language or the origin of semiosis is without any doubt the presence of Chomsky's linguistic theory in the language sciences.[1] In a Chomskyan perspective "language" is conceived of as a cognitive system of the human mind, its main function is not communication but cognition, it is a mental activity, not a phonetic one, and its main features are innate to the human brain, not acquired by social practice:

> [...] we may say that the basic properties of cognitive systems are innate in the mind, part of human biological endowment, on a par with whatever determines the specific internally-directed course of embryological development, or of sexual maturation in later years. (Chomsky 1991a: 15)

This cognitive system has no intrinsic practical use, it is "unusable":

> The general conclusion that seems to come to the fore, [...] is that language is designed as a system that is "beautiful", but in general unusable. It is designed for elegance, not for use, though with features that enable it to be used for the purposes of normal life. (Chomsky 1991b: 49)

The traditional function of language, communication, is only a secondary possible usage "for the purposes of normal life":

> [...] language is not intrinsically a system of communication. (Chomsky 1991b: 51)

Pinker, Chomsky's successful prophet, summarizes the mental activity called "language" in the following way:

> The way language works, then, is that each person's brain contains a lexicon of words and the concepts they stand for (a mental dictionary) and a set of rules that combine the words to convey relationships among concepts (a mental grammar). (Pinker 1994: 85)

One of the leading semioticians of our time, Thomas Sebeok, subscribes to that conception of language as a cognitive and mental combinatorial mechanism innate to the human brain and distinguishes language sharply from semiosis and speech. Semiosis is communication and it starts with life, it is a feature of life in general, not only of human life. Speech on the other side is that phonetic activity of humans by which "language" is externalized with a communicative aim, i.e. by which "language" is used semiotically. Since in that theoretical perspective, language is neatly separated from semiosis and speech, the relation between glottogenesis and semiogenesis is a problematic one. If language has nothing to do with communication, glottogenesis might be completely separate from semiogenesis. This is exactly one of the most controversial issues of the new discussion on the origin of language. Philipp Lieberman for instance is passionately fighting against the separation of speech and language. For him, communication and vocalisation are intrinsic features of language and, hence, glottogenesis is a kind of semiogenesis.[2]

2

In the 18th century there was no such separation of language and semiosis and speech as in the modern theory. Language in the 18th century was clearly considered as a sign. The background of the 18th century debate was the traditional aristotelian conception of language: Language (or the word) is sign, i.e. it is (1) communicative, (2) sound, and (3) arbitrary (*katà synthéken, ad placitum*). This traditional conception may be schematized by the following figure (which uses the terms of the secular Latin reception of Aristotle's *De interpretatione*):

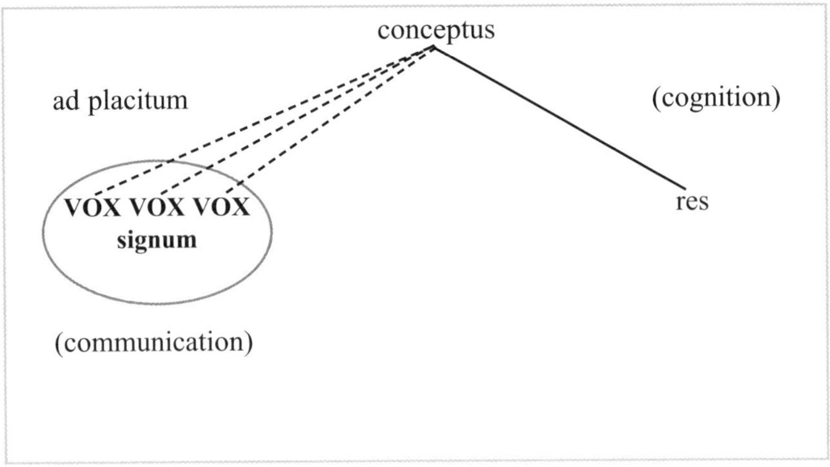

This aristotelian model of language (which was prevalent in medieval philosophy) had been reintroduced into the European tradition in the 16th and 17th century, in opposition to the humanistic language-conception of the Renaissance. In the so called *questione della lingua* in Italy and in France, the aristotelian language model served as the theoretical basis of the position of the Moderns who defended the usage of the "vulgar" languages for "higher" discourse, e.g. for scientific and philosophical uses. Since in that model words were only "arbitrary" phonetic devices to communicate a language-independent universal thought, the aristotelian theory could be used to legitimate the usage of the national languages instead of Latin. Latin had been defended by the humanists as a language with a special dignity and a very special semantic perfection. In the light of the semiotic conception of language this could not be maintained any longer: if languages are nothing but arbitrarily diverse sound there is no reason to prefer one language to another.

But now, in the 18th century, this rather generally accepted aristotelian theory will be questioned again, mainly because the European experience with a larger number of different languages of the world does not allow any longer to negate the semantic impact of languages. An increasing insight into the diversity of languages imposes the conclusion that languages do not only differ in sound (*voces*) but that they play a crucial role in the formation of thought, i.e. that the concepts (*conceptus*) depend upon individual languages and are not the same for all men. The method of criticizing the old semiotic conception of language is the research of "origins", the invention of a diachronical perspective. In that way, the philosophy of language of the 18th century develops, nearly as a whole, a critique of the semiotic conception of language, a critique of arbitrary reason. We will see that Vico attacks the aristotelian theory of language on all fronts: for him, language is not (only) communicative, it is not (only) sound, and it is not arbitrary. Condillac is the most traditional of the theoreticians, the closest to the semiotic conception of language, but also for him "arbitrariness" does not exclude iconicity. Rousseau changes the aristotelian model rather radically, he skips the relationship to the concepts: The word is communicative sound, but it is not a "sign" since it is not visual and has no "objective" reference but is the expression of subjective passions. Herder then is certainly the most radical critic of the aristotelian model: language is neither communicative nor sound nor arbitrary. He simply shifts language to the other part of the aristotelian model, to the right hand side of the aristotelian scheme: language to him is cognition, it is a mental and not a communicative activity, just as in Chomsky. By the end of the century language will not be a sign any more, but something else, namely language.

3

I will show this shift from semiogenesis to glottogenesis by reading some of the crucial passages of these four philosophers:

3.1. Vico

In order to understand Vico's semiogenetical scenario, it is important to know that his *Scienza Nuova* (1744) is a passionate *critique* of modernity.[3] Vico reconstructs what lies underneath the apparently rational and enlightened modern times. Human language also belongs to this modernity. Language seems to be, just as Aristotle had shown, rational, vocal, arbitrary and communicative, in short: *semeion*, sign. But Vico shows that underneath modern human language there is a wild and different past, a past that is still present in modernity.

> In harmony with these three kinds of nature and government, three kinds of language were spoken which compose the vocabulary of this Science: (1) That of the time of the families when gentile men were newly received into humanity. This, we shall find, was a *mute* language of *signs and physical objects* [*cenni o corpi*] having natural relations to the ideas they wished to express [*significare*]. (2) That spoken by means of *heroic emblems, or similitudes, comparisons, images, metaphors, and natural descriptions*, which make up the great body of the *heroic* language which was spoken at the time the heroes reigned. (3) *Human* language using *words* [*voci*] *agreed upon by the people*, a language of which they are absolute lords [...] (1) The *hieroglyphic* or sacred or secret language, by means of *mute acts*. This is suited to the uses of religion, for which observance is more important than discussion. (2) The *symbolic*, by means of *similitudes*, such as we have just seen the heroic language to have been. (3) The *epistolary* or vulgar, which served the *common uses of life*. (SN44: 32)[4]

The first element of Vico's critique of the semiotical language conception is his theory of the three languages according to the three ages of mankind. Human semiogenesis starts with visual signs and objects which signify "naturally". Those first "poetic characters" are, hence, no signs in the aristotelian sense (signifying *ad placitum,* arbitrarily) but rather images, icons. The second semiosis (for which Vico uses also the Greek term *sémata*) is a still predominantly visual semiosis, where the "natural" relationship between the signifier and the signified shifts to similarity. The third semiosis, human language, then is vocal language, it is the "normal" rational, arbitrary, communicative language serving the "common uses of life".

The second important element of Vico's semiogenetical story is his claim that visual and vocal signs are created together – they are "twins" – and that visual signs are prior to vocal signs:

> [...] philologists have believed that among the nations languages first came into being and then letters; whereas [...] *letters and languages were born twins and proceeded apace through all their three stages*. (SN44: 33)

What Vico here calls "letters" and "languages" clearly refers to visual and vocal semiosis in a very general way, not necessarily to letters and languages in a narrow and modern sense. Visual and vocal signs are born together. But in the beginning the visual twin is the bigger one. We have already seen, that the first language was a language of "signs and physical objects" (*cenni, corpi*). This priority of the visual is meant when Vico utters the strange claim that humans began to speak by writing (*parlarono scrivendo*): they communicated by visual signs:

> [...] for all nations began *to speak by writing*, since all were originally mute. "*Character*", on the other hand, means *idea, form, model*. (SN44: 429)

The term which expresses the visuality of the first signs in an unmistakable way, is the term "character".

The semiogenetical twins do not develop in the same way: the bigger twin, the visual one, becomes less and less important, while the vocal twin enhances its importance during the historical evolution. "Articulation", i.e. sound and the phonetic side of semiosis, eventually prevails:

> [...] the language of gods was *almost entirely mute, only very slightly articulate*; the language of heroes, *an equal mixture of articulate and mute*, and consequently of vulgar speech and of the heroic characters used in writing by the heroes, which Homer calls σηματα; the language of men, *almost entirely articulate and only very slight mute*, there being no vulgar language so copious that there are not more things than it has words for. (SN44: 446)

The term "character" refers not only to the visual materiality of the first sign, but also to the kind of "idea" or "model" that it creates: As a "poetic character" is not only a "sign or object" but also a figure with a specific personal story. The poetic characters are the first mythical persons: they are the gods. And since the first semiosis appears as semiogenetical twins, those divine characters are at the same time also phonetic events. Jupiter is the divine figure as well as an onomatopoetic sound: *Ious*:

> To follow up what has already been said: at the same time that the *divine character* of Jove took shape – *the first human thought* in the gentile world – articulate language began to develop by way of *onomatopoeia*, through which we still find children happily expressing themselves. By the Latins Jove was at first, from the roar of the thunder, called *Ious.* (SN44: 447)

The poetical characters are not creations of reason but of that more fondamental and "wilder" faculty which governs the humans of the premordial times: of *fantasia*. The "poets" of the past create those characters by their imagination and not through reason, which is a later mental development.

As far as the function of those first signs is concerned, it is clearly cognitive. Communication is not the problem of early humans, they are living together by nature (they are "political" animals by definition). But the problem they have to solve first is to deal with the wild surroundings, with a dangerous world. Those first signs, hence, are created in order to overcome the terrifying strangeness of the objective world. Creating the first signs is taming the wildness of the world. Vico's glottogenetic story might then be summarized in the following schematical way:

	divine →	**heroic** →	**human**
signifiers:	cenni (atti), corpi (caratteri poetici)	σηματα	voci
significare:	natural	similar	conventional (not a placito)
materiality:	GRAPH phon	graph phon	graph PHON
faculty:	fantasia		ragione
function:	cognition (communication)		communication

It is important to note, that the evolution from the visual signs via the heroic *sémata* to the human "voices" (*voci*) is a story of progress, of human accomplishment. But it is also important to retain, that reaching the human age and with it human language is not only leaving the past behind: The "wild" past is still present in the human age and in the human language. Hence, underneath the – apparently aristotelian – human language which seems to be vocal (*voci*), arbitrary (*a placito*), phonetic, rational and communicative, we have the visual, non-arbitrary (iconic), graphical, phantastic and cognitive past.

3.2. Condillac

Condillac tells a more traditional aristotelian story: glottogenesis is progress, the invention of language is the crucial moment in the ascension of the mind from sensation to reason, and it is the transition from nature to culture. I will not report the complicated history of semiosis outlined by Condillac in the second part of his *Essai sur l'origine des connaissances humaines* (1746). I will only sketch the transition from natural to cultural or "institutional" signs as it is delineated in the famous language origin story. In the first part of his *Essai*, Condillac describes the history of the human mind, its ascension from sensation to reason, and thereby he appoints a systematical position to language: Language appears in that operation of the mind which Condillac calls "memory". Memory is the systematic semiotic faculty. And in that context he distinguishes three sorts of signs:

> I distinguish three sorts of signs: (1) *Accidental signs* or the *objects* that some particular circumstances have connected with some of our ideas; (2) *natural signs*, or the *cries* established by nature for the emotions of joy, fear, pain, and so forth; (3) *institutional signs* or those we ourselves have chosen and that are *arbitrarily* related to our ideas. (Condillac 1746/1987: 476)

What has to be explained in this history of human intelligence is the transition from natural signs to institutional signs. This is what Condillac does by his famous story of the children living together in a "desert" and inventing arbitrary signs in their interaction.

> Living together, the children had occasion to give these first operations more exercise, for their interaction caused them to connect the *cries of each passion* with the perceptions of which these passions were the *natural signs*. They usually accompanied them with some *movement*, *gesture*, or *action* with an even more noteworthy expression. For example, the one deprived of *some needed object* was not satisfied just to cry out. He tried to obtain it, he moved his head, arms, and

> every part of his body. Touched by this sight, the other one looked at the same object. With feelings not yet understood, he or she suffered to see the discomforted companion suffer. From then on, he felt himself wanting to relieve his friend's discomfort, and he acted on this feeling as far as he could. Thus, just *by instinct*, the couple asked for and received each other's help. [...]
> The same circumstances could not often recur without the couple's eventually *getting used* to connecting the impassioned cries and various bodily movements with the perceptions so strikingly expressed. The more *familiar* they became with these signs, the more able they were to recall them *at will*. Their memory began to be exercised. They gained some *control* over their imagination, and gradually succeeded in doing *reflectively* what they formerly had done only *by instinct*. (Condillac 1746/1987: 525-526)

First one of the children exteriorizes his/her physical needs ("passion") by cries of distress. These "natural" signs are motivated by the lack of an object and express the desire to reach that object. The other child watches the expressive behaviour of his/her companion, and then, endowed with an innate instinct for help ("pity"), helps him/her to reach the desired object. This interactive behaviour is habitualized after a while ("getting used", "becoming familiar"), and by that habitualization the humans finally have control over their movements and cries. This transition from the instinctive pulsion to a reflexive voluntary activity is, in Condillac's glottogenetic story, the important transition, the transition to the "institutional" sign.

There is no critical intention in this glottogenetic story as in Vico. Condillac does not say: "Pay attention! Underneath all that reflective and arbitrary linguistic modernity you have the wild past." He tells the story of human progress. As far as the glottogenetic moment is concerned, we can summarize it by the following schematic representation:

	animals/humans		**humans**
accidental **signs**	natural **signs**	→	institutional **signs**
	cries/actions		words/gestures
	instinct		reflexion
	expression		communication

The story is about the transition from an expressive behaviour to a communicative behaviour which is also at the same time a "controlled" behaviour, i.e. "arbitrary" in the sense of "voluntary". Condillac explicitly specifies in a later text that "arbitrary" does not mean "non-iconic", on the contrary: the arbitrary ("artificial") signs of the origin will have been onomatopoetic signs. This iconic element as well as the intention of the story – how are material signs connected with "ideas" – show that even Condillac's story tends to criticize the aristotelian sign model of language. But the problem with Condillac's glottogenetic story is – and that flaw will be discovered by Herder's criticism – that he tells a communicative story which is not able to explain what he finally wants to explain, namely the *cognitive* impact of language in the development of the human mind. In Condillac's primordial scene, it is not clear how the expression of subjective physical need becomes the sign of the object to which the desire refers, of the objective "idea".

3.3. Rousseau

Rousseau, in his *Essai sur l'origine des langues* (first published posthumously in 1781), is not interested in the genesis of "ideas" or of signs which refer to objects. On the contrary, he even seems to regard objective reference as a pre-human "wild" and primitive faculty, which "real" language has to overcome. At the same time, Rousseau has a very clear but very limited conception of the term "sign". "Sign" in Rousseau means only a *visual* event or object which refers to another object, and it is opposed to the term "word": "What the ancients said in the liveliest way, they did not express in *words* but by means of *signs*. They did not say it, they *showed* it" (Rousseau 1781/1966: 6). Objective knowledge is not the motivation for the creation of language for Rousseau. Language is not reference or a cognitive relationship to objects, language is a purely communicative event, and as such its task is that of "stirring the heart and inflaming the passions" (Rousseau 1781, 1966: 8).

Since stirring the heart and inflaming the passions is the main function of language, Rousseau cannot accept the glottogenetic story of his friend Condillac: Condillac presupposes, what, according to Rousseau's conception of humans, cannot be presupposed, namely an instinct for pity, i.e. for a loving recognition of the other who suffers. According to Rousseau, humans are not naturally endowed with such an innate social instinct, but, on the contrary, in the first age they are living as separate individuals with no interest for the other, roaming around in a natural world – a kind of paradisiacal eternal spring – which makes social contact unnecessary. The interest for the other has first to be created. Therefore, Rousseau introduces natural catastrophes which cause changing climates. Changing climates create the need for a collective economy, for acting together in order to survive. Thus, in the savanna and warmer climates of the globe, people have to cooperate in order to dig wells for the watering of the cattle. Around these waterpoints a "moral need" (*besoin moral*) i.e. the recognition of the other, comes into being:

> From this alone it follows clearly that the origin of languages is not at all due to the first *needs* of humans. It would be absurd to suppose that the means of uniting them derived from the cause of their separation. Whence then this origin? *From moral needs, passions*. All the passions tend to bring people together while the necessity of seeking a livelihood forces them apart. (Rousseau 1781/1966: 11/12)

Condillac's "physical needs" do not explain the union of and the communication between human beings, but only "moral needs" which have to be invented first – around the wells where humans of both sexes come together:

> That is where the first ties were formed among the families; there were the first rendezvous of the two sexes. Girls would come to seek water for the household, young men would come to water their herds. There eyes, accustomed to the same sights since infancy, began to see with increased pleasure. [...] Under old oaks, conquerors of the years, an ardent youth will gradually lose its ferocity. Little by little they become less shy with each other. *In trying to make oneself understood, one learns to explain oneself*. There, too, the original festivals developed. Feet skipped with joy, earnest *gestures* no longer sufficed, being accompanied by an *impassioned voice*; pleasure and desire mingled and were felt together. There at last was the true cradle of nations: from the pure crystal of the fountains flow the first fires of *love*. (Rousseau 1781/1966: 44/45)

The "moral need" created around the well is love, and its expression is a vocal event: language. The voice is the means for the expression of moral needs (Condillac's pity will be felt in Northern climates). Sound is the materiality by which one can stir the heart and inflame the passions of the other. Language is hence a purely communicative, subjective, passionate and vocal event:

pre-human	human
Sign ⟶	Word
visual	auditory
need	passion
objective	subjective
communicative	communicative

3.4. Herder

The three stories of Vico, Condillac and Rousseau are stories of transitions from a pre-human to a human stage: In Vico we have a very complicated bundle of transitions from the divine to the human language, in Condillac the very core of the transition is the passage from instinctive to voluntary behaviour, in Rousseau it is the transition from need to passion and from the visual to the acoustic dimension. But in all three we still have a very clear connection to the traditional aristotelian conception of language. Vico does not deny that, eventually, language is – or at least seems to be – what Aristotle had said. Condillac even tells the story of the invention of the aristotelian communicative sign, and also Rousseau has, in a certain way, an aristotelian conception of language (communication and voice) but without any connection to the cognitive side of the aristotelian scheme. The new and revolutionary aspect of Herder's glottogenetic story is, that he does neither tell a story of transition nor of communication. On the contrary, he negates the possibility of any transition from a pre-human or animal state to a human state. His story is one of a revolutionary invention which leaves the aristotelian model behind. He explicitly states that language is not communication and that language is not an exterior communicative event, that it is not the vocal sound. Language is a purely cognitive event, and a completely interior one. Thus he shifts language from the left side of the aristotelian scheme to the right side. We might even say that language is primarily the creation of the *conceptus*, and not *vox*, the material (vocal) signification of the *conceptus* with the purpose of communicating it.[5]

> *While still an animal, man already has language.*[6] All violent *sensations* of his body, and among the violent the most violent, those which cause him pain, and all

> strong *passions* of his soul express themselves directly in *screams*, in sounds, in wild inarticulate tones. [...] So little did nature create us as severed blocks of rock, as *egoistic monads*! Even the most delicate chords of animal feeling [...] are *aligned* in their entire performance *for a going out toward other creatures.* (Herder 1772/1966: 87)

In this often quoted and often misunderstood beginning of his *Abhandlung* (1772) Herder passionately *dismisses* the communicative conception of language: as communication, language is an animal behaviour. Like all other animals, also humans express the sensations of their body and the passions of their soul by screams, and those screams are addressed to other animals. As expression of sensations addressed to other creatures of the same species, language is just like any other animal communication. But this animal behaviour is not that specifically human activity called "language" which makes the human being human. Now, for Herder there is no transition from that communicative vocal animal behaviour to language. Language is something completely different, and something completely human. Humans are endowed with a faculty which Herder calls *Besonnenheit* (reflection). *Besonnenheit* is the innate disposition for the creation of the knowledge of the world, it is a "need to know" (*Bedürfnis kennenzulernen*), a cognitive appetite which is at the same time the disposition for the creation of language. Its first activity consists in chosing a distinguishing mark within the surrounding reality. And that distinguishing mark will be an acoustic trait of the world: Herder's famous sheep represents the world which the human craves to know. The lamb presents itself in front of the *besonnene* human being who perceives it with his/her eyes and touch and ears. The acoustic impression is the decisive salient feature:

> The sheep comes again. White, soft, woolly – the soul sees, touches, remembers, seeks a distinguishing mark – the sheep bleats, and the soul recognizes it. And it feels *inside*, "Yes you are that which bleats." It has recognized it *humanly* when it recognized and named it clearly, that is, with a *distinguishing mark.* (Herder 1772/1966: 117)

The human mind creates a distinguishing mark out of an acoustic event. That distinguishing mark is an entirely mental thing within the human mind, and as such, i.e. as an interior cognitive mark it is language! Herder insists upon the fact, repeating it several times, that in order to create language, the human being does not need the society of other human beings and that he/she does not need the voice as the exteriorization of that distinguishing mark: The "inner bleating" is already language:

> The sound of bleating perceived by a human soul as the distinguishing mark of the sheep became, by virtue of this *reflection* [*Besinnung*], the name of the sheep, *even if his tongue had never tried to stammer it.* (Herder 1772/1966: 117)

In order to create language "neither society nor mouth" are necessary: "ohne Mund und Gesellschaft" (Herder 1772/1966: 119). Or, in another famous sentence: "The savage, the hermit living alone in the forest, would have had to invent language for himself, even though he had never spoken it" (Herder 1772/1966: 119). Herder's conception of language as cognition and interior mental activity can be summarized in the following figure:

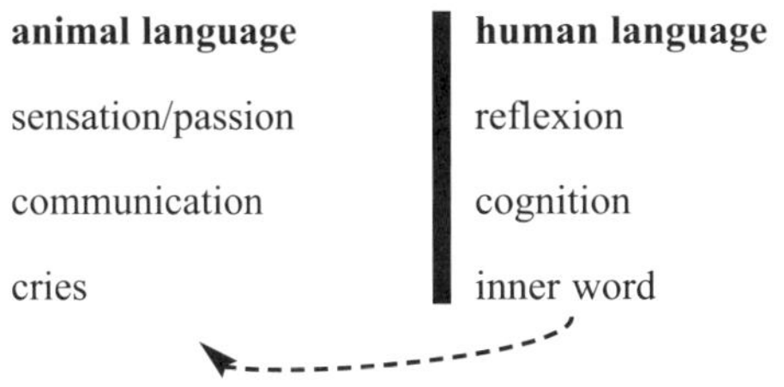

But, as can be seen by the arrow with its backward orientation toward animal language, there is nevertheless a connection between communication and cognition. Even if Herder has the revolutionary insight that language is mainly cognition, or, the other way round, that cognition is essentially language, he is however aware of the old aristotelian tradition. Therefore, he has to explain why that first human thought is "language" and not simply "thought". He does so by giving a communicative nature to the first thought itself: For Herder, the first thought is a communication of the human being with her/himself, a dialogue within her/his own soul. And only because this first interior word is already communicative thought, it tends to be externalized and communicated to others in a second step:

> Excellent how this new, *self-made sense of the mind* is in its very origin again a *means of contact*! – I cannot think the first human thought, I cannot align the first reflective argument without *dialoguing* in my soul or without striving to dialogue. The first human thought is hence in its very essence a preparation for the possibility of dialoguing with others! The first distinguishing mark which I conceive is *a distinguishing word for me and a word of communication for others*! (Herder 1772/1966: 128)

After those transitional stories, told by Vico, Condillac and Rousseau, Herder's story certainly presents the most modern scenario insofar as it tells a cognitive story, and not a communicative one. It is the most Chomskyan story in a way, even if Herder does not deny language its communicative function: "it is a distinguishing word for me and a word of communication for others" (128). By the end of the 18th century, hence, the origin of language is no longer told as a semiogenetical story but as a glottogenetical story.

4

At the basis of the 18th century debate about the origin of language there are, of course, different conceptions of the essence of language, the main opposition being certainly that of its communicative or its cognitive essence. The main issues in today's discussion about the origin of language are structurally still very much the same: The opposition of cognition vs. communication as well as the opposition of emergence vs. transition are at the very centre of the actual debate. Therefore, besides the historiographic interest, the – simpler – stories of the 18th century might possibly help to locate and understand the more sophisticated modern scenarios: Thus, e.g. Herder's glottogenetic story might shed some light on the Chomskyan position (cognition, emergence). Or, to allude to another scenario, Terrence Deacon tells a language origin story that is structurally quite close to Condillac's: his primordial scene is a scene of communication, but the aim of that communicative event is, eventually, the creation of a cognitive device. Furthermore, the communicative problem in Deacon's scenario is quite close to a fundamental social problem which is crucial for Vico's first humans, namely the problem of securing the sexual relationships or as we will say today: of securing the selfish genes. Deacon writes in the final chapter of *The Symbolic Species*:

> The first requirement, then, is that there must be a means for marking *exclusive sexual relationships* in a way that all members of the group recognize. [...]
> This information can only be given *symbolically*. [...]
> For a male to determine he has exclusive sexual access, and therefore *paternity certainty*, requires that other males also provide some assurance of their future sexual conduct. [...]
> What I am essentially describing is, of course, the skeleton of what we recognize as *a marriage agreement*. [...] Unlike what is found in the animal world, it is a *symbolic relationship*. (Deacon 1997: 399/400)

The problem of marking exclusive sexual relationships and of determining "paternity certainty" is also the first problem in Vico's story of the creation of human society. After wandering around in the big forest of the world, the *bestioni*, i.e. the wild men of the past, have to find hidden places where they can have "certain children" (*certi figlioli*) with certain women (*certe donne*):

> [...] and went into hiding in *certain* places. There, settled with *certain women*, through fear of the apprehended divinity, in religious and chaste carnal unions they solemnized *marriages* under cover and begat *certain children* and so founded families. (Vico SN44: 13)

And also as far as the material signifiers are concerned, Deacon is quite close to Vico: the first signs are, in Vichian terms, *cenni o corpi* (signs or physical objects):

> The earliest forms of *symbolic* communication were therefore likely not speech-like or manual sign language. They almost certainly included *vocalizations along with conventional/ritual gesture, activities, and objects*. (Deacon 1997: 407)

The only difference between Vico and Deacon in that regard seems to be that Deacon wants to establish a "symbolic", i.e. a non-iconic relationship, while in Vico the signification in the first sign is "natural", i.e. iconic.

> That [language] of the time of the families when gentile men were newly received into humanity. This, we shall find, was a *mute* language of *signs and physical objects* having *natural* relations to the ideas they wished to express. (Vico SN44: 32)

"Scenarios" are, as Ernst Mayr has shown in a very interesting recent paper,[7] heuristic instruments for modern scientific research. We cannot deny this important function to the scenarios of the past. Why smile about Vico, Condillac, Rousseau and Herder, why smile about *bestioni* in the big forest of the world, children on desert islands, wild boys and girls dancing around a well in the savannah, lambs on primordial meadows, when in biological research today stories of a similar kind are still told? Of course, we know much more about the brain, about the evolution of genes, about our animal parents etc. But when it comes to the very core of the question of the origin of language, stories still seem to be the adequate scientific instrument, the real mistery has still to be resolved through narration.

Notes

[1] For further – also bibliographical – information on the actual state of the discussion, cf. Trabant 2001. As far as the secular tradition of the question of the origin of language is concerned, cf. Gessinger/von Rahden (eds.) 1989.

[2] Cf. Lieberman 1991 and 1998. For further developments of that discussion cf. Trabant/Ward (eds.) 2001.

[3] For further details cf. my book on Vico's sematology Trabant 1994.

[4] The emphases in the quotes are all mine.

[5] Cf. my Herder studies Trabant 1990, 1992 and 2000.

[6] I am not quite sure whether that translation really renders the famous first sentence of Herder's *Abhandlung*: "Schon als Tier hat der Mensch Sprache" ("Already as an animal man has language").

[7] Mayr 1998.

References

ARISTOTLE
1962 *The Categories. On Interpretation. Prior Analytics,* Harold P. Cook/Hugh Tredennick (eds.), London/Cambridge, MA: Heinemann/Harvard UP.

CHOMSKY, N.
1986 *Knowledge of Language. Its Nature, Origin and Use*, New York: Praeger.
1991a "Linguistics and adjacent felds: A personal view", in Asa Kasher (ed.), *The Chomskyan Turn*, Cambridge, MA/Oxford: Blackwell: 3-25
1991b "Linguistics and cognitive science: Problems and mysteries", in Asa Kasher (ed.), *The Chomskyan Turn*, Cambridge, MA/Oxford: Blackwell: 26-53

CONDILLAC, E.B. DE
1746 *Essai sur l'origine des connaissances humaines*, Charles Porset (ed.), Auvers-sur-Oise: Galilée 1973 (English tr. in Condillac, *Philosophical Writings*, Vol. 2, Hillsdale/London: Erlbaum, 1987).

DEACON, T. W.
1997 *The Symbolic Species. The Co-evolution of Language and the Brain*, New York/London: Norton.

GAIER, U.
1988 *Herders Sprachphilosophie und Erkenntniskritik*, Stuttgart-Bad Cannstatt: Frommann.

GESSINGER, J. & W. VON RAHDEN (EDS.)
1989 *Theorien vom Ursprung der Sprache*, 2 vols, Berlin/New York: de Gruyter.

HERDER, J.G.

1772 *Abhandlung über den Ursprung der Sprache*, Wolfgang Proß (ed.), München: Hanser 1978 (English tr. in John H. Moran/Alexander Gode (eds.), *On the Origin of Language*, Chicago/London: University of Chicago Press 1966).

LIEBERMAN, PH.

1991 *Uniquely Human. The Evolution of Speech, Thought, and Selfless Behaviour*, Cambridge, MA: Harvard UP.

1998 *Eve Spoke. Human Language and Human Evolution*, New York/London: Norton.

MAYR, E.

1998 "Was ist eigentlich die Philosophie der Biologie?", in *Berlin-Brandenburgische Akademie der Wissenschaften. Berichte und Abhandlungen*, Vol. 5, Berlin: Akademie Verlag: 287-301.

PINKER, S.

1994 *The Language Instinct*, New York: Morrow.

ROUSSEAU, J.-J.

1781 *Essai sur l'origine des langues*, Charles Porset (ed.), Paris: Nizet 1981 (English tr. in John H. Moran/Alexander Gode (eds.), *On the Origin of Language*, Chicago/London: University of Chicago Press 1966).

SEBEOK, TH.A.

1991 *A Sign is Just a Sign*, Bloomington/Indianapolis: Indiana UP.

1996 "Signs, bridges, origins", in Trabant (ed.): 89-115.

TRABANT, J.

1990 "Herder's discovery of the ear", in Kurt Müller-Vollmer (ed.), *Herder Today*, Berlin/New York: de Gruyter: 345-366.

1992 "Language and the ear: From Derrida to Herder", in *Herder Yearbook* 1: 1-22.

1994 *Neue Wissenschaft von alten Zeichen: Vicos Sematologie*, Frankfurt am Main: Suhrkamp.

2000 "Inner bleating. Cognition and communication in the language origin discussion", in *Herder Jahrbuch*, Stuttgart/Weimar: Metzler: 1-19.

2001 "New perspectives on an old academic question", in J. Trabant and S. Ward (eds.): 1-17.

TRABANT, J. (ED.)

1996 *Origins of Language*, Budapest: Collegium Budapest.

TRABANT, J. & S. WARD (EDS.)

2001 *New Essays on the Origin of Language*, Berlin/New York: de Gruyter/Mouton.

VICO, G.

1744 *Princìpi di scienza nuova d'intorno alla comune natura delle nazioni*, A. Battistini (ed.), Milano: Mondadori 1990 (English tr. *The New Science of Giambattista Vico*, Ithaca/London: Cornell UP 1986).

R. Howard Bloch

ETYMOLOGIES AND GENEALOGIES: HISTORY, WORDS, AND THE WORLD

My thesis director used to tell me that I could expect a long life. "Medievalists don't die," he confided, "because they have never lived. "What he meant, of course, was that I would not have much pleasure, as I believe he did not. Unless, of course, that pleasure were somehow entwined with philology itself. Now, it has often been said that philology leads to crime, but rarely that it leads to pleasure. The violence latent in philological science, as it came into being after the Franco-Prussian war, is something that Anatole France picks up on in *Le Crime de Sylvestre Bonnard* whose protagonist, modeled in part on the wickedly exacting Paul Meyer, found fun in finding fault: "[...] I began to read a journal," says the narrator, "which, despite the fact it is run by young people, is excellent. The tone is rough, but the spirit enthusiastic. The article that I read examines with precision and critical rigor all that went on in my younger years. The author of the article, M. Paul Meyer, marked each error with a sharp rap of the finger nail" ("un coup d'ongle incisif.") (France 1961: 256)[1] The pleasure of the real-life Paul Meyer was more nationalistic in spirit and consisted in winning editorial battles against the Germans long after the guns of war fell silent. He is delighted when he is able to save a manuscript from the clutches of the Germans. "[...] les allemands vont se jeter dessus," he warns in 1879 à propos of a version of the *Vie de Saint Grégoire*. "Je fais copier cette vie pour pouvoir la sauver des griffes rapaces de ces harpyes" (BN, n.f. a. 24448, fol. 336).[2]

In some more enduring sense the pleasure of the medievalist, like that of the Classicist, is attached to the search – always Oedipal – for origins, though to say that it is Oedipal is merely another way of saying that it is pleasurable. And now that the taboo connected to origins, banished by the world systems of the 1970s and 1980s, seems to have been lifted, or at least to have waned with the end of the Cold War and the return of the referent, history, memory, and the subject, now that it is safe to speak again about origins, I confess to the secret pleasure attached to the period known as the High Middle Ages which has to do with the discovery of those moments when, if things do not begin in some absolute sense, as they never do, at least they begin again. Such discovery is, of course, illusory: even the earliest objects of human knowledge no doubt have a prehistory and are, therefore, little more than a screen beyond which we cannot see. But the pleasure of grounding our understanding in a place, investing our desire in an original object, is, as the medievals knew very well, akin to finding a pleasurable place – a "locus amoenus" – where the mind's anxious quest comes to rest for as long as such rest does not itself become an object of longing.

One such place is to be found in the "Prologue" to the *Lais* of Marie de France which reads like an Ars Poetica of the twelfth century and a virtual program of reading:

> Custume fu as ancïens,
> Ceo testimoine Precïens,
> Es livres que jadis feseient,
> Assez oscurement diseient
> Pur ceus qui a venir esteient
> Et qui aprendre le deveient,
> K'i peussent gloser la lettre
> Et de lur sen le surplus mettre. (*Lais*, vv. 9-16)

The "Prologue" to the *Lais* is one of those founding texts which appears at a liminal moment in the history of the West, what beginning with Charles Homer Haskins in the 1920s has been referred to as the "Renaissance of the twelfth century."

Marie's intervention lies, first, in her awareness of the importance of the subject. The passage contains as clear a statement as imaginable of the role of the subject in the interpretation of his or her world; and such a shift is part of what can be seen to be a moralizing or psychologizing of reality from third decade of the twelfth century on. The letter, once written, circulates: that is, finds its meaning in he or she who understands, as meaning becomes a function of the subject, an active subject, a "writerly reader" in R. Barthes's phrase. Moreover, the notion of surplus, the sense added by the reader, always exceeds that of the writer, if only because it never quite fits, something always spills over the edges, is inappropriate, does not match up. This much is banal. That which is not banal, indeed that which joins the pleasure of wallowing in origins, has to do with where it does not fit, how it does not fit; for it is there that we detect not only the presence, but the specific shape of the subject's *desire*. The excesses of meaning interjected by the reader are never arbitrary, but are motivated. "Gloser" means "to gloss" or "to interpret," which in medieval poetics is also always eroticized. "To gloss the letter" is "to desire" or "golozer" (>Lat. *glutio*) the letter, as in the Patristic association of letters with the corporeal. Then too, the "surplus of sense" that gloss produces sustains such a gloss on gloss. For *sens* can mean in Old French "sign," "sense," but also "seed" or semen (>Lat. *semino*); and the word "surplus" as "excess" and a spilling of seed equivalent to the much abused French "jouissance," is regularly used in Old French to indicate the sexual act, pleasure which exceeds language.[3]

The "Prologue" to the *Lais* of Marie de France defines perhaps better than any other work in medieval French literature the extent to which medieval writers in the vernacular conceived of their own task in philological terms, for even a so-called naïve reading suggests a historical paradigm according to which the relationship between past and present is cast in terms of a certain linguistic usury.

One of the differences between the Ancient and the medieval world is that where in the former history was cast in terms of "short wave" regenerative cycles (which might even include "long years"), the medievals cast the fate of man in broader, linear, degenerative terms.[4] Christian history, from the time of Augustine's elaboration of Eusebius's *Chronographia*, was considered to represent a long-range course of decline, a process of continual erosion according to specific periods – the *articuli temporum sive aetatum* – prior to final redemption at the end of human time. Further, if men evolve through time away from God, language – that which is *proper* to man and, indeed, for thinkers from Cicero to Aquinas, the condition of the possibility of human society – language is conceived to devolve (through use, catastrophe, translation, poetry [especially pagan verse]) away from an original state of proper meaning. According to the early medieval sense of history, a primary instance of signification – the moment against which everything else as a dissemination of men and of sense will be measured – occurred in the Garden of Eden. Adam is said to be the first to speak and the inventor of names: "omne enim quod vocavit Adam animae viventis ipsum est nomen eius." Hebrew, the original language, is sacred because it was imagined to be as close as any tongue could be to the thoughts of God at the time of Creation, and, as Philo of Alexandria asserts, to the *matter* of Creation: "with Moses the names assigned are manifest images of the things, so that the name and thing are inevitably the same from the first, and the name and that to which the name is given differ not a whit" (1929, 2: 43).

This belief in the integrity of a primeval language – an *Ursprache* not unlike the Indo-European of the nineteenth-century comparative philologist – lasted for as long as the model of universal history prevailed, that is, almost a thousand years. Augustine posits the existence of an original single tongue but hesitates about what to call it, maintaining only that "if the language that Adam once spoke still survives today, it contains the sounds with which the first man named the earthly animals and the birds" (1972, 2: 23). Isidore of Seville follows the tradition of Alexandrian Judiasm according to which "words are the indices of things," and Hebrew "the mother of all tongues" (1911, 1: iii) John of Salisbury refers to Hebrew as the tongue "mother nature gave our first parents" (1929: 23). Bruno Latini considers it the "original natural language"(1948: 317).

The first namer imposed upon things names adequate to – or proper to – their nature. This founding linguistic moment constitutes, in fact, a primary instance of the proper, as the propriety of beginnings is stressed over and over again by theologians, grammarians, and rhetoricians. Cicero claims that "the proper and definite designations of things were born almost at the same time as the things themselves" (1948, 2: 118). Quintilian asserts that "words are proper when they bear their original meaning" (1969, 1: 110), Augustine that "signs are proper when they are used to designate the objects for which they have been created" (1949: 258). The initial fixing in language of the properties of things, or adequation between the properties of things and words, was, in turn, passed on, inherited, along linguistic lines that are also family lines. This is more than a question of assimilating metaphors of the family to those of grammar. On the contrary, language functions in a family way. For the basic conceptual framework for the evolution of language is one of biological reproduction. And if medieval linguists remain conscious of the degenerative nature of verbal signs, the devolution from the proper, they also conceive of this process in terms of familial accretion. Varro, for example, maintains gender to be a function of generation: "*Genera* 'genders' are named from *generare* 'to generate.' For whatever *gignit* 'begets' or *gignitur* 'is begotten,' that can be called a *genus* and can produce a *genus*." (1951: 602). Priscian assimilates linguistic and biological reproduction in the development of nouns: "Genders, which are masculine and feminine, are properly named from 'generating' since they can generate" (1961: 141). And, according to Isidore, word classes procreate because they are sexually defined; letters replicate within words to "engender" or alter their significance: "Genera verborum ideo dicta, quia gignant. Nam activo adicis 'R' et gignit passivum; rursum passivo adimis 'R' et parit activum" (1911, 1: ix, vii).

The association of linguistic and genealogical reproduction is nowhere more evident than in the area of patronymics, which serves, at least for Varro, as the basic model of nominal genesis:

> As among men there are certain kinships, some through the males, others through the clan, so there are among words. For as from Aemilius were sprung the men named Aemilius, and the clan-members of the name, so from the name of "Aemilius" were inflected the words in the noun-clan: for from that name which was imposed in the nominal case as "Aemilius" were made "Aemilii," "Aemilium" "Aemilius," "Aemiliorum," and in this way also all the other words which are of the same line. (1951: 63)

In the name of the father lies the origin of names, and in fact, pure origin. As the 1st century grammarian explains, if Jupiter was once called *Diovis* and *Diespater* ("Father Day"), "they who come from him are called *dei* 'deities' and *dius* 'god' and *divum* 'sky'..." (*ibid.*: 63).

Priscian, in discussing the ways in which secondary words are derived from words of first imposition, begins with the patronym, which is deeply rooted in the proper: in contrast to derivation according to the principle of possession, which from common nouns yields all manner and gender of things, patronymic derivation from a proper noun is appropriate only to men and only to those in a direct line of descent. He thus poses the possibility within grammatical theory of something resembling the rule of primogeniture. Isidore shows a similar associative nexus in his search for the first roots of words (*primogenia*) as well as in the analogy which he establishes between the ways fathers and sons are related and the way they are named: "natura, imitatione, adoptione, doctrina." And as late as the fourteenth century, the author of the Provençal *Leys D'Amors* offers a systematic elaboration of the link betweens the modes of paternity and lexical derivation. Words are related, he maintains, by sound and meaning, by sound alone, or by meaning alone. If by sound and meaning (e.g. *amors* from *amar*) "this is the equivalent of a natural and legitimate son born within the bounds of legal wedlock." If by sound alone (e.g. *contrafar* from *contrari* and *far*), "this is the equivalent of a natural son, otherwise called a 'bastard.'" And if by meaning alone (e.g. *huey* from *jorn*), "this is equivalent to an adopted son" (1841, 2: 24).

If the prime model of linguistic derivation is that of paternity, that of historical linguistics is also one of genealogical succession. Jerome insists upon the coevolution of families and of tongues (1959: 11). Augustine, in dealing with the problem of continuity despite the linguistic catastrophe of Babel, associates the "House of Heber in which the primitive language of the race survived" and Hebrew (1924, 2: 204). Isidore, evoking a false etymology, renders the name "Heber" synonymous with inheritance: "Heber means passage. Its etymology is mystical, since through his lineage passes God; nor does it adhere in them, but is transmitted to the chosen people. From that one comes the Hebrews" (1911: 9, i, i). Linguistic continuity thus insures genealogical continuity, as language determines race: "...ex linguis gentes, non gentibus linguae exortae sunt" (*ibid.*: 9, i, xiv). For Isidore, the history of mankind is essentially that of its diverse tongues. From Hebrew stem Greek and Latin; from Greek, the five divisions of common, Attic, Doric, Ionic, and Aeolic; from Latin, the four subspecies of early, true, Roman, and corrupted. And from corrupted, we can only posit, as did Dante, the diverse vernacular tongues.

It is, in fact, in the *De Vulgari Eloquentia* that we find the most complete model of historical linguistics. Dante's search for beginnings leads him back through "the first form of speech created by God together with the first soul" to the first Hebrew word, and beyond words to the sound *El* "which," he maintains, "is neither question nor answer." Meaning everything and excluding nothing, the primal moment of signification is both divine presence and a potential mirror of the created world – an undifferentiated utterance, absolute vocative, whose subsequent division into syllables, words, parts of speech, languages, regional tongues, city dialects, and intramunicipal patois serves as a reminder that the degenerative history of language parallels that of humanity. Not only parallels it, but is itself inscribed within an unbroken chain of paternal relations, since for Dante the rapport between the illustrious vernacular and other more particular tongues is that of father to son:

> For as the whole door follows its hinge, so that whither the hinge turns the door may also turn, whether in or out, in like manner also the whole head of municipal dialects turns and returns, moves and pauses according as this illustrious language does, which really seems to be the father of the family. (1896: 16)

The history of human language is that of genealogical succession: from the first universal syllable, the name of God, to the most particular patois; and from God the universal father to the last sons of his line.

And just as men evolve through time away from God, words devolve from their original and proper meaning. From an original univocal signification stems the multiplicity of tongues; and from the unity of the original couple stems the multiplicity of the races of men. Both history and grammar are bound by a common sense of loss and dispersion, by a common nostalgic longing for beginnings, and by a set of ontologically similary strategies for return

The primacy of origins is an important – yea, the defining – characteristic of early medieval grammar; and it produced a problematic of loss, or a split between what writers and thinkers *knew* about human language as an essentially flawed, irrecuperable, conventional (socially determined) medium and what they *felt* as a deep nostalgia for beginnings. This split was expressed in a variety of discourses including those of theology, philosophy, and poetry in addition to that of grammar. The wish to begin again, to return to the "time before Babel," shapes early medieval sign theory. It accounts for the identification of linguistics with semantics and for a certain nostalgic "theology of words." Thus, the grammar of the period between Prisician and his twelfth-century commentators was dominated by the concept of signification and definition – by emphasis of the object of meaning over its mode; by insistence upon "real" definition based upon physical property; and, where grammar and theology coincide, by a certain over determined belief in the transparency of signs. Grammarians stress the originality – the determining efficiency – of the signified over its signifier. And the logician's technique of definition, transformed into the handmaiden of grammar, makes it possible to locate through language the proper significations of things that are rooted in (determined by) the properties of things, that are, to use Isidore's term, the "causes" of things. To signify properly is, within the recuperative, semantically oriented grammar of the period between Donatus and Abelard, to recapture the essence of things before the Fall. The science of straight connections, or grammar, enables an undoing of the dislocations – obliquities, circumlocutions, distortions – of sense that characterize the history of human speech, and hence to restore a proper or original meaning. This is why the practice of etymology is so important and, in fact, constitutes a branch of scientific knowledge until the fourteenth century.

In Classical rhetoric, etymology is one of the intrinsic arguments developed out of the meaning of a word and translated from Greek to Latin by *veriloquium* (true speech) because, in the phrase of Cicero and Quintilian, "words are the tokens [*notae*] of things." (Cicero: 1976: 408). Here, I insist both upon the notion of intrinsic and that of topic. All arguments are, for the rhetorician, intended to persuade. But an intrinsic plea is one which does not depend upon outside authority. The notion of topic (*topos*), which Cicero inherited from Aristotle, denotes a proper place from which to speak, a place from which arguments can be made and as such can be equated with the final product of the etymological process. End point of the attempt to reverse linguistic chronology, it implies a place where arguments end, where sound gives way to silence, motion to rest, and where words begin to border on meaning and meaning on things.

The positing of a place at which words and things converge serves to transform etymology into geography, *topoi* into a typology of spatially defined relations between fixed meanings; and it accounts for the disproportionate role which geography plays in early etymologies. Varro, in whom the principle of etymology reaches its Classical apogee, depicts the rooting of words in things in terms of territorial relations between neighboring properties: "We shall follow them [etymologies]," he promises, "to wherever the kin of a word under discussion is, even if it has driven its roots beyond its own territory. For often the roots of a tree which is close to the line of the property have gone out under the neighbor's field." (1951: 13) The majority of the derivations in the surviving fragments of *De Lingua latina* involve the names of places, the *loci*, which Varro associates with the first property of things, location. The notion of a verbal typology is subsumed by that of *locus*, the first of the four truly subsistent universal categories of the real equated with physical fixation: "*Locus* is where something can be *locatum* 'placed,' or as they say nowadays, *collocatum* 'established.' ...Where anything comes to a standstill, is a *locus* 'place'"; and "he who speaks [*loquitur*] with understanding puts each word in its own place..." (*ibid*.: 14, 222, 224).

In Isidore's *Etymologiarum sive originum libri XX* etymology becomes the defining principle of both grammar and rhetoric, "the exclusive source," in the phrase of the late Paul Zumthor, "of an entire learned culture" (1975: 149). Isidore consistently equates the qualities of things and their origin, conflates logical and chronological categories, a tendency attested throughout the *Etymologies* by the numerous causal connectives *causa, ratio, quia, quod* used interchangeably alongside of the prepositions *ex, a, ab*. Relations assumed to exist in nature (e.g., that man springs from earth [*homo* from *humus*], become the equivalent of those which are a function of language [*prudens* from *prudentia*], and even of language's lowest common denominator, sound (an *etymology ex vocibus*). For Isidore there can be no difference between speech and its referent, between the arts of language and the physical sciences. Things come into being with names, and without them consciousness would vanish: "Nisi enim nomen scieris, cognitio rerum perit" (1911, 1: vii,i).

Whether or not Isidore's faith in the essentially verbal nature of cognition represents an extreme, the fact remains that in an age which believed words to represent a merely tarnished mirror of the universe, knowledge of the world is essentially lexical. The more we know about the sources of words, the faster we can penetrate the nature of things: "Nam dum videris unde ortum est nomen, citius vim eis intellegis." (*ibid.*, 1: xxix, ii). Etymology represents a basis for the intelligibility of the earthly realm and a defining principle of scientific inquiry. Nor, as a tool of inference, is its domain restricted to the discipline of grammar and rhetoric but extends virtually everywhere – to metallurgy, geography, gardening, law, the arts of war, navigation, and agriculture. Even astronomy is ruled by etymology according to Isidore's practice of a mode of knowledge in which the causes of physical events matter less than the cause of their designation: "Nam Astronomia caeli conversionem, ortus, obitus motusque siderum continet, vel qua ex causa ita vocentur." ("For astronomy embraces the revolution of the heavens, the rise, setting, and motion of the heavenly bodies, and the origin of their names") (*ibid.*, 3: xxvii, i). The ultimate consequence of the *Etymologiarum sive originum libri XX* is the recuperation of philosophy by grammar, and even by a lexicology which takes on metaphysical proportions.

Among the Early Church Fathers, attitudes toward the practice of etymology are necessarily ambiguous because of conflicting attitudes toward language in general. Origen, for example, correctly situates the source of etymological thinking in Stoic doctrine, and he relates the wider debate about whether verbal signs signify naturally or conventionally to the efficacy of etymology: "The problem is whether, as Aristotle thinks, names were given by arbitrary determinations; or, as the Stoics hold, by nature, the first utterances being imitations of the things described and becoming their names (in accordance with which they introduced certain etymological principles.") (1953: 23).

Augustine's position is attenuated by his distrust of all verbal signs; yet he distinguishes between a belief in the continuity of linguistic evolution and the originally motivated quality of signs. Words change according to regular laws of resemblance (analogy), proximity (metonymy), and contrariety (antimony). And though it is not always possible to retrace their history, to arrive at the "resemblance of sound to things," such a quest can, in the best of cases, lead to a fuller knowledge of the earthly realm (1879, 32: col.1413).

It is in the realm of Biblical exegesis that the conflict between a knowledge of the degraded and illusory status of verbal signs as opposed to the regularity of their development along with the existence of an original text "sprung from a single tongue" (Augustine, 1949: 244) will partially be resolved. According to Augustine, the solution to the dilemma of the loss of intelligibility lies in a limited recourse to philology. The exegete, "armed with the science of languages," becomes capable of restoring the diminutions of sense implicit to translation and thus of discovering the proper meaning of the divine will inherent in Biblical discourse:

> The great remedy against ignorance of proper signs is a knowledge of languages. In fact those of the Latin tongue, whom I have undertaken to instruct, need two other languages in order to understand the holy Scriptures, namely Greek and Hebrew. These will permit them to appeal to older examples in cases where the infinite variety of Latin translators places them in doubt. (*ibid.*: 244)

Books 2 and 3 of the *De Doctrina Christiana* contain a series of philological principles by which to distinguish literal from figural expression and thus to recuperate Biblical allegory within the realm of the proper. And if Augustine's immediate goal in interpreting *Genesis* is, as he states, "to understand all these passages not in their figural but in their proper sense," his final aim is a recuperation – through philology – of the laws of linguistic evolution, a reversal – through charity – of the history of humanity, a reversal of history as dispersal, and thus a restoration of the One, a restoration of man to God.

It is, however, Jerome, the translator, who most systematically exploits etymology as a principle of exegesis which again relies upon a family model. For Jerome proper names are genetically prescriptive, the equivalent of a genealogical program, and the alternation of such a name is tantamount to a rewriting of the future. When, for instance, Abram's name ("quod interpretatus pater excelsus") is changed to Abraham ("pater multarum [gentium]"), his abundant progeny is both understood from the new name and prospectively inscribed in history. Jerome believes not only in the original propriety of Hebrew names but in the grounding of Hebrew roots in eternal truth. The name "Israel," for instance, is composed of the triple root for "man" ("uir ex tribus literis scribatur, 'aleph' 'iod' 'sin,' ut dicatur 'eis'"), the triple root for "seeing" ("uidens ex tribus, 'res' 'aleph' 'he,' et dicatur 'raha'"), plus the combined letter *el* from "aleph" and "lamed" and meaning "God without luck." Thus "Israel" means "one who sees God or the mind seeing God" ("uir uidens deum siue mens uidens deum") (1924: 41). Jerome's *Liber Interpretationis Hebraicorum Nominum* is nothing more than an alphabetical list of the etymological roots of Biblical names, which makes it clear that the search for linguistic beginnings and the mysticism of Hebrew roots are merely two sides of the same coin: in one meaning is read through the history of the name; and in the other, the name is read in terms of the historical genesis it prescribes. Jerome announces at the beginning of *the Hebraicae Quaestiones in Libro Geneseos* that his purpose in writing is to restore the lost (translated) truth, hence the authority of the Bible through a study of the sources of things, names, and places.

Nor is Jerome alone. Augustine participates in the mysticism of proper names; and the program of human history that he conceptualizes according to discrete evolution of moral and family lines is contained in the names of the founding fathers of the two cities [Cain and Seth] (1924: 41). Isidore understood the close connection between generation and appellation. "Sem," he tells us," means *named*, since the name is understood through a perception of future generations" ("Sem dicitur nominatus, quod nomen ex praesagio posteritatis accepit.") (1911: 7). Isidore seems to be aware that the Hebrew *Shem* means "name." Yet he also plays somewhat gratuitously, as in the example from Marie de France with which we began, on the resemblance between seed (*semen*) and sign (Greek *sema*, Latin *semanticus*); and such play reveals the extent to which genealogy is encoded in the name that is "borne out" – understood – through genealogically conceived time. For the Bishop of Seville, there is no distinction between the name "Sem," the engendering of his line, and its meaning; nor can these elements – Sem, insemination, and semantics – be distinguished from their culmination in the dissemination through Christ, "whose name is greatly on the lips of men," of the Word.

For Augustine, naming, reproduction, understanding, and preaching are bound within an essentially verbal epistemology based upon the mediatory power of signs. Prophecy, promise, and progeny are all allied:

> [...] from the very beginning of the human race, God, in his prescience, graciously inscribed in his works that which would come to fruition in centuries hence; he wanted for these things, revealed and written down at the opportune time – whether by the succession of men, or by his Spirit or by the ministry of angels – to bear witness to those who serve him of the promise of future events and of the knowledge of their completion. (1972, 2: 122)

Names, as signs, bear prospectively the mark both of their meaning and of their historical effects. Understood through time, they fulfill the promise – complete the genealogy – that they contain.

The etymological search for first words – *primogenia* – finds theological expression in the doctrine of the Incarnation, which, within a Christian economy of salvation, is experienced as a drama of language and of lineage. There is, first of all, much in Classical sign theory to suggest the permeation of paternal and linguistic functions. The notion of the *logos* is associated with paternity; and, according to a certain hermeneutic tradition, it is Hermes, the son and messenger of the gods, who lends his voice (*hermeneutikos*) to Zeus, the father (*logos*). Further, the Christian notion of the Word is, regardless of variations in trinitarian doctrine, also conceptualized in genealogical terms. The New Testament designation of Christ the Son as the Word made flesh is echoed among the Church Fathers. The Apologist Justin calls the Christian Word the "first-born of God"; Origen's pupil Denys of Alexandria claims that "the Father, who is divine and universal mind, has primarily the Son for his Word, his revealer and messenger." Eusebius maintains that "the Father murmurs in the ear of man by means of his only son."[5] But even more important, it is Christ, the voice of the Father, who permits a return to pure origin. As the "perfect expression" and source of knowledge of God, Christ the Word restores man to Him.

The drama of the return to the Father through the Son is crucial for Augustine's theology of history, which is indissociable from a theology of sacramental signs. Augustine thus distinguishes between the undifferentiated, immaterial, divine Word which, "engendered by the Father, is coeternal with Him," and corporeally articulated human speech. In some extended sense, however all words refer to the Word.[6] All language harks back to an origin synonymous with the Father who remains present in the objects of his Creation.

The desire to return to the father accounts for the centrality of memory and illumination in Augustine's verbal theology. And though, as we have seen, words per se cannot lead to truth in the first instance, memory functions in cognition to bind individual words perceived separately through time, and thus to create "a kind of artificial simultaneity" resembling God's coeternally present Word. God dwells in memory which is essentially of God. So too, the truth that does not belong formally to memory because it has always been there, the truth accessible only to the intelligence, points to the "Word of God coeternal with the Father." The Augustinian apotheosis – the transcendence of the illusory world of the senses – is, finally, a journey through perception and cognition toward the *intellectio* that he associates with a union between parent and child:

> In this arrangement, therefore, when we begin with the species of the body, and finally arrive at the species which is formed in the gaze of the thinker, four species are found; they are born, as it were, step by step, one from the other: the second from the first, the third from the second, and the fourth from the third. For the species of the body, which is perceived, produces the species in the memory; finally the species which arises in the gaze of the thinker. Hence, the will thrice unites, as it were, the parent with its offspring... (Augustine 1973: 456)

To transcend the body, to attain the inner truth beyond the temporal and beyond language, is to reverse an ontological genealogy whose highest term is God. It is to reunite the Father with the Son, the Speaker with the Word.

Augustine's goal, which is indistinguishable from the sacrament itself, is a convergence of the form of knowledge with its object, a recuperation of the names which are "the images of things." "Everyone," he affirms, "seeks a certain resemblance in his way of signifying such that signs themselves reproduce to the extent to which it is possible, the thing signified" (1949: 300). And not only does this doctrine of the Incarnation and of the sacrament justify the identification of etymology with genealogy, but it serves as a guide to Augustine's theological version of the Eusebius-Jerome model of universal history. The will for union between speaker and voice, sign and meaning, is, at bottom, linked to the dream of neutralizing the linguistic dispersion that characterizes the degenerative evolution of mankind. The desire for association between Father and Son represents a nostalgia for origins tied to the hope of undoing genealogical dispersion – to the abolition of history altogether, or the replacement of earthly chronology by eschatology. Though the Bishop of Hippo remains skeptical about the power of words – of etymology – ever to attain to the higher truth which only the intellect can provide, he nonetheless assimilates a reversal of the laws of language and of lineage that brings man closer to God.

Now, the medieval longing for the lost wholeness of a lineal and linguistic origin may seem like a distant and – well, the word itself has taken on a certain pejorative ring – "medieval" dream. And yet, it is neither so remote as it might seem, nor is it unrelated to the pleasures of philology with which we began. On the contrary, the dream of uniting the son with the father, or of retracing the history of humanity through the history of its tongues, resurfaces in the "philosophical anthropology" of the eighteenth century: in, say, Rousseau's equation of the three basic types of writing – allegorical figures, conventional characters, and alphabetic signs – with three corresponding types of social order: savage people, barbarians, and regulated societies ("peuples policés").[7] Giambattista Vico posits a similar linguistic trio corresponding to three stages of evolution and of political organization. The Age of Families at the dawn of humanity is characterized by "a silent language using signs or objects having a natural relation with ideas"; the Age of Heroes, by "heroic emblems founded on resemblances, comparaisons, images, metaphors, natural descriptions"; and the Age of Men, by "conventional signs appropriate to popular republics and monarchic states" (Vico, 1953: 163).

Though the first edition of *La Scienza Nuova* appeared almost a century before the constitution in the Romantic period of the discipline of comparative philology, Vico laid the foundation of historical linguistics and of history based upon linguistic study. Thus, in a move reminiscent of Dante, he attempts to prove that nouns existed before verbs since "in order to have a meaning...a sentence must start with a noun, either explicitly or understood, which governs it." (*ibid.*: 163). The Neapolitan philosopher's deduction of the development of language and of the individual from the logic of grammatical construction is crucial to the thought of the early comparative philologists, who seized upon the evolutionary significance of typological difference. But where Vico saw in the principles of internal structure an indication of the accretional ontogenesis of human language in general, F. Bopp, F. Schlegel, J. Grimm, and R. Rask, following the lead of comparative anatomy, found a key to the history of particular languages and to their genetic relation. Their attempt to establish a historical linguistics coterminous with the natural history of mankind obscured, in fact, the analogy between grammatical and political order.

Von Humbolt (*Über die Verschiedenheit des menschlichen Sprachbaues*, 1836), armed with the wealth of empirical data amassed ever since Sir W. Jones's positing of a common origin of Sanskrit, Greek, Latin, Gothic, and Celtic (1786), returned to the project of an assimilation of the formal structure of a particular language and, this time, the spirit of the people who speak it: "Ihre Sprache ist ihr Geist und ihr Geist is ihre Sprache." And it was his reformulation (from Schlegel and Bopp) of a tripartite system for the classification of languages according to morphology that spawned the outlandish articulations of Max Müller, who, retracing the history of mankind, assimilated isolating, agglutinating, and inflecting languages to societies built respectively around the institutions of family, tribe, and state. Thus, Family tongues, of which Chinese is the prototype, are ideally suited to conversation within the consanguineal group: "It is a style of thought and speech, not unusual between mother and daughter. The one generally knows what the other is going to say, and words are used more to indicate than to describe thought." Turanian or Nomadic languages, "which express in words not only ideas, but the relation of ideas," are suited to tribal organization. Finally, the so-called State languages are appropriate to life within the political community: "In the Arian and Semantic languages we find institutions, laws, and agreements, which, like the law of inheritance and succession at Rome or in India, show the stamp of an individual will impressed on the previous traditions of scattered tribes" (Müller, 1854: 1: 284, 285, 477).

Müller believes in the assimilation of language and race: "It is said that blood is thicker than water, but it may be said with even greater truth that language is thicker than blood," he writes in *The Science of Language*; "the blood which circulates in their grammar is Arian blood," he claims of the languages of Northern India (1899: 35). And though they are exaggerations, such statements serve nonetheless as a reminder of the extent to which the universalizing linguistics of the nineteenth century is, like the universal histories of the Middle Ages, defined by a family model. This is as true of the initial undertaking of comparative philology, the reconstitution of a lost original Indo-European ancestor. Historical linguistics, infused with the terminology of the family (e.g., mother and sister languages, families and subfamilies of tongues), depends upon the *Stammbaumtheorie* of Linnean biology for the classification of speech according to genera and species. That branch of philology concerned with the establishment of texts takes as its point of departure the organization of manuscripts into a pedigree (*stemma*) descended more often than not from a lost original prototype, as a genealogical model of poetic production mirrors that of historical linguistics. But most of all the abiding interest in etymology testifies to something more powerful at work than merely the history of words.

Etymology is a vexed undertaking: vexed, first, by the willingness of those who practice it to draw inferences – yea, lines – between discrete instances of words that may be separated by hundreds of years and bear only a minimal resemblance to each other, so great is the will for continuity; vexed, second, by the screen of a first origin behind which we merely cannot see and whose mystery I equated at the outset with Oedipal knowledge. (Here's a promising new field – "the erotics of etymology"!). What I suggest in closing is that the thrill of etymology is not unlike that discerned by Augustine whose "certain resemblance in the way of signifying such that signs themselves reproduce to the extent to which it is possible the thing signified" is equivalent to the sacramental return of the Son to the Father, a glimpse of the time before language or before being itself. A successful etymology produces a bit of a tingle, a thrill, a discharge akin to Goethe's "restoration of all things." And, so, to return to my thesis advisor's original hope and warning that I would have as little pleasure as he did, I can only reply that pleasure lies in recognizing the extent to which our own ways of understanding reproduce the object of our study and thus acknowledging the theological underpinnings of the philological enterprise. A successful etymology partakes of the divine not because it is right, but because it produces a feeling that meaning has come to rest, that language is superfluous to our being in the world.

Notes

[1] For a discussion of philology and war see my essay "The Siege of the Manuscripts: Military Philology between the Franco-Prussian and the First World War," *Aporemata*, ed. Most, Glenn W., 5 (2000): 1-15.

[2] Meyer's delight at beating the Germans to the text is doubled by the pleasure of seeing them fail because of internal rivalries among themselves: "Ces allemands qui sont ici se coupent mutuellement l'herbe sous le pied. Suchier et Ulrich se sont plaints… moi de Volmöller qui accapare tout. J'ai écrasé, Suchier de ma générosité, en lui anonçant… publier un texte provençal que j'avais tout près pour l'impression, et qui est intéressant. Il m'a dit tout confus: 'vous le publierez mieux que moi', ce qui est en effet possible" (BN, n.f. a. 24448, for. 305v.).

[3] "Ensemble gisent et parolent/ Et sovent baisent e acolent;/ Bien lur coviegne del surplus,/ De ceo que li autre unt en us" ("Guigemar," v. 531).

[4] The argument of this section follows closely that originally articulated in my *Etymologies and Genealogies: A Literary Anthropology of the French Middle Ages* (Chicago: University of Chicago Press, 1983), pp. 38ff.

[5] Eusebius, *Ecclesiastical History*, ed. E. Capps and T.E. Page (London: Heinemann, 1926), 2: 22.

[6] "Nothing then could be created which, if before time is not coeternal with the Creator, or creation – if the term 'reason' is not used improperly – in the partaking of a life coeternal in the Word of God coeternal to the Father. This is why Scripture, before enumerating each creature in the order of its creation, refers to the Word of God..." (*De Genesi*, 1: 164).

[7] "Ces trois manières d'écrire correspondent assez exactement aux trois divers états sous lesquels on peut considérer les hommes rassemblés en nation. La peinture des objets convient aux peuples sauvages; les signes des mots et des propositions, aux peuples barbares, et l'alphabet aux peuples policés" (J.-J. Rousseau, *Essai sur l'Origine des langues* in *Oeuvres complètes*, éd. P. R. Anguis [Paris: Dalibon, 1825], 1: 488).

References

AUGUSTINE

1879 *De Origine Verbi,* J.-P. Migne (ed.), *Patrologia latina*, Paris: Garnier.

1924 *De Civitate Dei*, in J. Welldon (ed.), London: Society for Promoting Christian Knowledge.

1949 *De Doctrina Christiana*, G. Combès & J. Farges (eds.), Paris: Desclée de Brouwer.

1972 *De Genesi ad litteram*, P. Agaësse & A. Solignac (eds.), Paris: Desclée de Brouwer.

1973 *De Trinitate*, G. Beschin (ed.), Rome: Città Nuova, 1973.

BLOCH, R.H.

2000 "The siege of the manuscripts: Military philology between the Franco-Prussian and the First World War", in G.W. Most (ed.), *Aporemata*, 5 (2000): 1-15.

1983 *Etymologies and Genealogies: A Literary Anthropology of the French Middle Ages*, Chicago: University of Chicago Press.

CICERO

1948 *De Oratore*, E. W. Sutton and H. Rackham (ed.), Cambridge: Harvard University Press.

1976 Topics, H. M. Hubbell (ed.), Cambridge: Harvard UP.

DANTE

1896 *De Vulgari Eloquentia*, P. Rajna (ed.) Florence: Le Monnier.

EUSEBIUS

1926 *Ecclesiastical History*, E. Capps & T.E. Page (eds.), London: Heinemann, 1926.

FRANCE, A.

1961 *Le Crime de Sylvestre Bonnard*, Paris: Gallimard.

ISIDORE OF SEVILLE

1911 *Etymologiarum sive originum libri XX*, W. M. Lindsay (ed.), Oxford: Oxford UP.

JEROME

1959 *Hebraicae Quaestiones in Libro Geneseos*, in *Corpus Christianorum*, Turnholt: Brepols.

JOHN OF SALISBURY

1929 *Metalogicon*, C.I. Webb (ed.), Oxford: Clarendon Press.

LATINI, BRUNETTO

1948 *Li Livres dou tresor*, F. Carmody (ed.) Berkeley: University of California Press.

MÜLLER, M.

1854 "The last results of the researches respecting the non-Iranian and non-Semitic languages of Asia or Europe, or the Turanian family of language", in C.C.J. Bunsen, *Outline of the Philosophy of Universal History*, London: Longman, Brown, Green, and Longman.

1899 *The Science of Language*, Chicago: Open Court.

ORIGEN

1953 *Contra Celsum*, H. Chadwick (ed.), Cambridge: Harvard UP.

PHILO

1929 *On the Cherubim*, F. H. Colson (ed.), London, Heinemann.

PRISCIAN

1961 *Institutionum Grammaticarum libri XVIII*, H. Keil (ed.), Hildesheim: Georg Olms.

QUINTILIAN

1969 *Institutio Oratoria*, H. E. Butler (ed.), Cambridge: Harvard UP

ROUSSEAU, J.-J.
1825 *Essai sur l'Origine des langues* in *Oeuvres complètes*, P. R. Anguis (ed.), Paris: Dalibon.

VARRO
1951 *De Lingua latina*, R. G. Kent (ed.), Cambridge: Harvard UP.

VICO, G.
1953 *La Science Nouvelle*, A. Doubine (ed.), Paris: Nagel.

ZUMTHOR, P.
1975 "Etymologies", in *Langue, texte, énigme*, Paris: Seuil.
1841 *Leys D'Amors*, in M. Gatien-Arnoult (ed.), Toulouse: Bon et Privat.

Winfried Nöth

SEMIOGENESIS IN THE EVOLUTION FROM NATURE TO CULTURE

1. Adam's navel and the semiotic thresholds

The problem of the origins of semiosis confronts us with an aporia similar to the one which once puzzled our medieval forefathers when they debated the question "Should Adam be depicted with or without a navel?" (Kirchner 1903: 18-19). Drawn with a navel, as in Albrecht Dürer's *Fall of Man*, Adam could not have been the first of humankind. Drawn without a navel, as in St. Hildegard's medieval prayer book, Adam was not a complete human being.

In our search for the *Origins of Semiosis* (Nöth, ed. 1994), Adam's navel is the sign, and the parallelism between the medieval paradox concerning the origins of humans and our problem concerning the origins of semiosis can be stated as follows: "Did the first sign in the evolution of the universe have a sign producer as its cause, or was there a first sign which originated spontaneously without a sign producer as its cause?"

Unless we follow St. John's account of semiogenesis, according to which the first sign was uttered by God in the form of a word (St. John 1.1), logic obliges us to conclude with the medievals that the first sign could not have been the first had it been uttered by a sign producer, since nobody can produce a sign without knowing signs. However, without an utterer, the first sign cannot yet have been a proper sign either, since no sign is a real sign unless it has a sign producer. Apparently, the first sign cannot have been a conventional nor an arbitrary sign either, because semiotic convention and arbitrariness presuppose signs. Even if we conceive of the first sign as a natural sign and concede that such sign can be without an utterer, we are confronted with the mystery of the interpreter of this first sign and the enigma of the sudden emergence of such spontaneous sign processing capacity. Does it make sense to postulate a first sign processor who is spontaneously able to interpret a sign without ever having interpreted any other sign?

In modern semiotics, the problem of Adam's navel is the problem of the semiotic threshold, as Umberto Eco (1976) has called it. The metaphor of the threshold suggests a division between a lower level without semiosis and a higher level where sign processes occur. The transition from the lower to the higher level promises to account for of the origin of semiosis. Many scholars have identified this semiotic threshold with the dividing line between nature and culture. The idea that there are two worlds in our universe, one of a semiotic culture *with* signs, the other of a physical nature still *without* signs, looms at the foundations of semiotic and cultural theory, but the theory of the two worlds, one of *mind*, the other of *matter*, has meanwhile been discredited as the great Cartesian error. In order to escape the blame of Cartesianism, modern semiotics has opted for a gradual extension of the semiotic field and hence for a gradual lowering of the semiotic threshold.

Let us investigate some of the thresholds of modern semiotics which localize the origins of semiosis at different stages in the evolution of our universe. How were they lowered, and with which result? We have to restrict ourselves to four major paradigms of twentieth century semiotics which differ with respect to their view of the semiotic threshold and hence as to their view of the scope of the semiotic field. Following Thomas Sebeok, I will call the first three of them anthroposemiotics, zoosemiotics, and biosemiotics. The semiotic agents associated with these paradigms are humans, animals, and biological microorganisms. The fourth paradigm dares to lower the semiotic threshold beneath the level of life into the sphere of lifeless matter. Ultimately it proposes to abolish the threshold altogether in favor of a theory of continuity from nature to culture. John Deely (1990) has dubbed this paradigm *physiosemiotics*, but I will call it *physicosemiotics* (Nöth 2000: 248) in order to express more transparently that semiosis, according to this perspective, is not restricted to the *physis* of organisms, but has its origins at the level of inorganic physical matter. – Physicosemiotics, by the way, is not be same as *semiophysics*, an approach to semiotics outlined by René Thom (1988) and Jean Petitot (1992) as a theory of "significant forms" and "semantic fields" common to both language and cognition on the one, and processes in organic and inorganic nature on the other hand.

2. Anthroposemiosis

The highest semiotic threshold is the one postulated by those semioticians who restrict semiotics to anthroposemiotics. The origins of signs in this perspective, coincide with the origins of humans. Let us briefly consider two modern theories of semiotics with this perspective, structural semiotics in the Saussurean tradition and phenomenological semiotics.

2.1. Semiosis according to structural semiotics

Structural semiotics in the tradition of Saussure and Hjelmslev is by definition anthroposemiotic. The point of departure is one of transsemiotic agnosticism, since thought, considered before language, in Saussure's (1916: 113) words, "is only a shapeless and indistinct mass, [...] a vague uncharted nebula." The transition from prelinguistic nature to language in this nebula must hence remain a semiotic mystery.

In sharp contrast to Peirce, Greimas, a protagonist of this paradigm, redefines semiosis in the logocentric categories of structural linguistics: "Semiosis," we read in his semiotic dictionary, "is that operation which, by setting up a relationship of reciprocal presupposition between the expression form and the content form (in Hjelmslev's terminology) [...] produces signs: in this sense, any language act implies a semiosis" (Greimas & Courtés 1979: 285). The origins of semiosis are hence the origins of language, whose semiotic essence consists in arbitrariness and conventionality.

Nevertheless, Greimas also postulates a semiotics of the natural world, but this semiotics of nature is not a theory of prehuman semiosis, but a theory of how human culture interprets nature. The natural world, according to this interpretation, is merely "a place for the elaboration and practice of multiple semiotic systems" (*ibid.*: 375). Structural semiotics in this tradition is a semiotics without any evolutionary perspective.

2.2. Semiosis according to phenomenological semiotics

In phenomenological semiotics, as outlined by Husserl (1890), meaningful signs (*bedeutsame Zeichen*) are distinguished from indexical signs (*Anzeichen*). Only meaningful signs constitute a complete triad of sign, meaning and object, whereas indexical signs consist only of the dyad of sign and object. Husserl considers them as signs without meaning, since they require no intentionality and conscious thought. Such signs are both opposed to the world of physical objects and to an immediate and intuitive apprehension of the phenomena (cf. Nöth 1990: 35, 99, 108). The transition from a merely intuitive apprehension of the phenomena to meaningful signs takes place when human consciousness intentionally bestows meaning upon an object in a "meaning endowing act" of a sign producer and a "meaning-fulfilling act" of an interpreter. When this semiotic threshold is crossed, a phenomenon is no longer perceived "in itself," but with the awareness that it indicates something else.

Human consciousness, the necessary awareness of the otherness of a sign in contrast to its object, and the requirement of intentionality establish an extremely high semiotic threshold (Short 1981). The evolutionary implications remain unclear. Apparently, animals can process indexical signs, whereas meaningful signs presuppose a human mind. However, why should animal semiosis be without purpose and intentionality, and what is the evolutionary role of immediate and unreflected, in relation to mediated, cognition? Does one precede the other in the evolution of sign processing?

3. Zoosemiosis

The programmatic extension of twentieth century semiotics from human culture to animal nature begins with Charles Morris (cf. Petrilli 1999). With it, the origins of semiosis now coincide with the origins of animals. Sign interpretation is no longer a matter of humans, but of "organisms," as Morris's definition (1946: 366) states, which specifies semiosis as "a process in which something is a sign to some organism." In particular, Morris's semiotic pragmatics was destined to deal "with the biotic aspects of semiosis, that is, with all the psychological, biological, and sociological phenomena which occur in the functioning of signs" (Morris 1938: 30). Semiosis, according to Morris (1938: 4), is furthermore a process of a "mediated taking-account-of" in which the sign is a means for attaining a certain goal (Morris 1946: 368). With this account, Morris is not in disagreement with Husserl's view of the semiotic threshold between immediate and mediated perception, but in contrast to Husserl, Morris lowers the semiotic threshold from human to animal semiosis. That the life of an animal is presupposed for the life of signs, according to his semiotic paradigm, becomes apparent when we consider the behavioristic categories in Morris's descriptions of sign processes: s*timulus, response, behavior, reaction,* or *receptor of the living organism* are clearly categories referring to animal semiosis (Morris 1946: 360-67).

4. Biosemiosis

The further development of zoosemiotic research and its extension to microbiological processes within the still more encompassing framework of biosemiotics has been Sebeok's major contribution to the history of semiotics (Kull 1999; Sebeok 2001). Semiosis, according to Sebeok (1986: 15), "is what distinguishes all that is animate from the lifeless." The origins of semiosis are hence also the origins of life. Semiogenesis coincides with biogenesis.

Jesper Hoffmeyer (1993: 94) is hopeful that the biosemiotic paradigm is likely to overcome the Cartesian dualism between mind and matter, although he does not himself attempt to extend the scope of the semiosphere to the inorganic world. Sebeok (2001: 68), by contrast, definitely rejects the idea of a semiosphere preceding life. His argument is: "Because there can be no semiosis without interpretability, [...] semiosis presupposes the axiomatic identity of the semiosphere with the biosphere." The semiotic threshold hence separates biogenesis from inorganic cosmogenesis. However, Sebeok discerns a quasi-semiotic bridge from the semiosphere to inanimate matter. This bridge is information: "Before semiosis," says Sebeok (1986: 15), "there was information. According to the standard (big bang) theory of cosmic genesis, the universe began totally devoid of information, but it quickly evolved out of that initial state as a measure of the multiform. The essence of information is change, the prerequisite of semiosis is life."

I cannot say how the evolutionary quantum leap from information to semiosis could have occurred, but the paradigm of physicosemiotics, which I want to consider next does not require an answer to this question. It takes semiosis or something that we might also call proto- or quasi-semiosis below the threshold of biosemiosis for granted.

5. Physicosemiosis

Physicosemiotics is the scandal of anthroposemiotics and of biosemiotics in the narrower sense. The idea that semiosis should be possible in the inorganic world is a contradiction in terms to all those who postulate that human intentionality or at least life is the essential semiotic threshold. There are two versions of physicosemiotics, a more moderate and a radical one. The former defines semiosis as a semiotic potential which natural signs have even before they meet an interpreter. The latter defines physicosemiosis as a teleological process which takes place in nature before an animal sign interpreter emerges.

5.1. Physicosemiosis as the semiotic potential of natural signs

Based on the semiotics of the late Scholastic semiotician Poinsot, Deely (1990: 90-91; 1994: 198) develops the more moderate version, which postulates physicosemiosis in the context of natural signs. One of Poinsot's semiotic maxims was: "It suffices to be a sign virtually in order to signify in act." From this principle, Deely derives the argument that not only the interpreted, but also the uninterpreted nature is endowed with semioticity and that this semioticity is a virtual one. Semiosis in the physical world is hence a "virtual semiosis." The "action" of the virtual sign is directed towards its interpretation somewhere in the future, but its effect, namely an actual interpretation, depends largely on chance (Deely 1994: 199-200). A still undiscovered fossilization of a dinosaur bone in my garden would be such a virtual sign, says Deely. It is, so to speak, dormant until it comes to life in an actual instance of sign interpretation, but it is nevertheless a sign. Deely (1994: 174) even attests a triadic nature to this natural sign: A, the sign, is the bone of the dinosaur. B, its object, is the once living dinosaur to which it belonged. C, its interpretant, is the present geological stone formation which was once a real bone.

However, if semiosis exists already in a natural phenomenon *before* it is interpreted as a natural sign, such a virtual sign is really defined independently of its actualization in a future interpretation, and in fact, Deely (1994: 174) goes so far as to argue that the undiscovered fossil in my garden already constitutes a semiotic triad before, and independently of, its future interpretation: this triad consists of the ancient bone as a sign, the dinosaur as its object, and its present state of fossilization as its interpretant. It is hard to see in how far this triad is more than a concatenation of two dyads of a very different kind, namely a cause-effect relationship, which connects the present fossil with the bone seventy million years ago (see also Short 1998: 48), and a part-whole relationship between the bone and the animal, whose bone was later fossilized.

5.2. Physicosemiosis as a process in the evolution of nature

There are not many semioticians who subscribe to an apparently pansemiotic theory of semiosis as a genuinely triadic process in nature before life can interpret signs. Nevertheless, Charles Sanders Peirce is the crown witness of both the advocates and the opponents of this theory: Thomas Short (1998: 49), the renowned specialist in Peircean semiotics, affirms that semiosis, according to Peirce, can only be anthropo- or zoosemiosis, because there is "no basis for the assertion that semiosis occurs outside of living things." On the other hand, no less renowned Peircean scholars such as Helmut Pape (1989), Klaus Oehler (1993), and Lucia Santaella-Braga (1994, 1996, 1999) affirm that the origins of semiosis, according to Peirce, begin before life. Between the two camps we find Felicia Kruse (1990: 220). She gives evidence of many instances of Peirce's extension of the theory of semiosis from living nature to the physical universe, but believes that it remains unclear whether Peirce actually wanted to extend the theory of semiosis from the living to the material world or whether he merely wanted to point out analogies between processes in the organic and the inorganic world.

No doubt, Peirce was a biosemiotician, as Hoffmeyer (1993) has convincingly shown, and Peirce's semiosphere certainly includes the whole biosphere. However, among the agents involved in processes of semiosis, Peirce does not only mention animals, such as "a chameleon and many kinds of insects" (MS 318: 205-206), microorganisms, such as "a little creature" under a microscope (CP 1.269), but also "plants that make their living by uttering signs, and lying signs, at that" (MS 318: 205-206). Furthermore, semiosis, and with it, also "thought," occurs even "in crystals, and throughout the physical world" (CP 4.551), and finally, the whole "universe is a vast representamen" (CP 5.119). With his bold extension of semiotics from the biosphere to the sphere of the inanimate world, Peirce ultimately crosses the threshold from physics to metaphysics, as we will see, but let us first examine the reasons he gives for such extensions of the semiosphere to the physical world. There are three keys to Peirce's extension of the semiosphere from the organic to the inorganic world: (1) the theory of final causation, (2) Pierce's broad concept of mind, and (3) his theory of evolutionary continuity from mind to matter.

5.2.1. Teleology (final causation)

Final causation or teleology is Peirce's common denominator of antroposemiosis, biosemiosis, and processes which also occur in the inorganic world (Short 1983; Pape 1993; Santaella 1999b). In human semiosis, it appears in the form of intentionality and self-correction in the effort to approach the dynamic object of the sign to which we can never have any ultimate access.

Anthroposemiotic teleology appears, as Peirce puts it, "in the purpose of signs – which is the purpose of thought – to bring truth to expression" (CP 2.444n). The principle of teleology in human semiosis is rather evident in the case of *communication* between a sender and a receiver, where we have the purpose of a sign producer and some effort of the receiver to understand the message correctly.

But does teleology also apply to signification, when a human observer interprets a natural sign, such as the smoke that indicates fire? The mere potentiality of a natural object to be interpreted some day as a sign, in which Poinsot saw a source of semiosis, is not a final cause. There is no other relationship between a potential sign and the actual sign which it may one day become than chance. Chance, however, belongs to the category of secondness. It can only be the source of efficient causality, which is dyadic, not of final causality, which is necessarily triadic. Hence the so-called potential sign is not a sign at all.

On quite different grounds, Stuart Kauffman (1995) has given evidence that the origin of life cannot be accounted for in terms of chance. His evidence comes from mathematics, where the improbability of the chance encounter of elements of matter to create life has been demonstrated. If life did not originate from chance, it is equally improbable that semiosis might have its origins in chance.

But how can teleology otherwise be at work in the interpretation of natural signs without a sender? In semiosis, the effect of teleology is one of a semiotic control that the object of the natural sign exerts on the outcome of sign interpretation, the interpretant. The object imposes, so to speak, cognitive constraints on the interpreter and thus restricts the possibilities of interpretation. Ransdell (1977: 173) illustrates such an effect of semiotic teleology in the interpretation of a natural sign with the example of traces on the ground which indicate the presence of a tiger. The control of the (dynamical) object on the interpreter, says Ransdell, occurs "by further signs the unquestioned interpretation of which can go towards determining the correctness or incorrectness of the interpretation in question. Such further signs might be, for example visual percepts of the animal, its smell, its roar [...] and so on."

Such goal directed semiotic behavior in communication and signification is most certainly also apparent in animals and below the biological threshold of zoosemiotic organisms (Hoffmeyer 1993). In biosemiosis we find teleology furthermore in all cybernetic processes of control and regulation within organisms which lead to its homeostasis (Nöth 1977).

Below the threshold of the living, where we certainly do not find communication and signification, in the sense of structural semiotics, the discoveries of dynamic systems theory and the theory of complex systems have meanwhile shown that teleology also exists in physical and chemical processes. Spontaneous self-organization occurs in dissipitative structures, and *Order out of Chaos,* becomes possible, as Prigogine & Stengers (1984) have shown. Other evidence of the possibility of growth of complexity in physical nature, which was previously thought to be a characteristic of life only, has been provided by Stuart Kauffman's (1995) research in autocatalytic processes. According to Bruce Weber and Terry Deacon (2000), there is even evidence of *memory* in physical chaotic systems (cf. Weber & Depew 1999: 56). Memory, of course, is an even higher form of semiosis than mere teleology, since it implies self-reference.

Peirce was himself involved biophysical research of teleological processes, where – as he wrote – a "tendency toward bringing about an ultimate state of things" (CP 7.471) and the fact "that chance begets order" (CP 6.279) can be shown (Santaella 1999b). He did not use the term physicosemiosis to describe these processes, but one of his conclusions was that "mind acts on matter" (CP 7.370, 8.259; Santaella 1999a: 513; and see 5.2.2).

Short (1998: 45) underlines that teleology is not a sufficient, but only a necessary criterion of semiosis, but more important than this difference between the processes in the inorganic and the organic world is what they have in common: a tendency towards self-control, self-reference, growth towards future states independent of initial states, but with a telos from the beginning on.

In spite of their common foundation in teleology, there are, of course, also differences between anthroposemiosis and physicosemiosis (or -quasisemiosis), but these difference are only a matter of degree: "Human acts of cognition differ from other self-referential and self-correcting processes by virtue of their greater degree of self-reference and self-correction. Human beings achieve this superiority through the creation of symbols, which represent and control our habits of action" (Oehler 1995: 269).

5.2.2. The origin of mind and the continuity of its evolution

Mind, thought, and semiosis are basically synonyms for Peirce (Santaella Braga 1994). The origin of semiosis is hence the origin of mind. But where does mind come from? Did it not evolve from matter? Peirce did not believe in a dualism between mind and matter and defended the general principle of a continuity between both, which he called synechism. Instead of a spontaneous origin there must have been a continuity between mind and matter, but which came first in cosmic evolution?

Peirce's answer to this riddle concerning the origin of mind is a metaphysical one: mind comes first, matter last. Semiosis is hence the origin, matter the end of cosmic evolution. The logic behind this metaphysical cosmology derives from the order of the three universal categories. Mind, considered as the pure possibility of thought (Potter 1967: 17, 135), not yet as a real event of thinking or even reasoning in a human being, must come first because it belongs to the category of firstness, of possibility, and spontaneity. Matter can only come last because it belongs to the category of thirdness, which is the one of habit and necessity.

Peirce's metaphysical account of evolution describes the beginning as a chaos, a state of qualitative continuities still without regularity (CP 1.412, 6.215). This state of pure continuous firstness was then interrupted by discontinuities, which entered the scene as instances of secondness like "flashes" (CP 1.412). The ensuing repetition of such singular occurrences of chance lead to habits, regularity, order, hence to thirdness (CP 1.414). Some irregularities were eliminated in evolution, others became more and more regular.

This is why Peirce can say that matter is mind frozen "to regular routine" (CP 6.277). Peirce's logic of evolutionary cosmology urges the conclusion that the end of the universe is reached at a point where matter is completely bound in regularity, resisting any spontaneous variation and influence by chance. This end state of order is by necessity the end of evolution.

Since mind, and with mind, semiosis, *is* at the origin of cosmic evolutions and does not evolve *from* matter, Peirce's metaphysical answer to the question of the medievals is clear: Adam must have had a navel from the moment of his creation on. But even, if we are unwilling to accept Peirce's metaphysical account of the origins of semiosis, we have to acknowledge the importance of his semiotic discovery of the principle of teleology and growth as an essential bridge that leads from the inorganic to the organic world and ultimately from nature to culture.

References

DEELY, J.
1990 *Basics of Semiotics*, Bloomington: Indiana UP.
1994 *New Beginnings: Early Modern Philosophy and Postmodern Thought*, Toronto: UP.

ECO, U.
1976 *A Theory of Semiotics*, Bloomington: Indiana UP.

GREIMAS, A.J. & J. COURTÉS
(1979) 1982 *Semiotics and Language*, Bloomington: Indiana UP.

HOFFMEYER, J.
(1993) 1996 *Signs of Meaning in the Universe*, Bloomington: Indiana UP.

HUSSERL, E.
(1890) 1970 "Zur Logik der Zeichen", in Husserl, E., *Gesammelte Werke*, The Hague: Nijhoff, vol. 12: 340-373.

KAUFFMAN, S.
1995 *At Home in the Universe*, Oxford: UP.

KETNER, K.L. (ED.)
1995 *Peirce and Contemporary Thought*, New York: Fordham UP.

KIRCHNER, J.
1903 Die Darstellung des ersten Menschenpaares, Stuttgart: Enke.

KOSLOWSKI, P. (ED.)
1999 *Sociobiology and Bioeconomics*, Berlin: Springer.

KRUSE, F.E.
1990 "Nature and semiosis", *Transactions of the Charles Sanders Peirce Society* 26: 211-224.

KULL, K.
1999 "Biosemiotics in the twentieth century", *Semiotica*, 127: 385-414.

MORRIS, CH.W.
(1938) 1970 *Foundations of the Theory of Signs*, Chicago: UP .
(1946) 1971 "Signs, language, and behavior", in C.W. Morris, *Writings on the General Theory of Signs*, The Hague: Mouton: 73-398.

NÖTH, W.
1977 *Dynamik semiotischer Systeme*, Stuttgart: Metzler.
1990 *Handbook of Semiotics*, Bloomington: Indiana UP.
2000 *Handbuch der Semiotik*, Stuttgart: Metzler.

NÖTH, W. (ED.)
1994 *Origins of Semiosis,* Berlin: Mouton de Gruyter.

OEHLER, K.
1995 "A response to Habermas", in K.L. Ketner (ed.): 267-272.
1993 *Charles Sanders Peirce*, München: Beck.

PAPE, H.
1989 *Erfahrung und Wirklichkeit als Zeichenprozeß*, Frankfurt/Main: Suhrkamp.
1993 "Final causality in Peirce's semiotics and his classification of the sciences", *Transactions of the Charles Sanders Peirce Society*, 29: 581-605.

PETITOT, J.
1992 *Physique du sens*, Paris: Centre National de Recherches Scientifiques.

PETRILLI, S.
1999 "Charles Morris's biosemiotics", *Semiotica*, 127: 67-102.

POTTER, V.S.
(1967) 1997 *Charles Peirce on Norms and Ideals*, New York: Fordham UP.

PRIGOGINE, I. & I. STENGERS
1984 *Order out of Chaos*, New York: Bantam.

SANTAELLA BRAGA, L.
1994 "Peirce's broad concept of mind", *European Journal for Semiotic Studies*, 6: 99-411.
1996 "Semiosphere: The growth of signs", *Semiotica*, 109: 173-186.
1999a "A new causality for the understanding of the living", *Semiotica,* 127: 497-518.
1999b "Peirce and biology", *Semiotica*, 127: 5-21.

SAUSSURE, F. DE
(1916) 1969 *Course in General Linguistics*, New York: McGraw Hill.

SEBEOK, TH.A.
1986 *I Think I am a Verb*, New York: Plenum.
2001 "Biosemiotics: Its roots, proliferation, and prospects", *Semiotica*, 134: 61-78.

SHORT, TH.L.
1983 "Teleology in nature", *American Philosophical Quarterly*, 20: 311-320.
1981 "Semeiosis and intentionality", *Transactions of the Charles Sanders Peirce Society*, 17: 197-223.
1998 "What's the use?", *Semiotica*, 122: 1-68.

THOM, R.
(1988) 1990 *Semiophysics: A Sketch*, Redwood City: Addison-Wesley.

WEBER, B. & T. DEACON
2000 "Thermodynamic cycles, developmental systems, and emergence", *Cybernetics and Human Knowing*, 7.1: 21-43.

WEBER, B. & D.J. DEPEW
1999 "Does the second law of thermodynamics refute the neo-Darwinian synthesis?" in P. Koslowski (ed.): 50-75.

Thomas A. Sebeok

ORIGINS: SEMIOSIS THE DOMAIN VS. SEMIOTICS THE FIELD*

> Cognition is simply a development of the selective attitude of an organism toward its environment and the readjustment that follows upon such a selection. This selection we ordinarily call "discrimination", the pointing-out of things and the analysis in this pointing. This is a process of labeling the elements so that you can refer to each under its proper tag, whether that tag is a pointing of the finger, a vocal gesture, or a written word. (Mead 1936: 350)

Throughout Western intellectual history, most semiotic theories and their applications have focused on messages – whether verbal or otherwise – in circulation among human beings, generally within their cultural setting. This kind of semiotic inquiry, characterizable as anthropocentric or, even more circumscribed, as logocentric, has been the rule since ancient times.

A partial if conspicuous, yet until recently by and large undeclared, exception to this tradition has been iatric semiotics, concerned with the arts of healing (symptomatology, diagnostics, prognostics, and the like), practiced and written about by physicians such as Hippocrates of Cos (BC 460-377) – called by many the Father of Medicine but by some also "der Vater und Meister aller Semiotik" (Kleinpaul 1972: 103; on medical theory and sign theory in Pre-Alexandrian times, see Langholf 1990: 57-68, 82-93, 150-164); or the great Neoplatonist Galen of Pergamon (AD 129-c200) (Sebeok 1996). As Baer observed of the Greeks: "Signs [*semeia*] are here construed as bodily clues that allow inferences based on observation" (1988: 47).

Iatric semiotics persevered with numberless modern successors of these venerable figures, to name only a few, through Thomas Sydenham (often called the "English Hippocrates") in the 17th century; F.G. Crookshank, also of London, emphatic about "the necessity to Medicine of a Theory of Signs" (1938: 354); Harley C. Shands, a distinguished New York cardiologist turned bountiful semiotician; F. Eugene Yates, a Los Angeles specialist in medical engineering who contends that science in general "has been permeated with semiotic issues all along" (1985: 359); and a host of other contemporaries.

But no pillar of the medical establishment would more crisply and trenchantly discern and signal a crucial paradigm shift in, or a consistently comprehensive semiotic overview of, the intellectual landscape than Thure von Uexküll [hereafter in this text: Thure]. To be sure, his familial as well as medical credentials are unique. So it is apposite and was presumably perhaps foreordained that he would most explicitly pinpoint *Biosemiotics* as the underlying exemplar for medicine, especially so in its aspect as a natural science concerned with "illness as a disturbance of a complicated physio-biochemical machine" (1982: 206; 1991).

A few years later, he spelled this out further: "The overwhelming majority of objective evidence of a disease belongs to those types of processes taking place within the body, which, in turn, are divided into subsystems (organ systems, organs, tissue, cells, cellular organelles)" (1986: 204). Just as, on the macroscopic level, "evolution depends on setting up new systems of communication" (Jacob 1974: 308), so also within the organism, no less than between the organism and its *Umwelt*. The components listed are among the major participators in the interchange of signs that ceaselessly ebbs and flows on the interior plane; accordingly, the living things are indeed aptly regarded as a web of semioses. In 1976, I tagged such schemes "cybernetic systems within the body" and then termed their operations "endosemiosic" (1985: 3).

By 1993, the conceptual framework for internal somatic sign transactions was comprehensively expanded by Thure and two of his medical associates. Since, as these authors point out, all sign processes within "are indirectly linked to phenomena in the organism's environment...these endosemiotic signs which belong to an 'inner world' have to be translated into the codes of other...sign systems" (1993: 5-7). Such other codes belong to those exosemiosic transactions which were described by means of what Jakob von Uexküll [hereafter in this text: Jakob] named a functional cycle (cf., e.g., 1973: 151-156; see also Thure 1987: 166-169).

"Medicine," as Thure highlighted, was ever "a semiotic discipline" (1992: 455). And, as the historian Carlo Ginzburg pointed out, this "model of medical semiotics or symptomatology," and "the 'semiotic' approach, a paradigm or model based on the interpretation of clues, had become increasingly influential [in the 19th century] in the field of human sciences". But in fact its "roots...were far more ancient." They can be traced to Mesopotamian forms of knowledge and beyond (1983:87-91). The medical crafts should thus be seen as the ultimate cradle of – and a lengthy if tacit prologue as well as a vivid backdrop to – not merely endosemiotics but its comprehensively encompassing domain that has become increasingly known in the last quarter of our century as *Biosemiotics*. This embraces, according to one recent exposition, "all processes that take place in animate nature at whatever level, from the single cell to the ecosystem," as "concerned with the sign aspects of the processes of life itself, not with the sign character of the theoretical structure of life sciences" (Hoffmeyer 1998: 82). In a different but equally valid formulation, "the socio-semiological limits of intentional communication...are largely overcome [by means of biosemiotics] as we are introduced to the global logic of the great ecosystem named Gaia where conceptual boundaries finally open up to the encounter between semiosis and life" (Petrilli 1999: 316). Furthermore, as Thure affirms, biosemiotics remains "of central interest for the biosciences and medicine" (1992: 456; for his most extended relation to-date, cf. 1997; for an early map of this then still ill-defined territory, see the collection by Sebeok and Umiker-Sebeok 1992). In short, the province of biosemiotics coincides in its entirety with that of the biosphere, which, in this context, is tantamount to the "semiosphere" (but in a sense far vaster than in Lotman's usage).[1]

Terminological issues abound, but this is hardly the place to rehearse the attendant philological niceties beyond acknowledging that the very label of this emerging domain of knowledge seems to have been claimed independently – at least twice in the U.S. and once in the former Soviet Union – over the past few decades. What remains important is to corroborate that the *domain* of biosemiotics and the *field* of biosemiotics[2] surfaced a long time *avant la lettre*; and that, furthermore, its ripeness did not just happen in a simple linear progression but surged by fits and starts as a convoluted affair, winding its long but episodic way through at least three successive 20th century iterations: I register these, respectively, with the names of J. von Uexküll [1864-1944], Heini Hediger [1908-1992], and Giorgio Prodi [1928-1987]. In the telling, I must make it clear that I intend to proceed not as a professional historian but rather as an implicated deponent, a predisposed witness, variously involved in the unfolding chronicle. The following account will therefore have an arguably autobiographical tinge

Jakob spent his student days at the University of Dorpat, in Estonia (1884-1888). But all pilgrims' paths eventually lead to Germany – according to the canonical version of his triumphant trajectory – where he became a citizen in 1918, joining (when already in his 60th year)

the University of Hamburg in 1924. He founded and led the Institute for Umwelt-Research there from 1925 to 1940. Although he produced the 1st edition of his *Theoretische Biologie* in 1920, he prepared a thoroughly revised 2nd edition in Hamburg, to appear eight years later then to be posthumously reprinted in 1973. The only English translation, published in 1926, was thus calamitously based on the 1st edition. This circumstance, aggravated by the poor quality of this rendering, alas retarded the appreciation (especially so, deplorably enough, in the Anglo world) of his *Umwelt*-science – and, correspondingly, the flowering of biosemiotics – by about half a century. Thomson, in his review of the English version, chose, ambivalently, to "congratulate Dr. D.L. Mackinnon on her remarkably successful translation of what we know to have been very difficult German. No one but an organically philosophical biologist could have achieved such a conspicuous success. Not the book can ever be easy-reading, in the most lucid translation". Yet, on the other hand, he grouses that "an unnecessary difficulty seems to be raised by the use of difficult terms, which perplex the reader gratuitously" (1927: 419, 415).

I myself first read the book in English in 1936, finding it bafflingly murky; but then I read the 2nd German edition in 1976, and found that, if not pellucid, nonetheless electrifying (Sebeok 1998a: 32-34). Some time later still, this experience led me to instigate and arrange for the publication of two of Uexküll's shorter monographs in English (1982 and 1992).[3]

But long before then, in the mid-1970s, I resolved to investigate Jakob's writings for my own edification, and to look at what others had written about them.[4] These exploratory readings resulted in a paper titled "Neglected Figures in the History of Semiotic Inquiry: Jakob von Uexküll," which I first presented in an abridged version in August 1977 at the III Wiener Symposium über Semiotik (Borbé 1978); the final, much longer version appeared in a book of mine, *The Sign & Its Masters* (1979, 1989: 187-207, 290-291). This chapter, my personal appreciation of Jakob and his principal works, was widely noticed, despite the fact that it was in the main researched and, foremost, composed to educate myself. So one needs to ask: just what did this piece accomplish for my readership? The answer is: it redefined and relocated a nonpareil pioneer investigator of a *domain* (= *Umweltlehre*) and sanctioned his having done so in a *field* (= Biosemiotics) appropriate to and by that time at last receptive of his creative achievement.[5]

Thure was among my audience in Vienna. He reacted to my paper about his father with no cavils, indeed, with enthusiasm. We had an extended talk over an ensuing dinner, in consequence of which, as a next step a few months afterwards, Thure came to call on me at my Bloomington home for a further lengthy evening's discussion. These two talks gave early impetus to, then came to decisively shape, the subsequent unfolding of biosemiotics. Among other things, it was during these initial dinner meetings that the two of us hammered out concrete publication plans in English of several works by both Jakob and Thure himself. Most of these eventually appeared in *Semiotica*, or in other series under the auspices of Walter or Mouton de Gruyter, or were issued by other houses in Germany and the U.S. (Representative items are listed among the References below.)

There were some other far-reaching consequences that flowed from our talks, two among them being especially worth some comments here.

First, the idea of launching a series of annual international conferences devoted to biosemiotics was broached and soon realized by Thure. Repeated about five or six times in the late 80s and early 90s, these were held on the premises of the Glotterbad Clinic for Rehabilitative Medicine in Glottertal, Baden-Württemberg, Germany, under his leadership, with the signal cooperation of Jörg M. Herrmann, M.D., the Clinic's Director. Thure, in his Introduction to one of the sessions, on "Models and Methods in Biosemiotics," succinctly stated the aims: "to support the experiment of bringing together Humanities, represented by semioticians; Natural Sciences, represented by experts in molecular biology; and Medicine, a science with an uncertain position between both of them, represented by internists, psychiatrists, and clinical psychologists." He depicted the topic of the conference as "the proposition of an order in nature which has nothing to do with causality, but which canalizes causal processes between living systems and their environment as well as in and between these systems. We maintain," he concluded, "that this order is a semiotic one or at least can be described in semiotic terms" (1990: 1).[6]

Secondly, Thure made arrangements for me to spend a week or so visiting him in Freiburg (in part intended to coincide with Rowohlt's publication of my German paperback, *Theorie und Geschichte der Semiotik*, where I characterized Jakob as "einer der gröβten Kryptosemiotiker seiner Zeit" [1979: 10].) Our Freiburg discussions about multifarious biosemiotic topics were carried out, with rare intensity, from morning late into every night, and were happily augmented by the continuous participation of Giorgio Prodi, Director of the Institute for Cancer Research of the University of Bologna. Prodi, an astounding polymath (Eco 1988) who had become my friend several years earlier, encountered Thure for the first time on that occasion; the two of them met only twice more, first in Palermo in the Summer of 1984, then the last time in Lucca in the early Fall of 1986 (Sercarz 1988). Prodi sparked the third biosemiotic iteration, to which I shall return below after sketching the second.

One of the sundry riddles that mar the gradual coming into view of modern biosemiotics – the second iteration, if you will – is the neglect of Heini Hediger, whose lifelong attempt to understand animals surely marked a milestone in the elucidation of this domain, providing it with a particularly beneficial empirical footing. This seeming indifference – or is it blindness? – to his capital achievements is the more puzzling in the light of Hediger's manifest admiration for Jakob, whose *Umweltlehre* clearly had a decisive influence on his own highly original analyses of the psychology and biology of animal flight response (or negative territoriality). For instance, touching on his 1932 dissertation and work resulting therefrom, he wrote: "This work was surprisingly successful; it was especially well received by J. von Uexküll at the Institute for Environmental Studies in Hamburg, where I met both him and his successor, F. Brock. For my part, I was extremely impressed by von Uexküll's Umwelt-Lehre... Consequently, I dedicated another paper following that on my flight work, a study of tameness, to von Uexküll...these two subjects formed the basis for my later investigation concerning the relationship between animals and man, especially in the zoo. In addition, they led to the founding of zoo biology..." (1985: 149). Hediger's seminal discoveries of the concepts of individual and social space in application to animals of many kinds were later applied to humans and further fruitfully elaborated under such labels as "proxemics" in anthropology (Hall 1968).

Some years afterwards, I myself discussed nine specific circumstances (among no doubt several others) in which man may have "semiotic encounters" with animals (Sebeok 1988: 68-71). These juxtapositions include taming, training in several interdependent variations (*apprentissage, dressage*, domestication, and the like). My understanding of such procedures was immensely enriched by

Hediger's wealth of experiences in shaping behavior, especially in zoos and circuses. Hediger totally accepted the principles of zoosemiotics – which of course constitutes a substantial segment of biosemiotics – " [the two of us] have been working together for some time" (Hediger 1985: 151; see further his 1980 book, with numerous examples and references under this heading).[7] As he noted, we "often met in Zürich or Amsterdam," and, in 1980, he was my guest in New York City. In all these venues, we frequented zoos and watched the training and performances of animals in circuses, some large enterprises (like Barnum & Bailey) and others small (such as the Swiss Circus Knie). His powers of observation and their subtlety far exceeded mine, so he taught me many things about applied biosemiotics which I could never have learned on my own (see, e.g., his stunning 1974 article, with striking illustrations, on reciprocal semiosis between man and wild animals, viz., panthers, elephants, etc., in the circus). Hediger's appreciation of the quintessentially biosemiotic constitution of the Clever Hans phenomenon was also uncommonly insightful (Sebeok and Rosenthal 1981: 1-17). He foretold "that eventually an explanation for the extremely complex and, so far, underresearched problem of the relationships between man and animals will be obtained by means of signal study or semiotics, specifically zoo-semiotics" (1985: 177). Over all, his legacy is a many-sided, profuse research program for biosemiotics that can easily extend for several generations ahead; (his 1980 book is a veritable treasure house for a research agenda).

Hediger was a visionary innovator who reached from the inside outwards. He felt entirely comfortable within Jakob's *Umwelt* paradigm, but, implicitly, with (zoo)semiotics too, which he came increasingly and quite explicitly to embrace and profitably apply in his later years. Giorgio Prodi, to the contrary, was a maverick: a prolific physician and experimental oncologist by profession, a novelist by avocation, but also an intermittent if resolute contributor to biosemiotics. However radically idiosyncratic, Prodi's recreation of a domain for biosemiotics was with little hesitation matched up with an existing field, or academic niche, a luxury not enjoyed by Jakob and only indirectly so, and only after his mid-60s, by Hediger.[8] His first major book on the subject – which claimed to deal with "la preistoria nelle sue pesanti conseguenze sulla storia e sulla teoria della semiosi" (1977: 5) – was promptly accepted for publication by Umberto Eco; he was asked to deliver a paper on the topic at the Third International

Congress of the IASS in 1984 (1988b); and invited to prepare a long English version of the former to appear in *Semiotica* (1988a). He was also chosen to be a key participant in the 1986 workshop on immunosemiotics, organized by Sercarz and others, where he spoke on "Signs and codes in immunology" (1988: 53-64).[9] Here he took a decided position against "semiotics as a pure human domain," in contrast to his own perspective of "a general semiotic domain," and introduced the notion of a "protosign", which belongs to "proto-semiotics... the basic feature of the whole biological organization" – protein synthesis, metabolism, hormone activity, transmission of nervous impulses, and so on (1988: 63, 55).

More extensively, he labeled the domain, over-all, "natural semiotics" (1988c: 149-170), which seems to be roughly equivalent to mathematician Kergosien's "nature semiotics" (1992: 145), as well as to the phrase "semiotics of nature," occasionally used by Hoffmeyer and Emmeche (1991: 117-118) (but who currently seem to favor "biosemiotics").

In my judgment, these quasi-synonymous terms are poor substitutes for "biosemiotics." There are several reasons for this, some narrow, others broader. The narrow reason is that the word "nature" is used with quite different technical connotations by Jakob, as explicated in Thure's Glossary: "Systematically ordered and complete structure of all UMWELTS whose meaning is sought in overlapping composition" (1987: 236). Yet, at other times, Jakob equated "nature" with "true reality": "Da die Tätigkeit unseres Gemüts das einzige uns unmittelbar bekannte Stück Natur ist, sind seine Gesetze die enizigen, die mit Recht den Namen Naturgesetze führen dürfen" (Jakob 1973: 40).

The over-arching context for biosemiotics is our biosphere in sense of the organic whole of living matter (cf. fn. 2, below); and this is the only geosphere, which contains living matter. Because there can be no semiosis without interpretability – surely life's cardinal propensity – semiosis presupposes the axiomatic identity of the semiosphere with the biosphere. As Short persuasively argued, "there is no basis for the assertion that semiosis occurs outside of living things" (1998: 49) (except, one may add, man's inert extensions, such as automata, computers, or robots). Local nature (Gaia), however, additionally comprehends the inorganic matrix for the place wherein organisms dwell – the enveloping gaseous mass, waters, and rocks; while cosmic nature further includes the totality of extraterrestrial objects (Sebeok 2000).

Another eccentricity of Prodi's is his avoidance of references to the works of others. For example, in his English article, although dealing with intrinsically biosemiotic issues, viz., of "natural semiology" (1988: 206), he cites only Frege and the 1923 edition of Ogden and Richards. While this composition style perhaps adumbrates Prodi's striking originality, it fails to align him with any predecessors or successors in semiotics, so his untutored readers may flounder for lack of familiar signposts. But having said this, it was also the case that, during the week we spent together in our open-ended 1979 "intensive seminar" in Thure's company in Freiburg on the practical and conceivable ins and outs of biosemiotics, the three of us got along extremely well; as I commented afterwards, "this uniquely stimulating experience enabled me to enhance my writing and teachings...in biosemiotics in its various topical subdivisions" (Sebeok 1998b: 34-35).

In 1988, some months after Prodi's untimely death at the age of 59, I received an invitation from the officers of a medical association in his country to attend a sizable memorial gathering at an isolated resort in Southern Italy, where I was to delineate Prodi's contributions to biosemiotics. As it turned out, my fellow participants were all physicians or biologists. His colleagues seemed genuinely respectful of, indeed, fascinated by, the semiotic side of Prodi's scholarly endeavors, yet none publicly declared a commitment to his line of research.

Such appear to me to have been the three principal biosemiotic iterations of our century. But these evidently do not exhaust the prehistory of this domain. Other creative figures could be named (although, arguably, in a minor key): for one, Kenneth Craik [1914-1945], the reclusive don of St. John's College, Cambridge, who independently invented "another kind of *Umwelt* theory" (Craik 1943; see Sebeok 1991: 104); and for another (if perhaps tangentially) René Thom [b. 1923], the mathematician whose catastrophe-theoretical excursions into areas of biological morphogenesis were powerfully impacted by Jakob's theorems of the dynamic of life (Thom 1975, *passim*).

Biosemiotics tends sometimes to be promoted, though I think mistakenly, to contrast with cultural semiotics. But "culture" is not much more than that realm of nature where the logosphere – Bakhtin's dialogic universe – impinges in infant lives then comes to predominate in normal adult lives. Yet in fact even mainstream semioticians range over a wide spectrum of attitudes toward biology. Ernst Cassirer's writings are, for instance, saturated not just by biological intimations – Jakob's impress is palpable throughout (e.g., 1944: 23-26; cf. Thure in

Jakob 1992: 311, fns. 2 and 3). For A.J. Greimas, zoosemiotics looms somewhere in a hazy if rosy future: "it is destined to become a genuine semiotic realm, both autonomous and promising," he once declared (1982: 376). Umberto Eco, who once banished zoosemiotics to "il limite inferiore della semiotica" (1975: 21), now concedes that "in the depth of biological processes lie the elementary mechanisms from which semiosis springs" (in Sercarz 1988: 15). Louis Hjelmslev remains silent on the matter. And so on...

In an attempt to ascertain dispositions in some depth rather than by a mere impressionistic sampling, I was able to persuade an array of colleagues to scrutinize the *oeuvre* of five pre-eminent semioticians of yore – Peirce, Lady Welby, Charles Morris, Roman Jakobson, and Yuri Lotman – "for harbingers of biosemiotic discernments, judgments, prognostications, or at the very least congeniality" (from my Foreword to Hoffmeyer and Emmeche 1999). Readers interested in pursuing the fascinating results of these searches are referred to *Biosemiotica*, constituting Part I of Vol. 130 (1999) of the journal *Semiotica*.[10]

In some crudely simple quantitative terms, biosemiotics can certainly be said to have proliferated over the past decade: for example, as compared to the Sebeok-Umiker volume on *Biosemiotics* (1992), which ran to less than 500 pages, the Hoffmeyer-Emmeche volume *Biosemiotica* (1999), ran to 660 pages; but that was, as well, shortly preceded by another over 250 page double issue of the same journal devoted to a closely kindred topic, "Semiotics in the Biosphere" (Vol. 120 [1998]); plus it is to be closely followed by another volume of *Semiotica* (early in 2001), to be dedicated to the memory, appreciation, and influence of the domain's chief architect, Jakob. Single-author book-length publications in biosemiotics, like Merrell's (1996) or Hoffmeyer's (1993) or Kalevi Kull's (for Mouton, in preparation), are multiplying, as are collections such as the one by Van der Vijver, *et al.*, with yet others in sight. Significantly, new reference books are now routinely graced by separate, sometimes even multiple entries, as in Walter de Gruyter's *Handbook on the Sign-Theoretic Foundations of Nature and Culture* (Posner, *et al.* 1997: 1: 436-591), the Oxford University Press's *Encyclopedia* (Hoffmeyer 1998: 82-85), Icon Books' *Icon Critical Dictionary of Semiotics and Linguistics* (Paul Cobley, ed., 2000), the University of Toronto's *Encyclopedic Dictionary of Semiotics...* (Marcel Danesi 2000), and the expanded 2nd edition of Nöth's *Handbuch der Semiotik* (2000, Section IV). Too, I have already listed (in fn. 6, below) scores of recent conventions on biosemiotics, of diverse sizes and varying composition, assembled at venues over four continents.

It is on the other hand also true that biosemiotics – as general semiotics itself – has not typically become a conventional university-based discipline, nor, in my view, should it have.[11] This is not the place to document, or argue again for, my preference, but it is clear that such formal units of knowledge production are by no means the only possible, let alone the most desirable, type of reputational system of work organization and control. Semiotics, and, *a fortiori*, biosemiotics, is, or should be, a field committed to producing novelty and innovations, not much else. Whitley rightly emphasized (1984: 13) that there exists an "'essential tension' between novelty and tradition, or co-operation and competition," a notable feature of certain kinds of modern scientific works, surely inclusive of biosemiotics. He observed that a "broader and more general social unit of knowledge production and co-ordination is the intellectual field." Such fields, conceived as "relatively well-bounded and distinct social organizations which control and direct the conduct of research on particular topics in different ways," possess identities that are by no means always identical with employment or education unit boundaries. They "vary in the degree of cohesion and autonomy from other [academic] structures, but constitute the major social entities which co-ordinate and orient research across a wide variety of situations.... They reconstruct knowledge around distinct 'subjects' and their organization and change are crucial aspects of intellectual work and knowledge production in the modern, differentiated sciences" (Whitley 1984: 7). By "science," Whitley has of course in mind all forms of modern scholarship, not than just the natural sciences; and each intellectual field, or craftwork, he stresses, "has a distinctive language for describing cognitive objects and communicating task outcomes which reduces lay participation in the assessment of contributions and enables results from different production sites to be compared and co-ordinated" (Whitley 1984: 34). In a useful tabular form, he differentiates between scientific fields, in which biosemiotics obviously belongs under his type (e) (Whitley 158, Table 5.2).

Note that each of our three biosemiotics trailblazers was an intrinsically unconventional academic. Jakob, in support of his consecutive faculty engagements in Germany, was, in addition to his affiliation with the Zoological Center in Naples, particularly active in his own Institute for Umwelt-Research at the University of Hamburg. Hediger was, to be sure, a Professor of Psychology at the University of Zürich, but his concentrated intellectual efforts radiated out of a succession of zoological gardens, first at Dählhölzli (Bern), then Basel, finally, effective 1954, his beloved Zürich Zoo. Prodi, who held the Chair in Experimental Oncology at the University of Bologna's School of Medicine, worked out of his own Instituto di Cancerologia. The functions of these distinctions, which may seem to academic outsiders mere subtle refinements, or frosting atop of a cake, are perfectly understood by professors like me, for I too was the chairman of a Research Center at my institution for 37 years. This is also why the University of Tartu's Jakob von Uexküll Center – a modernized reincarnation (under Kalevi Kull's direction) of the Hamburg prototype – is fraught with such promise of new research departures, supplementing his university's time-honored departmental structures necessarily dedicated to upholding traditional paths of teaching and learning propagation.

An interesting condition specified for the establishment of scientific fields as distinct systems of work organization is that "each field has to control a separate communication system", that is, a benchmark set of shared vocabulary items of its own that differentiates this field from all others as a sort of monopolistic exclusion device (Whitley 1984: 29, 31-32). This is why Jakob's seemingly arcane terminology, often remarked on by biologist commentators and other readers, is so advantageous, even when – or especially because – it provokes an often felt need to have recourse to an accompanying formal Glossary (e.g., in 1982: 83-87). This was pointed out by Thure himself when he insisted that the differences in Jakob's "terminology are not to be regarded simply as a source of difficulty; they may also prove helpful where the various semiotic theories diverge." Here he surely refers to the unavoidable disparities between his father's idiom and Peirce's and Saussure's (1987: 148; see also Krampen 1997: 512).[12]

Although Jakob's research interests in principle encompassed the comportment of *all* organisms, he in fact spun his theory of models and of the attendant functional cycle almost entirely out of his observations of "the worlds of animals and men," particularly marine animals (jellyfish, sea-urchin, octopus, trout) and insects (annelids, ticks, dragonflies). He is therefore justly to be counted among the founders of ethology (Bleibtreu 1968: 13), for this "certainly owes more to his teaching than to any other school of behaviour study" (Lorenz 1971: 277); and many of the phenomena and operational concepts that "gave focus to classical ethology were first described, or at least anticipated" by him (Dyer and Brockman 1996: 529). His design was also commonly used by early investigators of synchronic animal communication processes, as well as for the testing of the hypothesis of "ritualization" – or what I have elsewhere called "the semiosis of *gene-dependency"* – an intriguing special case of diachronic sign science (Sebeok 1989: 29-30, Fig. 2-1). Inasmuch as any animal's communication system must be a natural extension of its sensorium, which invokes an understanding of its *Umwelt*, it is easy to appreciate how indispensable Jakob's insights were to the origins and development of zoosemiotics (Sebeok 1972: 61). Doubtless, the most cited example of the zoosemiotic aspects of Jakob's explorations is his fabled scrutiny of *Ixodes rhitinus*, the cattle tick (whose story Bleibtreu opens his 1968 book with), often revisited, and reinterpreted in a Dresden lecture by Udo Figge as recently as February 1999 in strictly semiotic terms (cf. now Figge 2001).

Hediger had a sweeping yet intimate knowledge of the behavior of an exceptionally wide range of animals – especially terrestrial vertebrates – based on extensive field work as well as acute observations both in and far beyond the zoo. At the very outset of his remarkable book he specifies: "Insbesondere werden wir uns mit der Zoosemiotik zu befassen haben, also mit den Signalen, die zwischen Tieren und besonders zwischen Tier und Mensch in beiden Richtungen wirksam sind, gewissermassen hin und her schwingen." Later he adds: "Der Zoosemiotik bleibt noch ein weites Feld zu bearbeiten" (1980: 10, 144), but already Hediger himself impressively contributed to this field. Following in Jakob's footsteps, he consistently applied both biological and semiotic criteria to the study of animal communication. Jakob did so implicitly, Hediger eventually in quite categorical terms.

Some have suggested that "Biosemiotics has evolved from the study of animal communication to more general considerations of biological codes" (e.g., Peter Cariani in Van de Vijver 1998: 360). This, however, simplifies, even skews, an in truth far more labyrinthian sequence of events culminating in biosemiotics to which zoosemiotics is but one contributing factor (Sebeok 1998: 10). This notwithstanding, zoosemiotics is doubtless "a particularly rich branch of biosemiotics because animals are in some sense semiosic mediators between creation and decay. On a macroscopic scale, they can be viewed as transforming agents fixed midway between the 'composer' plants, organisms that set interpretants in motion, and 'decomposer' fungi, which break them down," viz., between phytosemiosic and mycosemiosic operations. Too, in their role as go-betweens, animals process signs through media embracing the entire sensory spectrum, each – in conformity with Jakob's teachings – according to, but only commensurate with, its specific array of sense organs (Sebeok 1988: 65, 1997: 116).

Others chose to pursue different pathways to stoke the biosemiotic superstructure, an enticing case in point deriving from some casual remarks of Jakob's to the effect that plants lack a function cycle. Krampen has shown the predominance of indexicality in plant semioses, that plants none the less do have feedback cycles connecting sensors and regulators, and how "meaning factors" function in the vegetal (vs. animal) realm – or, in a nutshell, how phytosemiosis differs from zoosemiosis (1981, 1997).

Not surprisingly, the guiding preoccupation of medical practitioners from Hippocrates to our day, notably including both Thure and Prodi, has focused on endosemiosis or "protosemiosis" from the cell to the highest integration level, up to the sphere where the non-conscious inner world may in humans and certain other animals become transmutable, by means of sign connections via neurotransmitters, neurohormones, and other neurobiological processes still far from understood, into consciously experienced reality.[13]

Researches at the ephemerally woven frontiers of biosemiotics – evolutionarily the highest and the lowest planetary limits of which are circumscribed by two suggestive metaphors (both, as it happens, of Canadian vintage) – are of quotidian concern. The upper periphery, a virtual community, was dubbed a *global village* by Toronto' Marshall McLuhan (1962: 31). This electronically mediated global forum, located nowhere on the superhighway called the Internet, is a very real, if volatile, network of networks. It is populated by biomimetic creatures with unconventional communication schemes and emotive manifestations actualized by media embodiments, such as animation, robot languages and robot speech, and text. Regular and occasional users are subject to the vagaries of cybersemiotics (cf. fn. 7, below). (According to a report just issued by the Department of Commerce, 67% of Americans still do not use the Internet.)

The scalar opposite metaphor was coined by Montréal's Sorin Sonea: the *global organism*. Nor did the similitude with the Internet escape him, as he notes: "Like an electronic communications network the bacterial world possesses an enormous data base, in this case in the form of bacterial genes... This biological communications network, which possesses more basic information than the brain of any mammal, functions in a manner that sometimes resembles human intelligence" (Sonea and Panisset 1983: 85). Furthermore, the ensemble of bacteria resemble "a vast computerized communications network – a superorganism whose myriad parts shift and share genetic information to accommodate any and all circumstances" (Sonea 1988: 45). The smallest known autopoietic entity is a single self-maintaining bacterial cell, the "biosemiotic atom."

The analogy is powerful, yet not absolute. While being wired is optional – we, who are nonusers, think we have rational grounds for our skepticism – the global prokaryotic community inescapably perfuses the Earth. In a way that is literally mind-boggling, all of us eukaryotes are fashioned of bacteria; we are both their habitats and vehicles for further dispersal. In particular, our central nervous system may be characterized as a colony of interactive bacteria. For this reason alone, any biosemiotic theory failing to take into account the multiform data of bacterial semiosis is as flawed as would be one that ignored the complexities of the verbal code in its social ramifications (Sebeok 1997: 114).

Notes

[*] This paper exists in three different versions, of which this is the most substantial. The materials on which it was based were both presented orally in two successive, interconnected segments at the University of Dresden respectively in mid-February and on October 8th, 1999, the latter at the 7th Congress of the International Association for Semiotic Studies A ms. with a different emphasis is slated to appear in a collection dedicated to the memory of Jakob von Uexküll (ed. by Kalevi Kull), under the title, "Biosemiotics: its roots, proliferation, and prospects" (2001).

[1] For the contrast between Y.M. Lotman's anthropological usage and V.I. Vernadsky's global usage, see Sebeok 2000.

[2] For this important distinction – which is particularly pertinent to biosemiotics – between "domain" and "field," see Csikszentmihalyi 1986.

[3] Ironically, Klopfer and Hailman wrote of his earliest classic work, the *Umwelt und Innenwelt der Tiere* (1909, 1921), that this has "had relatively little effect on animal behavior studies compared with the great originality of its content" (1967: 126). One reason for this seems to have been that it was far ahead of its time; or, in Csikszentmihalyi's parlance, that there was no field competent in the domain to take control over it: "There are several ways that domains and fields can affect each other. Sometimes domains determine to a large extent what the field can or cannot do... No matter how much a group of scientists would like their pet theory accepted, it won't be if it runs against the previously accumulated consensus" (1996: 44).

[4] That research was in large part conducted at the Netherlands Institute for Advanced Study, where I was a Fellow during 1973-1974.

[5] See again Csikszentmihalyi (1986). Note my continued emphasis on the availability of a responsive field, which was by no means at hand in 1934, when Bühler first recognized the semiotic character of the *Umweltlehre*, "welcher von vornherein in seiner Grundbegriffen 'Merkzeichen' und 'Wirkzeichen' sematologisch orientiert ist" (1965: 27).

[6] Those attending the Glottertal conferences one or more times included, besides many Germans, Swiss, Danes (e.g., Hoffmeyer), Estonians (e.g., Kull), and myself from overseas. A prominent German semiotician whom I remember being there on each occasion was Martin Krampen, who substantiated *phytosemiotics*, i.e., the semiotics of plants, putting this then novel domain on an equal footing with other recognized branches of biosemiotics (1981: 187; see discussion above). A large wind-up gathering in this series was organized in the 90s by Hoffmeyer; this took place in Denmark, with an expanded attendance on the part of Scandinavian semioticians as well as natural scientists. More recent locations for biosemiotics get-togethers (enumerating here only those which I myself was asked to participate in, several repeatedly) were scheduled in Berkeley, Denver, Dresden, Gaithersburg, Imatra, Guadalajara, Las Cruces, Sao Paulo, Tartu, and Toronto.

[7] At the risk of being overcome by terminological surfeit (or vertigo), I can offer the following non-exhaustive rundown – with a basic reference or two – of the currently labeled component branches of biosemiotics that I am aware of: protosemiotics ("the basic feature of the whole biological organization [protein synthesis, metabolism, hormone activity, transmission of nervous impulses, and so on]," cf. Prodi in Sercarz 1988: 55); microsemiotics (in prokaryotes, cf. Sonea 1988, 1990, 1995); cytosemiotics (in cells, renamed microsemiotics by Yates 1997); endosemiotics (in the *milieu intérieur*, Thure 1993); phytosemiotics (plants, cf. Krampen 1981, 1997); zoosemiotics (speechless animals, cf. Sebeok 1972, 1990); mycosemiosis (fungi, Kraepelin 1997); and cybersemiotics (cf. Sebeok 1997: 116; androids, robotics, cyborgs, sensor and muscle augmentation, prostheses [eye-glasses, hearing aids, dentures, artificial limbs, mirrors, etc., cf. Eco 1986: 220-222]). "The new science of pharmacosemiotics" refers to the fact that therapeutic drugs, being atoms and molecules, "convey messages to the complex biochemical systems of a patient by acting as lexical units in a chemical language that can be 'understood" by cells in a living organism" He also introduces the expression "semantic chemistry"(Yates 1998: 86, 92). Anthroposemiotics (speechifying animals) is usually excluded. Exosemiotics has been used in two different senses: as the opposite of endosemiotics, or in passing reference to the sign behavior of putative extraterrestrial creatures.

[8] A reminder: one of the central components of creativity is the *field*, "which includes all the individuals who act as gatekeepers to the domain. It is their job to decide whether a new idea or product should be included in the domain." Publishers and journal editors figure prominently among the "field of experts" who recognize and validate innovation, as are academic administrators, officers of public and private sources of financial support, or, to put it briefly, persons with control over access to critical resources (cf. Csikszentmihalyi 1996: 28, 6).

[9] Tomio Tada's definition of immunosemiotics is: "the study of the general principles underlying the structure of sign systems perceived by different cells of the immune machinery," according to which "restrictions in partner cell interactions must exist as part of an intercellular semiotic system" (Sercarz 1988: vii).

[10] Two among these subjects were my former teachers. To gain a still more rounded historical perspective of this cardinal domain of learning, we hope to arrange for similar probes of writings by other such respected figures, for instance, Susanne Langer.

[11] For glimpses of the relation of semiotics and biosemiotics, see Thure 1998: 2189-2190.

[12] There is no evidence that these three masters of the sign were aware of one another.
The meandering, diffuse arguments at last June's Uexküll-related twin meetings (Tartu, Imatra) over matters of basic terminology underline these points. There were sharp debates about the meaning even of such a pivotal term as *Umwelt* and its correct rendering into English, ranging from such approximations as "perceptual universe," "self-world," or "phenomenal world," to such absurdities as "environment" (but see Immelman and Beer 1989: 88) or "niche." Despite the fact that the closest English equivalent is manifestly "model," the only palpable group consensus reached was the unhelpful surrender, that the German word should be retained in English. Nevertheless, seemingly recondite concerns about technical vocabulary, leading toward a standardized symbol system, tend to reinforce the unity of a field like biosemiotics.
Two marginalia to the *Umwelt* concept may be tentatively ventured here, the first pointing toward the historical past, the second toward the nebulous future.
The relations of Jakob's *Umwelten* to Leibniz's monads are yet to be clarified. I had briefly alluded to this before (Sebeok 1986: 13), pointing out that all living beings are immersed in an "impalpable bubble," delineated and defined by the special possibilities allowed each organism by its unique means of sensual perception; and that such constructs may hark back to Leibniz's fundamental ontological thesis as formulated in his *Monadology* (1714). For Leibniz, monads are embodied in the real world, yet are non-extended – i.e., lacking spatial-temporal parts– hence immaterial entities.
My second observation, much more tenuous (and subject to empirical verification), relates to a recent extension of superstring theory in modern cosmology designed to include vibrating mem*branes* – hence termed *brane theory* (chiefly associated with he names of Lisa Randall and Raman Sundrum; cf. Johnson 2000) – which may have many dimensions. In brane-theory, it is proposed that our universe is just one of many three-dimensional bubbles, or "branes," afloat within a four-dimensional hyperspace. An implication of the theory is the possibility that there are countless brane worlds floating in the megaverse, constituting, as it were, neighboring islands separated by the a fourth-dimensional divide communication, if any, across which could be, if but dimly, sensed.

[13] *On nitric oxide,* that "pantheon of messenger molecules," and so-called "hedgehog genes," cf. Sebeok 1997: 120, fn. 13.

References

BAER, E.
1988 *Medical Semiotics*, London: University Press of America.

BLEIBTREU, J.N.
1968 *The Parable of the Beast: An Exploration of the Frontiers of Biological Knowledge*, London: Gollancz.

BORBÉ, T.
1978 *Semiotik III: Zeichentypologie*, München: Wilhelm Fink.

BÜHLER, K.
1965 [1934] *Sprachtheorie: die Darstellungsfunktion der Sprache*, Stuttgart: Gustav Fischer.

CASSIRER, E.
1944 *An Essay on Man: An Introduction to a Philosophy of Human Culture*, New Haven: Yale UP.

CRAIK, K.J.W
1943 *The Nature of Explanation*, Cambridge: Cambridge UP.

CROOKSHANK, F.G.
1938 "The importance of a theory of signs and a critique of language in the study of medicine", in C.K. Ogden & A. Richards (1938).

CSIKSZENTMIHALYI, M.
1996 *Creativity: The Flow and Psychology of Discovery and Invention*, New York: Harper Collins.

DYER, F.C. & H.J. BROCKMAN
1996 "Sensory processes, orientation, and communication: Biology of the *Umwelt"*, in L.D. Houck and L.C. Drickamer (eds.), *Foundations of Animal Behavior*, Chicago: University of Chicago Press.

ECO, U.
1975 *Trattato di semiotica generale*, Milan: Bompiani.
1986 "Mirrors", in P. Bouissac, M. Herzfeld, and R. Posner (eds.), *Iconicity: Essays on the Nature of Culture: Festschrift for Thomas A. Sebeok on His 65th Birthday*, Tübingen: Stauffenburg.
1988 "Una sfida al mito delle due culture", *Saecularia Nona* 2, January-February, Bologna.

FIGGE, U.L.
2001 "Jakob von Uexküll: 'Merkmale' und 'Wirkmale'", *Semiotica*, 134.

GINZBURG, C.
1983 "Clues: Morelli, Freud, and Sherlock Holmes", in U. Eco and Th.A. Sebeok (eds.), *The Sign of Three*, Bloomington: Indiana UP.

GREIMAS, A.J. & J. COURTÈS
1979 *Semiotics and Language: An Analytical Dictionary*, Bloomington: Indiana UP.

HALL, E.T.
1968 "Proxemics", *Current Anthropology*, 9:83-108.

HEDIGER, H.
1974 "Communication between man and animal", *Image Roche*, 62:27-40.
1980 *Tiere verstehen: Erkenntnisse eines Tierpsychologen*, München: Kindler.
1985 "A lifelong attempt to understand animals", in D.A. Dewsbury (ed.), *Leaders in the Study of Animal Behavior: Autobiographical Perspectives*, Lewisburg: Bucknell UP.

HOFFMEYER, J.
1993 *Signs of Meaning*, Bloomington: Indiana UP.
1998 "Biosemiotics", in P. Bouissac (ed.), *Encyclopedia of Semiotics*, New York: Oxford UP.

HOFFMEYER, J. & C. EMMECHE
1991 "Code-duality and the semiotics of nature", in M.A. and F. Merrell (eds.), *On Semiotic Modeling,* Berlin: Mouton de Gruyter.

HOFFMEYER, J. & C. EMMECHE (EDS.)
1999 *Biosemiotica*, *Semiotica* 130. [Special issue].

IMMELMAN, K. & C. BEER
1989 *A Dictionary of Ethology*, Cambridge: Harvard UP.

JOHNSON, G.
2000 "Physicists finally find a way to test superstring theory", *Science Times,* April 4: D1, 10.

JACOB, F.
1974 *The Logic of Living Systems: A History of Heredity*, London: Allen Lane.

KERGOSIEN, Y.L.
1992 "Nature semiotics: The icons of nature", in Th.A. Sebeok & J. Umiker-Sebeok (eds.).

KLEINPAUL, R.
1972 *Sprache ohne Worte*, The Hague: Mouton.

KRAEPELIN, G.
1997 "Mycosemiosis", in R. Posner, K. Robering, and Th.A. Sebeok (eds.), *Handbuch der Semiotik*, Berlin: de Gruyte, 1.

KLOPFER, P.H. & J.P. HAILMAN
1967 *An Introduction to Animal Behavior: Ethology's First Century*, Englewood Cliffs: Prentice-Hall.

KRAMPEN, M.
1981 "Phytosemiotics", *Semiotica,* 36:187-209.
1997 "Phytosemiosis", in R. Posner, K. Robering, and Th.A. Sebeok (eds.), *Handbuch der Semiotik*, Berlin: de Gruyte, 1.

LANGHOLF, V.
1990 *Medical Theories in Hippocrates*, Berlin: Walter de Gruyter.

LEIBNIZ, G.W.
1898 [1714] *The Monadology and Other Philosophical Writings*, Oxford: Oxford UP.

LORENZ, K.
1971 *Studies in Animal and Human Behaviour*, Vol. 2, Cambridge: Harvard UP.

MCLUHAN, M.
1962 *The Gutenberg Galaxy*, Toronto: University of Toronto Press.

MEAD, G.H.
1936 *Movements of Thought in the Nineteenth Century,* Chicago: University of Chicago Press.

MERRELL, F.
1996 *Signs Grow: Semiosis and Life Processes*, Toronto: University of Toronto Press.

OGDEN, C.K. & I.A. RICHARDS
1938 *The Meaning of Meaning: A Study of the Influence of Language upon Thought and of the Science of Symbolism*, New York: Harcourt, Brace.

PETRILLI, S.
1999 "About and beyond Peirce", *Semiotica,* 124: 299-376.

POSNER, R., ROBERING, K. & TH.A. SEBEOK (EDS.)
1997 *Semiotics: A Handbook on the Sign-Theoretic Foundations of Nature and Culture*, Berlin: Walter de Gruyter.

PRODI, G.
1977 *Le basi materiali della significazione*, Milan: Bompiani.
1988a "Material bases of signification", *Semiotica* 69:191-241.
1988b "La biologia come semiotica naturale", in M. Herzfeld and L. Melazzo (eds.), *Semiotic Theory and Practice*, Berlin: Mouton de Gruyter.
1988c *Teoria e metodo in biologia e medicina*, Bologna: CLUEB.

SEBEOK, TH.A.
1972 *Perspectives in Zoosemiotics*, The Hague: Mouton.
1979 *Theorie und Geschichte der Semiotik*, Hamburg: Rowohlt Taschenbuch.
1985 [1976] *Contributions to the Doctrine of Signs*, London: University Press of America.
1986 *I Think I Am a Verb,* New York: Plenum.
1988 "*Animal* in biological and semiotic perspective", in T. Ingold (ed.), *What Is an Animal?*, 63-76.
1989[2] [1979] *The Sign & Its Masters*, London: University Press of America.
1990 *Essays in Zoosemiotics*, Toronto: Toronto Semiotic Circle.
1991 *Semiotics in the United States*, Bloomington: Indiana UP.
1996 "Galen in medical semiotics", *Interdisciplinary Journal for Germanic Linguistics and Semiotic Analysis,* 1:89-111.
1997 "Global semiotics", in I. Rauch and G.F. Carr (eds.), *Semiotics around the World: Synthesis in Diversity*, Berlin: Mouton de Gruyter.

1998a *Come comunicano gli animali che non parlano*, Bari: Edizioni del Sud.
1998b "The Estonian connection", *Sign Systems Studies*, 26: 20-38.
2000 "The music of the spheres", *Semiotica*, 128:329-337.

SEBEOK, TH.A. & R. ROSENTHAL (EDS.)
1981 *The Clever Hans Phenomenon: Communication with Horses, Whales, Apes, and People*, Annals 364, New York: The New York Academy of Sciences.

SEBEOK, TH.A. & J. UMIKER-SEBEOK (EDS.)
1992 *Biosemiotics*, Berlin: Mouton de Gruyter.

SERCARZ, E.L. *ET AL.* (EDS.)
1988 *The Semiotics of Cellular Communication in the Immune System*, Heidelberg: Springer- Verlag.

SHORT, T.L.
1998 "What's the use?", *Semiotica*, 122:1-68.

SONEA, S.
1988 "The global organism: A new view of bacteria", *The Sciences* 28(4): 38-45.
1990 "Bacterial (prokaryotic) communication", in Th.A. Sebeok and J. Umiker-Sebeok (eds.), *The Semiotic Web 1989*, Berlin: Mouton de Gruyter.
1995 "Oui, les bactérie communiquent!", *Débats Sémiotiques*, l(1):24-37.

SONEA, S. & M. PANISSET
1983 *A New Bacteriology*, Boston: Jones and Bartlett.

THOM, R.
1975 *Structural Stability and Morphogenesis*, Reading: W.A. Benjamin.

THOMAS, T.A.
1927 "Review of J. von Uexküll", *Theoretical Biology*, *Journal of Philosophical Studies*, 2(7):413-419.

UEXKÜLL, J. VON
1973 [1920, 1928] *Theoretische Biologie*, Frankfurt: Suhrkamp. (English tr. *Theoretical Biology*, D.L. Mackinnon, London: Kegan Paul).
1982 *The Theory of Meaning*, Thure von Uexküll (ed.), *Semiotica* 42(1):1-87.
1992 *A Stroll through the Worlds of Animals and Men*, Thure von Uexküll (ed.), *Semiotica*, 89(4):273-391.

UEXKÜLL, TH. VON
1982 "Semiotics and medicine", *Semiotica*, 38:205-215.
1986 "Medicine and semiotics", *Semiotica*, 61:201-217.
1987 "The sign theory of Jakob von Uexküll", in M. Krampen, *et al.* (eds.), *Classics of Semiotics*, London: Plenum Press.
1990 "Introduction to *Models and Methods in Biosemiotics*", Unpublished Manuscript.
1991 "Die Bedeutung der Biosemiotik für die Medizin", *Münchener medizinische Wochenschrift*, 133(41):601-602.
1992 "Varieties of semiosis", in Th.A. Sebeok and J. Umiker-Sebeok (eds.).

1997 "Biosemiose", in R. Posner, K. Robering, Th.A. Sebeok (eds.), *Handbuch der Semiotik*, Berlin: de Gruyter.
1998 "Jakob von Uexkülls Umweltlehre", in R. Posner, K. Robering, Th.A. Sebeok (eds.).

UEXKÜLL, TH. VON ,W. GEIGGES & J.M. HERRMAN
1993 "Endosemiotics", *Semiotica*, 96:5-51.

VAN DER VIJVER, G. *ET AL.* (EDS.)
1998 *Evolutionary Systems: Biological and Epistemological Perspectives on Selection and Self-Organization*, Dordrecht: Kluwer Academic.

WHITLEY, R.
1984 *The Intellectual and Social Organization of the Sciences*, Oxford: Clarendon Press.

YATES, F.E.
1985 "Semiotics as bridge between information (biology) and dynamics (physics)", *Recherches Sémiotiques/Semiotic Inquiry* 5:347-360.
1997 "Microsemiosis", in R. Posner, K. Robering, Th.A. Sebeok (eds.).
1998-1999 "Pharmacosemiotics: on the question of chemical languages", *Recherches Sémiotique/Semiotic Inquiry*, 18-19:79-92.

Maxine Sheets-Johnstone

ON BACTERIA, CORPOREAL REPRESENTATION, NEANDERTALS, AND MARTHA GRAHAM: STEPS TOWARD AN EVOLUTIONARY SEMANTICS

1. Introduction

The purpose of this introduction is threefold: to specify the particular evolutionary approach taken in this essay, to clarify thereby what it means to answer the question of the origin of semiosis from the viewpoint of intact, whole-bodied living creatures – in effect, from the viewpoint of species-specific modes of signification – and to show how this approach is vital to semiotic understandings in ways beyond an approach anchored in a Peircean semiotics. By taking these preliminary steps, I hope to situate the main text of the essay within present-day perspectives on the origin of semiosis.

Living creatures are animate forms geared in bodily meaningful ways to the world about them. They are geared according to the body they are. In the most basic sense, this is what natural selection is all about: those creatures who are most congenially attuned to the particular world in which they find themselves – those who are able actively to make sense of that world in continuously life-enhancing ways – are the creatures who survive and reproduce. But animate forms may also be semantically exploratory and creative; that is, they may create meanings as well as find them ready-made in an already existing world. They may thus affect the course of their evolution by new behaviors that maximize survival and reproductive capacities. Thus, to account for the origins of semiosis, one must account for "signs of meaning in the universe" – to use biologist Jesper Hoffmeyer's apt phrase (Hoffmeyer 1996) – not only as those meanings are found embedded in myriad ways in the world, but as those meanings are newly minted by animate forms themselves in the course of their evolution.

Spelled out in this way, the origin of semiosis demands a broader and deeper base than that offered by philosopher Charles Peirce's system of signs (for an introduction, see Peirce 1991, 1992). It demands this enriched perspective because a consideration of animate forms requires a point of departure different from a logic of signs; it requires a beginning in evolutionary history and the construction of an evolutionary semantics. The starting point from this perspective is not "the sign" but sense-making organisms themselves, in terms of both the bodily ways in which the world is meaningful to them and the bodily ways in which they go about making sense of the world. In each instance, sense-making is tied to animate forms in species-specific ways. It is thus tied to certain bodily conformations, markings, and colorations, certain kinetic dispositions and potentialities, certain sensory capacities and characteristic movement patterns, and so on (Sheets-Johnstone 1999a).

To approach the question of the origin of semiosis in this way is to set the answer within a bona fide epistemological framework. Though certainly pertaining and appealing directly at times to epistemological understandings, Peirce's referential categories have a basically ontological rather than epistemological status: categories rather than experience are the bottom Peircean line. His categorial grid sets the referential or representational record straight, so to speak, and does so according to law-like, ordered semiotic relationships. But the record is set straight at the price of deeper questions of meaning, notably, the living ways in which meanings are experienced and created across evolutionary time. What a phenomenological methodology and perspective allow is a forthright epistemological approach, and this because methodology and perspective are rooted in experience and in analyses of experience. Though characterizing his system early on as a phenomenology,[1] Pierce's system in large measure passes over an experiencing subject in favor of the semiotically known. A Husserlian phenomenology (Husserl e.g., 1980, 1983, 1989), in contrast, requires an account not just of the known – in quite general phenomenological terms, the object *as meant* (e.g., Husserl 1973: 36-37), in Peircean terms, *the sign* as a triadic function – but of the knower, the epistemological subject. It thus elucidates not only so-called contents of consciousness – what it properly recognizes as *objects* of consciousness and a Peircean semiotics recognizes as icon, index, or symbol, or as quality, relation, or synthesis, or finally and more remotely as Firstness, Secondness, or Thirdness, (see e.g., Peirce 1991: 180-85) – but acts and structures of consciousness itself. A concern with the subject of experience directs us naturally to these acts and structures. It does so in the present instance by directing our attention to both the ways in which, and the means whereby, living subjects – animate forms of life – constitute meaning. Animate organisms make sense of their environment at the very least. Within the kingdom Animalia, most make sense of other creatures, at minimum those that are edible and those that are harmful. In some instances, they make sense of their own bodies prior to and/or coincident with these sense-makings (Sheets-Johnstone 1999a). An appreciation of the ways in which and the means whereby meanings are constituted leads to an understanding of how sense-making itself has evolved in the course of evolution and of the diverse ways in which it is fundamental to life.

Though the constitutional facet of Husserlian phenomenology will not be taken up directly,[2] the constitution of meaning is important to recognize. One aspect of its importance is capsulated in primatologist Thelma Rowell's statement that "Once an intention movement has acquired meaning, or predictive value, *and this is a matter of the evolution of the receiver rather than the animal making the movements*, it may presumably come under selection pressure as a signal" (Rowell 1972: 94; italics added). The question of how a displayed-to animal comes to validate the movements or gesture of another as meaningful, how it acquiesces to meaning and thus officially instantiates a particular meaning in the repertoire of the species, is a constitutional question fundamental to the origin of semiosis. It is indeed a basic question within the larger framework of an evolutionary semantics (Sheets-Johnstone 1990, 1999a, 1999b). Of interest in this regard is how questions about origin cut across disciplines. How things come to have the meaning and value they do is a foundational question in phenomenology (Husserl 1970, 1973) and one quintessentially pertinent to understandings of the origin of semiosis in the sense Rowell's statement indicates.[3] As formatively realized over the course of evolution, sense-making has involved the constitution of new interanimate meanings on the basis of new corporeal acts, dispositions, discoveries, developments, and so on. Because in all such instances it is a question of meaning and not reference (or information, for that matter), understandings of the origins of sense-making necessarily require understandings of the living organisms that define natural history, in particular, understandings of the diverse ways in which they both move about in and experience the world.

A final clarification warrants attention. In this essay I draw a distinction between signs and symbols based on progressively more complex forms of responsivity and "agentivity" (to borrow a term from psychologist Jerome Bruner [Bruner 1990: 77]). An evolutionary semantics begins with living subjects – animate forms – not only in the Peircean sense of interpretants and in philosopher Susanne Langer's sense of active subjects who, in a manner akin to the semantically responsive displayed-to animal that Rowell pinpoints, *constructively* respond to the world (Langer 1948), but subjects who, as indicated, themselves actively create meanings, subjects who are creative agents of semantic novelty and change. The acknowledgment of creative as well as responsive subjects necessarily points us in the direction of an evolutionary semantics rather than to an origin of semiosis and this because fundamentally distinct ways of meaning evolved with species-specific forms of life. There is, in other words, not an origin of semiosis but origin*s* of semiosis; as this essay will show, different forms of semiosis evolved coincident with the evolution of a diversity of animate forms. This biological fact of life is true in a particularly strong sense with respect to symbol-making, for symbolization by definition is a creative act: to symbolize means to make one thing stand for another – conceptually, yes, as Langer (1948) would argue,[4] but conceptually not to the exclusion of bodily gestures and acts, or more precisely, to the exclusion of a *kinetic semantics*. We can exemplify the import of semantically creative subjects briefly but clearly by a consideration of anthropologist Terrence Deacon's account of the origin of human language.

Deacon attempts to show continuity from sign to symbol through a Peircean grid: the passage from indexicals to symbols is the result of "unlearning" indexical associations as such, i.e., the one-to-one correspondence between signs and their objects, and seeing them instead as functional units within a single system of symbolic reference, what Deacon terms token-token relationships (Deacon 1997: e.g., 87, 92-93). The problem is that if "[s]ymbols are learned by first establishing... indexical associations" (*ibid.*: 404), then the challenge of accounting for the origin of symbols remains. In broader terms, one cannot account for the origin of human language without accounting for the origin of words, and as Deacon himself seems to recognize, until words are "available" – "Probably not until *Homo erectus* were the equivalents of words available" (*ibid.*: 407) – words are not available. Indeed, they are not available until they are invented, and they are not invented until they are created by individuals who are aware of themselves both as sound-makers and as potential creators of sound (Sheets-Johnstone 1990, 1999a).[5]

This very problem threads its way through Deacon's account of language-learning by chimpanzees. However insightful and compelling his account, Deacon cannot properly make the analogy from chimpanzees to early humans precisely because in the latter instance, the invention – the *creation* – of linguistic symbols must be accounted for. Talk about teaching[6] and learning[7] "symbolic relationships" as Deacon does with respect to chimpanzee language-learning is not enough: again, until words are available, words are not available. Thus, however clear the case with respect to Kanzi and other chimpanzees for whom the learning of indexical associations was "kept up until the complete system of combinatorial relationships between the symbols was discovered" (*ibid.*: 402), the same case cannot be made for early hominids for whom there was no ready-made symbolic system, i.e., verbal language, and hence no ready made symbolic "combinatorial relationships" to be rehearsed over and over again to the point that a symbolic system of reference "was discovered."

A further point warrants mention. All the selection pressures in the world will not invent language. Neither will any particular kind of brain. What is wanted are living subjects. At some point, it is necessary to bring to the fore intact, whole-bodied organisms, animate forms, the actual creatures who themselves created verbal language by creating symbols that were not simply referential tokens but semantically rich sounds. Deacon's account of the origin of symbolic reference does not extend this far,[8] and the basic problem goes unacknowledged to the end. Even so, Deacon appears marginally aware of the problem when, toward the end of his book, he makes two startling and confounding statements. He declares that "The origins of the first symbolic communication have nothing intrinsically to do with language per se" (*ibid.*: 408-409) and that "The argument I have presented is only an argument for the conditions which required symbolic reference in the first place" (*ibid.*: 409), the conditions being basically the need for a marriage agreement which would cement a male provisioning and female reproductive arrangement. His second statement regarding the narrowness of his argument comes as a double surprise to the reader since *the origin of symbolic reference, not its original conditions*, has been at the forefront from the beginning, and since missing, but at the heart of the conditions he spells out, are living subjects. The first statement is doubly puzzling because, on the one hand, symbolic communication has similarly been at the forefront from the beginning and because, on the other hand, language in its social, communicative function has been the only linguistic function of concern. In sum, Deacon's "symbolic species" falls short of explaining the origin of symbols because it falls short of explaining the invention of something semantically new. In the absence of living subjects, there are no originating agents of semantic novelty and change.[9]

2. On bacteria

Stephen Jay Gould observed that:

> If we must characterize a whole by a representative part, we certainly should honor life's constant mode. We live now in the 'Age of Bacteria'. Our planet has always been in the 'Age of Bacteria', ever since the first fossils – bacteria, of course – were entombed in rocks more than three and a half billion years ago. (1996: 176)

Semiosis has a history in the life of living forms all the way back to bacteria. Accordingly, I begin with a description of the way in which bacteria move in recognition of their surrounds, namely, through surface recognition sensitivity, a fundamental biological capacity. Consider the following description taken from a standard biology text:

> Processing in a bacterium may be thought of as a sort of molecular polling... the positive 'votes' cast by receptors in response, say, to increasing concentrations of a sugar are matched against the negative votes produced by increasing concentrations of noxious compounds. On the basis of this continuous voting process, the bacterium 'knows' whether the environment, on the whole, is getting better or worse. The results of this analysis appear to be communicated by electrical signals to the response centers. The final stage, the response, consists of a brief change in the direction of rotation of the several stiff, helical flagella that propel the bacterium. The result is that the bacterium founders briefly and then strikes out in a new direction, once again sampling to see whether the environment is improving or deteriorating. (Keeton and Gould 1986: 452)[10]

Surface recognition sensitivity is a more precise way of characterizing what the text identifies as responsivity.[11] Surface recognition sensitivity is in the service of movement, movement toward and away from things in the environment. The sensitivity is essentially a *tactile* sensitivity; bacteria sample the environment through direct contact, by literally bumping into it, finding either propitious or noxious molecules in the process. While surface recognition sensitivity is commonly spoken of by scientists in terms of "mechanoreception" (Laverack 1976: 17), as if the organisms in question were machines, from the viewpoint of living forms, the sensitivity is more appropriately specified as a form of *tactile*-reception. The protozoan ciliate species *Stentor*, for example, uses its cilia to sweep away noxious particles and the *Stentor* itself bends away from the tactile disturbance (Curtis 1975: 311). Tactility in the service of movement, of recognizing something outside one's own body and moving accordingly, similarly describes the cilia-mediated tentacle movement of a sedentary hydrozoan polyp toward a food source. At the most fundamental level, organisms recognize particular things in their environment by touching them, and in touching them, pursue a certain course of action. To state the same biological truth from an opposite, Peircean-colored perspective, we can say that the world is replete with signs that signify for particular organisms depending on their surface sensitivities.

When biologist Jakob von Uexküll (1957) spoke of objects in an organism's *Umwelt* having particular functional tones – of an object being perceived as something to eat, for example, or something to shun, or something to climb, and so on – he implicitly acknowledged just such a relationship, what we may term a *kinetic semiotics*, the tone being created and established through a creature's possible movement in relation to the object. The basic dimension of a kinetic semiotics is surface recognition sensitivity. I might note that in acknowledging this signifying relationship between organism and surrounding world, von Uexküll gave a near Husserlian or phenomenological account of an object in that an object's functional tone is an aspect of *the object as meant* (Husserl 1973: 36-37), the object in terms of what it signifies to the perceiver.

3. Morphological corporeal representation

From a compound semiotic-evolutionary perspective, surface recognition sensitivity is related to corporeal representation,[12] *morphological* corporeal representation, or the formal means whereby one animal recognizes another as being of a certain age, as being male or female, and so on. Bodily conformations, patternings, and colorations signify. Biologist Adolf Portmann wrote of this morphological semiotics, though not terming it such. He described the way in which animals such as wild pigs and plovers recognize another's age and social status by its external patternings and colorings (Portmann 1967: 152, 156, 158, 159). He spoke explicitly of *form production* in this context, exemplifying across a vast range of species how an individual's bodily coloring, shape, conformations, and/or patternings are visually meaningful. In all such instances, Portmann affirmed, "form production may be termed *sematic*, since it has a striking, signal-like effect" (*ibid.*: 115). By the term *sematic* – not to be confused with *semantic* – Portmann means precisely a sign, not a symbol, function.[13]

It is important to emphasize that these built-in meanings of animate form derive not from what a particular animal does but directly from its morphology – its shape, conformations, patternings, and colorings as these formal features change or remain constant over time. It is thus understandable not only why Portmann conceived and subtitled his study "a study of the *appearance* of animals" – shape, conformations, patternings, and colorings are striking *visual* phenomena – but further, why his delineation of the inherently meaningful appearance of animate forms may be defined as morphological corporeal representation, and further, why morphological corporeal representation may be related to surface recognition sensitivity. The latter phenomenon specifies a tactile recognition of features and objects of the environment, as illustrated not only by bacteria and the protozoan ciliate *Stentor*, as we have seen, but by a locust's sensitivity to air currents, for example, and a spider's sensitivity to an object landing on its web; in these instances too, tactility is the primary sensory modality, a modality in the service of movement. Morphological corporeal representation specifies a different primary sensory modality, a modality also in the service of movement, but movement in relation to conspecifics. Concisely stated, surface recognition sensitivity is tied to tactility and to environmental features and objects; morphological corporeal representation is tied to vision and to other living creatures. In the one instance, the semiotic articulates a tactile organism-environment relationship; in the other instance, the semiotic articulates a visual organism-organism relationship.

Especially in the context of a morphological semiotics, it warrants mention that inquiries and studies of organic form[14] have all but disappeared. The pervasive concern in present-day Western science is not with morphology but with brains, and furthermore, not with meaning but with information. Bruner (1990), in tracing the rise of cognitivist science, has written eloquently of the displacement of meaning. Even without his narrative, one can readily appreciate how, with the shift to information, the epistemological terrain shifts: a concern with meaning gives way to a concern with mechanisms. Accounts of living creatures as living creatures – animate forms – and accounts of life as it is lived by living creatures – forms of life – become grist for mechanistic mills. Since a descriptive literature is no longer of value in itself nor directly relevant to an understanding of life, semiosis – the process of reading the environment and the process of reading other organisms – virtually disappears as a topic of concern within mainstream cognitivist science. When descriptive studies such as those of von Uexküll and Portmann are excised, however, so also is a critical dimension of biological research, namely, research into origins. We might recall that George Wald, Nobel prize-winning physiologist in 1967, remarked that there are three fundamental questions in biology: where does it come from? how does it work? what is its survival value? Contemporary cognitivist studies in Western science and philosophy are tethered almost exclusively to the second and third questions, thus on delineating causal relationships and specifying adaptive value. In these endeavors, explanation reigns supreme; description is minimal. To work back to origins and to trace the history of a biological phenomenon, however, requires detailed descriptions, precisely as Darwin's observational record of his travels aboard the Beagle decisively shows. Short of these detailed observations, the entire field of biology would in fact collapse; the observations are the backbone of evolutionary theory and evolutionary theory is the glue that holds the whole of biology together.

Study of the origins of semiosis from an evolutionary perspective necessarily involves the study of organic form, for organic form is a source of meaning. Indeed, a study of the origin of semiosis should eventuate in a descriptive account of how it is that organisms first came to read each other in meaningful ways. Morphological corporeal representation is an initial step toward this end. The term "reading," I might mention, is only partially used in a metaphoric sense. The etymology of *read* includes both the sense "to discern" and the sense "to discover the meaning or significance [of something]." Surface recognition sensitivity and morphological corporeal representation are both semiotic markers in this respect, markers that, we might explicitly note, are not extinct any more than bacteria or wild pigs are extinct.

4. Kinetic corporeal representation

The semiotic significance of tactility and vision is apparent in a further form of corporeal representation, one that is kinetic rather than morphological and symbolic rather than sematic. In this kinetic form of representation, animate bodies symbolize the spatio-kinetic dynamics of their own kinetic/tactile-kinesthetic experiences – or neuro-muscular corollaries thereof. The honey bee dance is a classic instance. The distance and direction of a sugar source, knowledge of which is conveyed by a dancing bee through her movement, is rooted in the dancing bee's tactile-kinesthetic experience of flying to the sugar source. Whether humanlike tactile-kinesthetic experience is characteristic of the bee or not is beside the point. There is a spatio-kinetic similarity between the actual flight of the bee and the dance by which she represents her flight. The similarity is one in which kinetic experience is iconically linked to spatio-kinetic correlates. This is true not only with respect to the bee's bodily orientation to the sun in her actual flight and her correlative orientation to gravity in her symbolic rendition of the flight, but with respect to other aspects of movement that strikingly point up the role of tactile-kinesthetic elements further. For example, if the flight is experimentally made more arduous, the dance reflects the greater effort; if the sugar concentration is high – basically a tactile datum – the vigorousness of the dance is greater. An iconic relationship clearly exists between tactile-kinesthetically experienced meanings and tactile-kinetically represented meanings. The tactile-kinesthetic dynamics of actual corporeal activity serve as a semantic template for the spatio-kinetic dynamics that constitute the dance.

We see a similar form of kinetic representation in the tongue-flicking behavior of female howler monkeys. As described by C. R. Carpenter, whose world-renown field studies seventy years ago established the basis for much of the subsequent work in nonhuman primate social behavior, the tongue-flicking behavior leaves no doubt but that tactile-kinesthetic analogues function symbolically. Carpenter (1963: 49-50) describes the behavior as follows:

> When approaching a male, [the female] will form an oval opening with her lips and her protruding tongue will rapidly oscillate in and out and up and down. It is clear to an observer... that the function of this gesture is to invite copulation... In a real sense the act is symbolic of sexual desire and readiness for copulation in the female and it stimulates appropriate responses in the male.

Tongue and mouth are in this instance[15] sexual analogues of male and female genitalia respectively. They are sexual analogues in the behavior of other primates as well. The tongue-smacking of some monkey species, especially *Macaca nemestrina* (Pigtailed macaque) in mating situations, is equally indicative of the genital/oral relationship (van Hooff 1969), for example, and in present-day hominids there is evidence of genital symbolization in the sexual tongue-flicking behavior of the !Ko Bushmen (Eibl-Eibesfeldt 1974). Even a ram, in his attempts to interest a ewe in being mounted, flicks his tongue in and out of his mouth as he thrusts his head forward, sidles up to, and nudges a ewe – as any sheep farmer will attest.

In sum, where interanimate meanings are represented, animate bodies represent them corporeally. In both their form and their movement, animate bodies are potential semantic templates. This is why a psychology, aesthetics, archaeology, and linguistics of symbolizing behaviors is possible – why pears and mountains can be interpreted to represent female breasts and umbrellas and tree trunks can represent penises, as in Sigmund Freud's psychology of dreams (Freud 1938, 1953); why traditional works of art can be understood as symbols, their dynamic forms being logically congruent to the dynamic forms of human feeling, as in Langer's analysis of aesthetic form (Langer 1953); why archaeological artifacts in their design features can be interpreted as representations of female and male genitalia, as in archaeologist André Leroi-Gourhan's analysis of paleolithic cave art (Leroi-Gourhan 1971); and why the articulatory gestures of primordial language can be shown to be tactile-kinesthetic analogues of their referents, as in anthropological linguist Mary LeCron Foster's analysis of the symbolic structure of primordial language (Foster 1978, 1994a, 1994b, 1996). In view of the commonly privileged status of human language, I will use the latter example – primordial language – to specify further the symbolic nature of kinetic corporeal representation, showing how, as with the honey bee dance, the articulatory gestures of primordial language were not arbitrary gestures but iconic counterparts of their referent.

5. Kinetic corporeal representation and the origin of language

Foster's global reconstruction of linguistic root forms demonstrates that primordial language was anchored in tactile-kinesthetic experience, an articulatory gesture being in each instance iconic with respect to its referent. For example, all root forms with *m* refer to some kind of bilateral relationship – "the fingers or hands in taking or grasping," or "two opposed surfaces in tapering, pressing together, holding together, crushing, or resting against" (Foster 1978: 110). The bilateral relationship is in each case isomorphic with the bilateral articulatory gesture that produces the sound *m*. Moreover as the examples suggest, and as Foster points out, meanings in primordial language tend to focus on "motional-relational complexes" rather than on discrete objects (Foster 1978, 1996). In just the same way, the honey bee dance represents not an objectified geographical location, or even an object per se, but *how far* and *in what direction* a sugar source is in relation to "home." In other words, primordial language was not a matter of *naming*, but a matter of indicating spatial relationships and bodily movement in relation to space. *Kinetic corporeal representation* indicates as much: it articulates a dynamic rather than static semantics; it is an analogically rather than arbitrarily formulated semantics; and it is a relational rather than object-tethered semantics.

There are further commonalities with the honey bee dance that warrant consideration. Representation in primordial language as well as in the honey bee dance is *meta*corporeal. The iconic articulatory gestures are in each instance a spatio/tactile-kinesthetic transcription of worldly experience or activity. That is, they specify something out in the world apart from the body yet iconically related to corporeal kinetic experience. This is of course immediately apparent in the case of the honey bee dance. But it is also apparent in the case of primordial language. The bilateral relationships *resting against, pressing together*, or *crushing*, for example, are primordial perceptual meanings anchored in what might aptly be termed *primordial bodily experiences*: *resting against* nest materials in sleeping or the earth in standing; *pressing together* in copulating or in producing the sound *m*; *crushing* in chewing food or pounding one thing with another. In effect, root forms of language were anchored in correlative root bodily experiences. Where the bees' dance and primordial language differ is in both mode of articulation and mode of communication. In a honey bee's dance, articulation is of the whole body and what is communicated is transmitted in a whole-body tactile-kinetic manner from dancer to potential recruit (in what linguist Philip Lieberman in a primatological context terms a "whole body gestural system"; see Lieberman 1983). In primordial language, articulation is of the supralaryngeal parts of the body and what is communicated is transmitted not tactilely, through intimate body-to-body contact of articulatory parts, but aurally, through a distinctively *second* sensory modality. Communication is in the one instance directly by way of the tactile-kinetic gestures themselves, and in the other instance, by way of the sounds the gestures create.

In each instance, however, articulatory gestures constitute meanings. What is interesting in this regard is that studies of human speech show that speech perception is actually speech *apperception*. The listener makes co-present with aural perception something that is not actually given in the perception, namely, the articulatory gestures that make the sound: "The listener responds as though he is interpreting the acoustic signal in terms of the articulatory gestures that a speaker would employ to generate the word" (Lieberman 1975: 535; see psychologists Alvin Liberman and Ignatius Mattingly 1985 for a detailed and more recent account of the research on which Lieberman's statement is based). There is thus a *tactile-kinesthetic decoding of speech*. From this perspective, the ultimate difference in mode of sensory communication between the honey bee dance and primordial and present-day human language is the difference between *actual tactile-kinetic* experience and *apperceived tactile-kinesthetic* experience, that is, between a recruit's actual tactile-kinetic experience of a dancing bee's movement and a listener's apperceived tactile-kinesthetic experience of a speaker's speech.

Now short of species-specific tactile-kinesthetic invariants, there could be no such intercorporeal communication. The honey bee dance, primordial language, the tongue and mouth movements of female howler monkeys, and all other forms of kinetic corporeal representation would in each instance be meaningless to the animal to whom the semantically-laden kinetics was addressed. This is precisely the import of primatologist Stuart Altmann's concept of *comsigns* (Altmann 1967). What the term *comsign* pinpoints is the fact that most primate signals are part of the repertoire of *all* members of the species or particular group in question, at the very least for some period in each animal's life. What is true of primates is in this instance also true of bees.

Potential recruits are potential dancers because tactile-kinesthetic invariants anchor interchangeability.

Before going on to show the relationship of tactile-kinesthetic invariants and iconicity to analogical thinking, I would like to interpose a question alluded to earlier: how are new interanimate meanings minted? In particular, how is it that one individual knows what another individual means when the latter individual does something the former individual has not seen done before? This question arises when we think seriously about the fact that it is the perceiving rather than acting individual who solidifies meaning. An individual can, after all, gesticulate or make all kinds of sounds for that matter, but unless and until the individual on the perceiving end responds, and responds in a way coincident with the intended meaning of the gestures or sounds, the intended meaning goes unrecognized. The passage from Rowell cited earlier makes this very point: unless and until the receiver certifies meaning, the gestures or sounds will not enter the communicative repertoire of the species or group in question. In Altmann's terms, the gestures or sounds will not become a comsign. The question of how a displayed-to animal comes to validate the movements or gestures of another as meaningful is thus of critical importance. A particularly graphic example will serve to highlight the possible complexity of a new interanimate meaning. The example comes from a book titled *Primate Cognition*.

> [T]he initiation of play often takes place in chimpanzees by one juvenile raising its arm above its head and then descending on another, play-hitting in the process. This then becomes ritualized ontogenetically into an 'arm-raise' gesture in which the initiator simply raises its arm and, rather than actually following through with the hitting, stays back and waits for the other to initiate the play, monitoring its response all the while...If the desired response is not forthcoming, sometimes the gesture will be repeated, but quite often another gesture will be used. In other situations a juvenile was observed to actually alternate its gaze between the recipient of the gestural signal and one of its own body parts; for example, one individual learned to initiate play by presenting a limp leg to another individual as it passed by (an invitation to grab it and so initiate a game of chase), looking back and forth between the recipient and its leg in the process. (Tomasello and Call 1997: 244)

The gesturing chimpanzee clearly intends a meaning, but why should the presentation of a limp leg and a direct gaze at a passing individual constitute an invitation to play chase? From the point of view of validated meaning, the question is more properly formulated in terms of the addressed individual, i.e., in terms of *how* the gestures come to be perceived as meaningful, and it is answerable precisely in terms of the fact that *validated* meanings are rooted in species-specific kinetic capacities, dispositions, and possibilities. An addressed individual comes to validate meaning on the basis of a fundamental kinetic/semantic relationship that is not arbitrary but iconic, a relationship based on a formal similarity between movement and meaning. In the present instance, the relationship is compound and might be glossed as "legs are to chasing as eye contact is to inviting." What grounds the compound relationship is a common body and a common body of movement linking the two individuals. In effect, an answer to the question "how?" rests on an acknowledgment of the corporeal underpinnings of comsigns. In the most fundamental sense, one body understands another body to the degree it not only resembles that body, but moves and gestures, or has the possibility of moving and gesturing, in ways similar to the ways in which that body moves and gestures; a body that, accordingly, has perceptual experiences that consistently combine certain tactile-kinesthetic/affective feelings with certain contextually situated kinetic-visual or kinetic-auditory or kinetic-tactile awarenesses. Meaning is thus in the most fundamental sense corporeally structured; it is articulated along the lines of species-specific bodies.

At minimum, tactile-kinesthetic invariants predispose organisms toward iconicity since the most easily formulated, consistently utilizable, and readily understood symbols are those structured in bodily movements and experiences shared by all members of the species – like the pressing together of lips to produce the sound *m*. It is important to emphasize, however, that the foundational disposition toward iconicity, as toward corporeal representation itself, is not necessarily a conscious disposition, nor are any of the associated kinetics necessarily consciously planned and executed. At the most basic level, tactile-kinetic symbols are structured not in reflective acts – such as "I think I'll make up a symbol" – but in prereflective corporeal experience; that is, they are the spontaneous product of certain species-specific bodily experiences. What Freud said of the dreamer is thus likely true of the symbolizing animal: "The dreamer's knowledge of symbolism is unconscious" (Freud 1963: 148). But while the symbolizing animal is, like the dreamer, unaware of its symbolizing behavior *as such*, *unlike the dreamer*, it is not unaware of its behavior. It is conscious of its own actions; it experiences its own body; it experiences its own appetites, desires, and proclivities toward movement and meaning. Its thinking is tied to these experiences, which are essentially kinetic experiences. A disposition toward iconicity is thus a disposition toward analogical thinking. To say that analogical thinking is at the root of kinetic corporeal representation is in turn to identify a process of thinking in which what is thought is thought along the lines of the body. Analogical thinking is foundationally a process of thinking not in words but in movement. Analogical thinking as a *reflective* act is an elaboration of this basic dispositional capacity.

In sum, kinetic symbols are spontaneously formed analogues of tactile-kinesthetic experience. They are anchored in the tactile-kinesthetic perceptual lives of the creatures and species concerned. That they are structured in prereflective rather than reflective acts is substantiated not only by studies of speech perception and by the honey bee dance but by Carpenter's untroubled interpretation of a female howler's tongue-flicking gesture: "It is clear to an observer who has seen this series of events," Carpenter writes, "that the function of this gesture is to invite copulation" (Carpenter 1963: 49). Carpenter was not puzzled by the behavior nor did he have to analyze it painstakingly either to determine its meaning or to justify that meaning to his readers. On the contrary, his brief verbal description suffices to convey immediately to the reader the same unequivocal meaning the actual behavior embodied for him in the flesh. Correlatively, our ready understanding of his description is a validation of our own basic and well-nurtured capacity to think analogically along the lines of our bodies and in turn, to think in movement (Sheets-Johnstone 1990, 1994, 1999a, 1999b). No one taught us to think in these ways. We think quite naturally along the lines of our bodies and in movement. By this very token, we can understand why a male howler monkey understands the behavior of a tongue-flicking female howler monkey: he too knows without instruction of any kind "that the function of the gesture is to invite copulation." Were this not so, the gesture would hardly "stimulate appropriate responses in the male."

That primordial language was structured analogically along the lines of the body should give pause for thought. Received wisdom urges us to think that language is made up of vocal sounds that are arbitrarily formed and arbitrarily linked to objects in the world, and that naming things and naming them by way of arbitrary sounds is the crowning mark of humans. However brief, the foregoing evolutionary perspective – from precambrian semiosis to morphological and kinetic corporeal representation – challenges the wisdom of this view. More than that, it challenges the empirical evidence – or in truth, lack of evidence – for this view. Indeed, taking a cue from Gould and Lewontin's critique of adaptationist stories with its cautionary emphasis against taking present-day utility of a trait or behavior as reason for its origin, we may similarly issue a cautionary note against taking the arbitrary counters of present-day human languages as the defining feature present at the origin of human language. Foster's comprehensive studies of languages worldwide point us in an exactly opposite direction and present us with a formidable array of evidence supporting the conclusion that the symbolic structure of primordial language was through and through analogical; particular meanings followed along the lines of the bodily dynamics constituted by particular articulations of the supralaryngeal tract.[16]

6. Neandertals

We can contrast the evidence for and the rigor of these findings – and in fact the whole of the foregoing evolutionary perspective concerning the origins of signs and the origin of symbols – with anthropologist Christopher Stringer and archaeologist Clive Gamble's thesis that symbols "arose with the flick of a switch," notably with the advent of *Homo sapiens sapiens* (Stringer and Gamble 1993: 203).[17] Their thesis is stated in the context of their investigation of Neandertals, specifically, in the context of their answer to the question of whether Neandertals are close kin or distant relatives. Their bias against Neandertals precludes not only a just evaluation of Neandertals; it precludes their own ability to think clearly and cogently both about symbols and how symbols arose. Their claim that symbols arose with the advent of modern humans is buttressed by the claim that the campsites of modern humans *were symbols*, that the tools of modern humans *were symbols*, and so on, and that such "symbolic behavior," as they term it, is antithetical to mere survival behavior, the behavior that they say characterizes Neandertals.[18] They state that "arranging symbolic behavior according to symbolic codes" defines the onset and nature of symbolism, and that "Symbolism involves making mental substitutions and appreciating associations between people, objects and contexts" (*ibid.*).

Now to begin with, to speak of campsites and tools as "symbols" generates conceptual muddles. What is a campsite a symbol of? The answer is nowhere to be found in Stringer and Gamble's account. The same may be said for tools crafted by modern humans; how they function as symbols is nowhere elucidated. When put to the test – *cashed in for real currency* – the words making up their claims fail to deliver. This is because campsites themselves are not symbols nor are items such as tools that are found within them, nor are what Stringer and Gamble designate "patterns of settlement" or "new habitats." These constructions achieve symbolic status only on the basis of *being currently read as symbols*; that is, they are symbols only from the interpretive perspective of Stringer and Gamble – and others – who read them as *symbols* of intelligence. Pits used for the storage of fuel at a campsite, for example, or stacked mammoth bones that form a hut (Stringer and Gamble 1993: 204), are not symbolic of anything. They refer to something beyond themselves only in the sense of referring to what Stringer and Gamble (and others) specify as "intelligence." Pits and huts may indisputably be regarded ingenious constructions, extraordinarily clever utilizations of the environment, and so on, but such positive regard does not make them symbols nor can it confer symbolic status upon the behavior of their makers. When Stringer and Gamble write that "architecture now embodies cultural, symbolic behaviour and not purely expedient survival behaviour" (*ibid.*: 204), they are confusing their own judgments with that which they are judging. Their attributions are conceptually muddled because they are projections of their evaluations and not descriptive of the things themselves. Their denigrating judgment of Neandertal language is indeed a classic case in point. After remarking that Neandertals "no doubt spoke, albeit simply and probably slowly" they write that "Neanderthals lacked complex spoken language because they did not need it" (*ibid.*: 217). Such judgments not only fail to elucidate the individuals we call Neandertals and to tell us anything about symbols and the origin and nature of human speech; they fail to be rational judgments in that no evidence is provided to substantiate them.

A crucially significant aspect of symbolizing activity can only remain hidden in these circumstances, namely, the variable relationship between analogical thinking and symbolization. Symbolization is fundamentally a form of analogical thinking, and analogical thinking is fundamentally structured in corporeal representation, representation that may or may not result in symbolization. In other words, analogical thinking does not *necessarily* eventuate in the production of symbols. Analogical thinking is basically a form of thinking that generates understandings on the basis of bodily experience, and these understandings may or may not eventuate in the production of symbols. Stone tools in fact provide an excellent example of how analogical thinking may *not* eventuate in the production of symbols.

That stone tools are an instance of analogical thinking is consistently attested to by anthropologists and archaeologists who, writing of the origin of stone tools, regularly state that stone tools replaced teeth; that is, like teeth, stone tools crush, tear, scrape, pierce, and so on.[19] That stone tools were functionally fashioned in the image of teeth, however, does not make them symbols of teeth; it makes them only analogues of teeth. But they are corporeal analogues in a further sense as well. The further analogy is implicitly adumbrated by anthropologist Paul Mellars in his article, "Technological Changes across the Middle-Upper Palaeolithic Transition: Economic, Social and Cognitive Perspectives." Mellars notes that "over large areas of Europe, the major changes in both the anatomy of the human populations, and the technology of the associated archaeological assemblages, can be shown to have occurred over at least broadly the same range of time – i.e., broadly between c. 40 000 and 30 000 BP" (Mellars 1989: 338; note: BP means "before the present"). The idea that morphology and technology are linked is in fact strongly suggested to any perceptive and non-Cartesian-thinking reader who compares two illustrations that Mellars includes in his article, one of European Neandertal (French Mousterian) tools, one of European modern human (Châtelperronian/Early Perigordian) tools. The former tools are squat, bulky, indeed, *robust* tools; the latter are lithe, elongate, indeed, *gracile* tools. With respect to bodily form the former tools were created more in the image of a body's bulk than in the image of its linear contours; the latter tools more in the image of a body's linear contours than in the image of its bulk. An analogical corporeal-lithic relationship is palpable in each instance.

Yet the archaeological situation is more complex than Mellars's illustrations of Western European artifacts indicate and would have us believe. Neandertals and modern humans, for example, produced essentially the same lithic technology in the Levantine Mousterian (Near East area, approximately 40 000 to 200 000 B.P), Neandertals actually producing a preponderance of blade tools – spear points – in comparison with those produced by modern humans (Shea, pers. com.; see Shea 1997, 1998 on Levantine spear point use by Neandertals).[20] Yet such evidence does not countermand a corporeal-lithic relationship. The corporeal-lithic analogy specifies a *basic* formal correspondence between body and tool. When stone tools are made, they are geared to do a certain kind of work. The work they do is contingent on ecological circumstances, including kind of prey available in a particular site, for example. But in the most fundamental sense they are geared to the kinetic dispositions and movement possibilities of the body making the tool, and it is in this fundamental sense that tools are crafted along the lines of the body. The tools one makes and wields are, in other words, tools congenial to the body one is: tools that fit one's grip (however large or small, powerful or weak, for example), that fit one's style of moving (however fleet or heavy, long or short in endurance, for example), that fit one's range of movement (however flexible or constrained, ample or small, for example) and so on. In short, what one conceives and elaborates in the way of a tool is patterned on the kinetic possibilities and dynamics of the animate form one is. Thus, given the extraordinary thickness of bone in Neandertals and given the extraordinary physical powers of Neandertals that were called on daily for their survival – "Tremendous strength, endurance, and fortitude exceeding those of any modern human life-style were required on a daily basis" (Trinkaus and Shipman 1993: 381) – it is likely that Neandertal spear points were in the service of close-up engagement with prey. In other words, Neandertals did not throw their spears but thrusted and pierced with them. Anthropologist John Shea has in fact remarked that the overall shape of Neandertal spear points "is more congruent with this kind of hunting tactic [thrusting] than it is with habitual long-distance throwing" (Shea, personal communication).

In the most fundamental sense, then, the body functions analogically as a semantic template. Archaeologists and paleoanthropologists tend to skip over the analogical relationship between body and tool and in doing so not only regularly skip over analogical thinking and the formidable question of the origin and nature of symbols, but regularly miss seeing the foundational connection between body and mind that would shed light on the origin and nature of symbols. To explain the difference between Upper and Middle Paleolithic tool-makers (modern humans and Neandertals), for example, Mellars vaguely speculates that modern humans "imposed form" on their stone tools and thus arrived at "symbolism and symbolically defined behaviour" or "symbolic meaning" (Mellars 1989: 358-60). The idea that thinking has something to do with the body – or the body with the mind – never surfaces in his account. In consequence, analogical thinking never surfaces nor does an awareness of the variable relationship between analogical thinking and symbolization.

7. Martha Graham's *Lamentation*: Analogical thinking and symbolization

To put the relationship between analogical thinking and symbolization in concrete present-day perspective, and to understand in finer terms why stone tools are the product of analogical thinking but are not thereby symbols, let us consider a contemporary instance of symbolization, a dance titled *Lamentation* that Martha Graham choreographed.

A figure is sheathed in a tube of jersey that reveals only feet, hands, and face. The upper open part of the jersey forms a triangle, with the apex at the head, and the base stretching from elbow to elbow; the lower open part stretches across the ankles. The figure is seated on a low platform and performs the dance almost in its entirety in that seated position. As the figure moves – twists, turns, extends obliquely, recoils, and so on – the jersey sculpts the moving torsions in conflicting lines that at times seem to pull the figure apart. The dance has been described as "a moving sculpture of grief" (Mazo 1977: 194). The bodily drama of grief is etched kinetically into the moving fabric as it is visibly animated by every move of the moving body within. Drawing lines that do not simply mirror the anguished lines of a living body in grief but magnify its contorted pains, the ensheathing jersey follows every twinge and wrenching of the body, bringing grief *as it is experienced – lived* – to visible form. In effect, the covering turns the body inside out: what we see is a shifting qualitative landscape of grief as it is lived from within. The smallest movement spreads itself over the whole, and not languidly like a ripple in a pond, but severely, burdensomely, drawing all parts of the ensheathing fabric with it, no dimension remaining apart. The head turns away, for example, and its turning reverberates in contorting lines; the foot arches and its arching reverberates in a tautness that stretches upward to the knee and beyond; the body bends over, hands clasped, arms hanging heavily between the legs and moving ponderously from one side to the other, the entire form reverberating in a brooding oppression. Whatever the movement, it reverberates dynamically and throughout.

What we see is thus not a story about grief, a tale of lamentation, but its felt form. The movement dynamics echo the bodily pangs of grief – the keening, wailing cries of a body that grieves, the felt spasms and warpings of a body in pain. Yet there is no actual lamentation. How is this possible?

The movement dynamics of the moving form are congruent with the affective dynamics of sorrow, of deep mourning. The formula, so to speak, for symbolizing feelings through movement is palpable in the movement of the sheathed animate form we see before us. What Langer terms a "logical congruity" between forms of human feeling and aesthetic form is in actuality a *dynamic congruity* (see Sheets-Johnstone 1999c). There is no mistaking the solo dance *Lamentation*, for example, with the title figure's dance in *Afternoon of a Faun* or with the dance of the Sugar Plum Fairy in *The Nutcracker*. What we see before us is a movement dynamics that is congruent with a form of human feeling that we either have lived through ourselves in everyday life or have empathically witnessed someone else living through. A recognizable bodily dynamics is amplified, all its grievings and moanings made visible, all its mournful feelings blown up in the full proportion of their felt, lived through reality.

Because dynamics themselves are not uncommonly complex phenomena, symbolizing the dynamics of a complex phenomenon may result in a complex mode of symbolization, more complex than the modes of iconic corporeal symbolization discussed earlier. The dynamic congruity epitomized by the dance *Lamentation* exemplifies this complexity. Its dynamics are a *qualitative* dynamics, an intricate tapestry of shifting intensities and energies that are spatially and temporally elaborated such that the dance symbolizes as a whole and is indeed a seamless whole that has no component symbolizing parts, as the honey bee dance, for example, has component symbolizing parts, direction being symbolized apart from distance, for instance. Formal congruency in Graham's *Lamentation* rests on an ongoing qualitative dynamic; formal congruency in the honey bee dance rests on discrete spatio-kinetic relationships – what might in quite broad terms be called discrete geometric corporeal/world relationships. Human feelings are complex qualitative phenomena whose forms could hardly be captured by discrete symbolizing geometries; on the other hand, *direction* specifies a particular kinetic-spatial relationship that could hardly be captured by ongoing qualitative dynamics. Nonetheless, *similarity of form* – analogy – structures both modes of symbolization; it is the basis of both the congruency of Graham's qualitative dynamics and of a honey bee's kinetic-spatial geometries. Indeed, formal congruency rooted in analogy between symbol and thing symbolized underlies the symbolic structure of a speaker's utterance in primordial language, and of a female howler's tongue-flicking movements no less than a honey bee's dance and the dance *Lamentation*. Moreover there are or may be aspects of the one mode of symbolization within the other. For example, while the shifting postures of the grieving figure in *Lamentation* do not at any moment symbolize anything by themselves, the bearing of the body at any moment, its spatial attitude, is an integral aspect of the feeling symbolized. Correlatively, a bee symbolizing the richness of a sugar source by the vigorousness of her movement approximates to the greater complexity of a qualitative dynamics, just as a speaker of primordial language might have approximated to it when, in making the sound *m*, he or she pressed his/her lips together with deliberate effort and intensity to signify crushing as distinct from resting against.[21]

In just this context, a distinction may be explicitly drawn between that which is symbolic and that which is not. The distinction, mentioned in passing in the earlier discussion of Neandertal stone toolmaking, lies in a further dimension of symbolization, a dimension in fact of all modes of symbolization whether a formal dynamic congruity undergirds them or not, that is, whether symbolization is the result of an iconic or of an arbitrary relationship. All symbols are created entities that refer to something apart from themselves. Cultural anthropologist Raymond Firth highlights the referential nature of symbols when he writes that the essence of symbolism lies "in the recognition of one thing as standing for (re-presenting) another" (Firth 1973: 15); Langer does the same when she writes that symbols "let us develop a characteristic attitude toward objects *in absentia*, which is called 'thinking of' or 'referring to' what is not here" (Langer 1948: 37). The defining referential aspect is succinctly specified by philosopher Albert Johnstone in his statement that a relation is a symbolizing one "if and only if it is a four-term relation of standing for, where in the eyes of a symbolizer something, the symbol, stands for some other thing, the symbolized, within the context of a particular activity" (Johnstone 1984: 167). As functionally fashioned in the image of teeth, stone tools are an instance of analogical thinking, but symbolization requires something further than analogical thinking. It requires a referent, precisely as the tongue-flicking movements of a female howler monkey, the movements of a dancing bee, the articulatory gestures of a speaker of primordial language, and the movement dynamics of *Lamentation* demonstrate. In other words, although stone tools replaced teeth, they do not *refer* to teeth; they do not in fact refer to anything at all. Indeed, as one anthropologist observed, "Stone tools that are regarded as symbolic are generally *not* functional as powerful instruments" (John Lukacs, pers. com.). That stone tools replaced teeth and in this sense were fashioned along the lines of the body, however, is a significant fact from the perspective of the evolution of symbols, for *the body is both at the origin of analogical thinking and the foundation on which symbolizing activity and symbols originate and evolve*. The implication is that a greater attention to bodies might lead us to deeper evolutionary understandings of the nature of thinking and of how symbolization arose.

In sum, the evolutionary history of signs and the evolutionary history of symbol-making form a continuous thread from the perspective of intact, whole-bodied living creatures – animate forms. Were we to trace this thread along all its corporeal lines, we would trace out the evolution of an evolutionary semantics, a semantics correlative to the evolution of animate forms, that is, correlative to the diversity of life as it has evolved from bacteria onward. The barest outlines of this semantics show that what begins in tactility, tactility in the service of movement, evolves into a visual morphology that enters into the behavioral ordering of social relationships, and that what begins in movement, in kinetic representations of experience, opens the way to a vast and boundless world of possible symbols. Living organisms – animate forms – are at the heart of this evolutionary semantics.

Notes

[1] For an excellent article comparing Peirce's and Husserl's phenomenology, see Spiegelberg 1956.

[2] The constitution of meaning is a complex phenomenon. Even to exemplify the phenomenon briefly would require showing how in the case of humans, for example, objects, others, and one's own body are not given fully and completely in one fell semantic swoop, but are built up and continue to be built up in the course of life experiences (Husserl 1973, 1977, 1983, 1989). It would require showing, through a phenomenological reading of animal behavioral studies, how the same is true for other animals such as dolphins, chimpanzees, and ravens, and not true to the same extent of animals such as annelids, and even less true of animals such as jellyfish, for example. It would require showing through the same kind of reading how other animals such as anemones make sense of their environment, and to some degree of other creatures such as starfish; and so on. In a word, it would require extensive investigations and analyses beyond the scope of this paper.

[3] Husserl's essay "The Origin of Geometry" (1970) shows in a particularly exacting way how a genetic Husserlian phenomenology is concerned with the origin and constitution of meaning and how the methodology is thus particularly suited to a search for origins. (To avoid possible misunderstanding, it should perhaps be noted explicitly that Husserl's term "genetic" has nothing to do with genes; it specifies origins, as does the common English word *genesis*, which derives etymologically from the Greek word *genesis*, which itself derives from *gignesthai*, meaning to be born: *OED*.)

[4] Langer's thesis, simply stated, is that signs signify: they are indicators that prompt action; symbols do not indicate but represent: they are "instruments of thought" that lead one to conceive of something not immediately present. It is this aspect – *conception* – that, according to Langer, essentially distinguishes signs from symbols.

I follow Langer's distinction only in part because a clean separation between sign and symbol is not wholly viable. In particular, a clean separation does not jibe with experience – any more than an air-tight separation of "humans" from "animals" via language (Langer 1948, 1972) jibes with research studies showing the ability of some chimpanzees to learn a symbolic language (Premack 1975; Savage-Rumbaugh and Lewin 1994). Sight of one's national flag, for example, a symbol of one's nation, prompts action of some kind – a salute, a hand over the heart, or at the very least, consummate attention. A national flag may also lose its symbolic status, becoming simply a piece of material, no longer standing for something to be honored and thus no longer eliciting ritual action. The smell or sight of smoke, commonly taken as a *sign* of fire – a natural sign – exemplifies the non-viability of the distinction from the other end. The smell or sight can lead one not to action but to conceive of the town hall burning, for example, and in fact can evoke an image of the town hall burning. Smoke may thus on Langer's definition shift from sign to symbol and slip over concretely into symbolic thinking. In short, a possible slippage is apparent from symbol to sign and from sign to symbol, which testifies to a less clean separation than that which Langer proposes. What leads us to conceive may well lead us to act and what leads us to act may well lead us to conceive. Conception and action are indeed most often experientially intertwined and separable only in analysis.

Langer's thesis, however, through its emphasis on conception and action (or more precisely, on conception and *act*; see Langer 1967), consistently presences a subject, a living intact organism, and this presencing, coupled with her analysis of discursive and non-discursive symbols and her notion of semblance with respect to the latter kinds of symbols, gives her thesis special evolutionary import in spite of its strong and rigorous insistence on evolutionary discontinuities.

[5] Vocalizations are inherently prosodic. Their pitch, timbre, intensity, length, rhythm, and so on, make them distinctive. These prosodic elements might well have been the source of discovery of oneself as a creator of sound. A number of Deacon's comments supports just such a linkage.

Deacon speaks of prosodic elements as a "system of indices" that "probably had the longest co-evolutionary relationship with language." In particular, he states that prosodic elements "are used both to direct attention to what the speaker deems to be more salient elements and to communicate correlated emotional tone" (1997: 364). He conjectures that this system, "a parallel channel to speech" was probably "recruited from ancestral call functions," and that the various prosodic features "are most often produced without conscious intention" but reflect the "arousal level, emotional states, and attention" of the speaker (*ibid*.: 418). Earlier, he has said that "many aspects of this speech melody have been shown to have features in common with the innate vocalizations of primates" (*ibid*.: 313), noting in particular that there is a correlation "of changing pitch, volume, and rate of production with the level of arousal"; that a change "in the quality of vocalization" is "an indication of type of interaction (hostile, submissive, etc.)"; and that rhythm or "overall phrasing" is correlated with "breath control" (*ibid*.: 314).

Though all these features are "most often produced without conscious intention" *in present-day human speech*, there are good reasons to think that at the dawn of verbal language, an initial and growing awareness of oneself as a creator of sound was linked to just these already existing prosodic features of vocalization: to intensities, timbre, rhythm, length – to the shortness, shrillness, softness, regularity, cadencing, and so on, of any particular vocalization – and to the way in which these already existing prosodic features not only combined to produce meaning but were latent with meaning. In other words, the first creators of verbal symbols, becoming initially aware of the prosodic features inherent in their vocalizations and of how these features were cognitively charged, became aware of the qualitative possibilities of sound and of their own possibilities for creating meaningful sounds.

[6] "How could a social environment have arisen spontaneously, which possessed the necessary supports for overcoming the immensely difficult and complicated task of teaching symbolic relationships to individuals whose brains were not only unprepared but resistant to learning them?" (Deacon 1997: 402).

[7] "Symbols refer to relationships among indices, and are learned by first establishing these indexical associations" (Deacon 1997: 404).

[8] Or rather, one might say that it extends quite sketchily this far in the form of a "story" (Deacon 1997: 407-408).

[9] It is of interest in this respect to note Borchert and Zihlman's thesis (Borchert and Zihlman 1990) that there is a difference between explaining the origin of language and

the evolution of language. In explaining the latter, they too, like Deacon, draw on Baldwin's notion of organic selection and Waddington's notion of genetic assimilation in their thesis that phenotypic change preceded genotypic change. Moreover they consult the same chimpanzee studies that Deacon consults, notably studies of Sherman and Austin and of Kanzi (Savage-Rumbaugh et al. 1978; Savage-Rumbaugh and Sevcik 1984)), but instead of concluding finally that a marriage agreement between consenting adults – the males in order to guarantee access to a female, the females in order to be adequately provisioned – was the precipitating cause of linguistic symbolization, Borchert and Zihlman find developmental phenomena to be precipitating events: "language evolved through changes in ontogeny" (Borchert and Zihlman 1990: 21). More specifically, they suggest that "the transition to vocal tool-using initially occurred not primarily because natural selection favored adults who were somehow more competent with symbols, but because it favored *infants* who were more successful at using vocalizations to manipulate their mothers' behavior" (*ibid.*: 34). ("Manipulate" is an unfortunate word choice that suggests fraudulent management of another; "solicit" would have been a better choice since soliciting the mother's attention is what appears of moment with respect to protection, affection, care, nourishment, and so on, precisely as Borchert and Zhilman go on immediately to specify: "Vocal symbolic tool-using [vocal symbolizations] may have increased infants' protection from predators and may have ensured them a reliable supply of food, water, warmth, affection, social interaction and cognitive stimulation" [*ibid.*].)

It should be noted too that in support of their thesis, Borchert and Zhilman call attention to the "Gestural Complex" (*ibid.*: 25 ff.) that emerged on the part of Sherman, Austin, and Kanzi, namely, the spontaneous use of pointing, and of showing, giving, and requesting objects in conjunction with their language-learning, a gestural complex that, they point out, is evident in language-learning in human infants and young children.

[10] Another biological text describes the responsivity of a bacterium more exactingly in terms of movement: "When the concentration of chemicals in the water is uniform, the cell [the bacterium] tumbles often, changing direction every time. By contrast, when the cell is moving along a gradient, there are fewer tumbles, so the cell continues longer in the same direction" (Curtis and Barnes 1989: 131).

[11] Responsivity is consistently identified in biological texts as "a fundamental and almost universal characteristic of life" (Curtis 1975: 28).

[12] For a full discussion of this term, see its introduction and original specification in Sheets-Johnstone 1990.

[13] Note, however, that in the discussion of Portmann which follows, I convert Portmann's term *sematic*, which is etymologically tied to signs, to *semantic*, which is tied to meaning, in order to highlight the sense-making activity of living organisms, animate forms.

[14] For an especially probing and informative example, see Sinnott (1963).

[15] I underscore "in this instance" (and include those further instances that follow in the text) in order to offset any misreading. In the oral version of this essay (presented at the San Marino Conference), I was mistakenly criticized by Philip Lieberman for making a hard and fast analogy between tongue and penis, and mouth and vagina. I was

then, and am now, making no such analogy. Other analogical uses of the mouth, for example, include the mouth-opening of an infant in conjunction with its attempt to open a matchbox (Piaget 1968). Why the infant opens its mouth is inexplicable apart from a certain corporeal conceptual relevance obtaining between the opening of its mouth and the opening of the matchbox, a relevance implicitly noted by Piaget, but only by accident, as it were, since the spatial tactile-kinesthetic analogy between the two movements (or "behaviors") is neither identified nor examined by him (see Sheets-Johnstone 1990: 337). The essential point is that thinking is fundamentally modeled on the body; bodies are sources of meaning and constitute semantic templates.

[16] See Sheets-Johnstone 1999b for a presentation and discussion of the fascinating and apparently little-known findings of Alfred R. Wallace on this very topic.

[17] For both a detailed and broader discussion of the controversy over Neandertals, together with its assumptions and implications regarding minds and bodies, see Sheets-Johnstone 1999a.

[18] The advent of symbolizing behavior – not symbolic behavior, as it is a times erroneously termed (e.g., Stringer and Gamble 1993; see Sheets-Johnstone 1999a for further clarification) – is the result of analogical thinking that eventuates in the creation of a symbol of some kind. To distinguish between symbolizing behavior and symbolic behavior, consider the following brief examples.

If one joins a march to protest the decimation of rain forests, one's marching may be termed *symbolic* in that one's marching is symbolic of one's values: the march makes active reference to those values or brings those values to the fore. In contrast, the tongue-flicking movements of a female howler monkey, the dancing of a bee to inform conspecifics of a sugar source, the utterances of a speaker of primordial language, and the choreographing of a dance such as *Lamentation* are not symbolic *behaviors*. If they merit the designation "behavior" at all (they are more properly and most exactingly specified in terms of movement, i.e., kinetic form), they may be designated *symbolizing* behaviors; that is, they result in the creation of a symbol or symbols. The fashioning of stone tools is neither a symbolic behavior nor a symbolizing behavior: the acts involved in fashioning a stone tool neither stand for something apart from themselves nor does the completed act of production – the tool – result in a symbol.

[19] For a fully detailed account of how stone tools are analogues of teeth, see Sheets-Johnstone 1990, Chapter I.

[20] I am grateful to anthropologist John Shea for calling my attention to Mellars's Eurocentric perspective on Neandertals and modern humans, to the more complex facts of Levantine Mousterian tools, to his own innovative research strategies, and to the present-day controversy in which Mellars is involved with other anthropologists concerning the European Neandertal toolkit.

[21] A bee who through her movement symbolized obstacles to be avoided along a certain directional path would give a qualitatively nuanced sense of the way to the sugar source. To the degree that a spatio-kinetic or geometrically-rooted symbol approximates to a qualitative dynamics, it necessarily becomes a more complex phenomenon.

References

ALTMANN, S.A.
1967 "The structure of primate social communication", in S.A. Altmann (ed.), *Social Communication among Primates*, Chicago: University of Chicago Press.

BORCHERT, C.M. & A.L. ZIHLMAN
1990 "The ontogeny and phylogeny of symbolizing", in M. LeCron Foster & L.J. Botscharow (eds.), *The Life of Symbols*, Boulder, CO: Westview Press.

BRUNER, J.
1990 *Acts of Meaning*, Cambridge, MA: Harvard UP.

CARPENTER, C. R.
1963 "Societies of monkeys and apes", in C.H. Southwick (ed.), *Primate Social Behavior*, New York: Van Nostrand Reinhold.

CURTIS, H.
1975 *Biology* (2nd ed.), New York: Worth Publishers.

CURTIS, H. & N.S. BARNES
1989 *Biology, Part I: Biology of Cells* (5th ed.), New York: Worth Publishers.

DEACON, T.W.
1997 *The Symbolic Species: The Co-Evolution of Language and the Brain*, New York: W. W. Norton.

DOLHINOW, PH.J.
1972 "The North Indian Langur", in P.J. Dolhinow (ed.), *Primate Patterns*, New York: Holt, Rinehart, and Winston.

EIBL-EIBESFELDT, I.
1974 "The myth of the aggression-free hunter and gatherer society", in R. Holloway (ed.), *Primate Aggression, Territoriality, and Xenophobia*, New York: Academic Press.

FIRTH, R.
1973 *Symbols: Public and Private*, Ithaca: Cornell UP.

FOSTER, M. LECRON
1978 "The symbolic structure of primordial language", in S.L. Washburn & E.R. McCown (eds.), *Human Evolution: Biosocial Perspectives,* Menlo Park, CA: Benjamin/Cummings: 77-121.
1994a "Symbolism: The Foundation of Culture", in T. Ingold (ed.), *The Companion Encyclopedia of Anthropology,* New York: Routledge.
1994b "Language as Analogic Strategy: Suggestions for Evolutionary Research", in L.H. Rolfe, A. Jonker and J. Wint (eds.), *Studies in Language Origins*, vol. 3, Amsterdam: John Benjamins.
1996 "Reconstruction of the Evolution of Human Spoken Language", in Andrew Lock and Charles Peters (eds.), *Handbook of Symbolic Evolution*, Oxford: Oxford UP.

FREUD, S.
1938 *The Basic Writings of Sigmund Freud*, New York: Basic Books.
1953 *Complete Psychological Works of Sigmund Freud*, vols. 4 and 5, J. Strachey (ed. and trans.), London: Hogarth Press.
1963 *A General Introduction to Psychoanalysis*, New York: Liveright.

GOULD, S.J.
1996 *Full House*, New York: Harmony Books.

HOFFMEYER, J.
1996 *Signs of Meaning in the Universe*, B.J. Haveland (trans.), Bloomington: Indiana UP.

HUSSERL, E.
1970 "The origin of geometry", in *The Crisis of European Sciences and Transcendental Phenomenology*, D. Carr (trans.), Evanston, IL: Northwestern University Press.
1973 *Cartesian Meditations*, D. Cairns (trans.), The Hague: Martinus Nijhoff.
1977 *Phenomenological Psychology*, J. Scanlon (trans.), The Hague: Martinus Nijhoff.
1980 *Ideas Pertaining to a Pure Phenomenology and to a Phenomenological Philosophy*, Book 3 (Ideas III), T.E. Klein and W.E. Pohl (eds.), The Hague: Martinus Nijhoff.
1983 *Ideas Pertaining to a Pure Phenomenology and to a Phenomenological Philosophy*: *Book 1 (Ideas I)*, F. Kersten (trans.), The Hague: Martinus Nijhoff.
1989 *Ideas Pertaining to a Pure Phenomenology and to a Phenomenological Philosophy*: *Book 2 (Ideas II)*, R. Rojcewicz and A. Schuwer (trans.), Boston: Kluwer Academic.

JOHNSTONE, A.A.
1984 "Languages and non-languages of dance", in M. Sheets-Johnstone (ed.) *Illuminating Dance: Philosophical Explorations,* Lewisburg, PA: Bucknell UP.

KEETON, W.T. & J.L. GOULD
1986 *Biological Science* (4th ed.), New York: W. W. Norton & Co.

LANGER, S.K.
1948 *Philosophy in a New Key*, New York: New American Library.
1953 *Feeling and Form*, New York: Scribner's Sons.
1967 *Mind: An Essay on Human Feeling*, vol. 1. Baltimore: Johns Hopkins UP.
1972 *Mind: An Essay on Human Feeling*, vol. 2. Baltimore: Johns Hopkins UP.

LAVERACK, M.S.
1976 "External proprioceptors", in P.J. Mill (ed.), *Structure and Function of Proprioceptors in the Invertebrates*, London: Chapman and Hall.

LEROI-GOURHAN, A.
1971 *Préhistoire de l'art occidental*, Paris: Mazenod.

LIBERMAN, A.M. & I.G. MATTINGLY
1985 "The motor theory of speech perception revised", *Cognition*, 21 (1): 1-36.

LIBERMAN, A.M., COOPER, F.S, SHANKWEILER, D.P. & M. STUDDERT-KENNEDY
1967 "Perception of the speech code", *Psychological Review* 74: 431-461.

LIEBERMAN, PH.
1975 "On the evolution of language: A unified view", in R.H. Tuttle (ed.), *Primate Functional Morphology and Evolution*, The Hague: Mouton Publishers.
1983 "On the nature and evolution of the biological bases of language", in E. de Grolier (ed.), *Glossogenetics*, New York: Harwood Academic Publishing.

MAZO, J.H.
1977 *Prime Movers*, New York: William Morrow & Co.

MELLARS, P.
1989 "Technological changes across the Middle-Upper Palaeolithic transition: Economic, Social and Cognitive Perspectives", in P. Mellars and C. Stringer (eds.), *The Human Revolution,* Princeton: Princeton UP.

PEIRCE, CH.S.
1991 *Peirce on Signs*, J. Hoopes (ed.), Chapel Hill: University of North Carolina Press.
1992 *The Essential Peirce*, vol. I, N. Houser and Ch. Kloesel (eds.), Bloomington: Indiana UP.

PIAGET, J.
1968 *La naissance de l'intelligence chez l'enfant* (6th ed.), Neuchatel: Delachaux et Niestlé.

PORTMANN, A.
1967 *Animal Forms and Patterns*, H. Czech (trans.), New York: Schocken Books.

PREMACK, D.
1975 "Language in chimpanzees?", *Science,* 172: 808-22.

ROWELL, TH.
1972 *The Social Behaviour of Monkeys*, Harmondsworth, England: Penguin Books.

SAVAGE-RUMBAUGH, S. & R. LEWIN
1994 *Kanzi: The Ape at the Brink of the Human Mind*, New York: John Wiley & Sons.

SAVAGE-RUMBAUGH, E.S. & R.A. SEVCIK
1984 "Levels of communicative competency in the chimpanzee: Pre-representational and representational", in G. Greenberg & E. Tobach (eds.), *Behavioral Evolution and Integrative Levels*, Hillsdale, NJ: Lawrence Erlbaum.

SAVAGE-RUMBAUGH, E.S., RUMBAUGH, D.M. & S. BOYSEN
1978 "Linguistically mediated tool use and exchange by chimpanzees (pan troglodytes), *The Behavioral and Brain Sciences*, 4: 539-554.

SHEA, J.J.
1997 "Middle Paleolithic spear point technology", in H. Knecht (ed.), *Projectile Technology*, New York: Plenum Press.

1998 "Neandertal and early modern human behavioral variability: A regional-scale approach to lithic evidence for hunting in the Levantine Mousterian", *Current Anthropology*, 39, Supplement, June: S45-S78.

SHEETS-JOHNSTONE, M.
1990 *The Roots of Thinking*, Philadelphia: Temple UP.
1994 *The Roots of Power: Animate Form and Gendered Bodies*, Chicago: Open Court Publishing.
1999a *The Primacy of Movement*, Amsterdam: John Benjamins.
1999b "Sensory-kinetic understandings of language: An inquiry into origins," *Evolution of Communication*, 3/2: 149-183.
1999c "Emotion and movement: A beginning empirical-phenomenological analysis of their relationship", *Journal of Consciousness Studies*, 6/11-12: 259-77.

SINNOTT, E.
1963 *The Problem of Organic Form*, New Haven: Yale UP.

SPIEGELBERG, H.
1956 "Husserl's and Peirce's phenomenologies: Coincidence or interaction", *Philosophy and Phenomenological Research*, 17: 164-185.

STRINGER, CH. & C. GAMBLE
1993 *In Search of Neanderthals: Solving the Puzzle of Human Origins*, London: Thames and Hudson.

TRINKAUS, E. & P. SHIPMAN
1993 *The Neandertals: Changing the Image of Mankind*, New York: Alfred A. Knopf.

VAN HOOFF, J.A.R.A.M.
1969 "The facial displays of the Catarrhine monkeys and apes", in D. Morris (ed.), *Primate Ethology*, Garden City, NY: Doubleday Anchor.

VON UEXKÜLL, J.
1957 "A stroll through the worlds of animals and men", in C.H. Schiller (ed.), *Instinctive Behavior*, New York: International UP.

Sherman Wilcox

HANDS AND BODIES, MINDS AND SOULS: WHAT CAN SIGNED LANGUAGES TELL US ABOUT THE ORIGIN OF SIGNS?

1. Cartesian roots: "I am truly distinct from my body"

For deaf people who use their hands and bodies to express their language, questions about the nature of their native signed languages and what it might tell us about the origins of semiosis are not merely academic questions. The status of signed languages is an issue that deeply affects deaf people. Only 100 years ago, questions about signed language centered around whether it was a true language and an appropriate instrument for use in teaching deaf children, or whether it was merely gesture. The debate over whether to use speech or signs in schools for the deaf was in a very real sense a battle for deaf people's minds and souls. As the title of this section suggests, this debate was grounded in Cartesian mind-body dualism.

Space does not permit a full exploration of the many philosophical and historical threads that make up the tapestry of thought that led to the rise of the Cartesian world view of the mind, the body, language, and cognition. Two excerpts from Descartes' "Meditations on First Philosophy" will, however, provide a glimpse of how Cartesianism is pertinent to the topic of this chapter and anticipate the subject to which I will soon turn: the nature of signed languages and what they can tell us about the origin of signs. The first excerpt concerns the relation between two modes of conceptualization: understanding or reasoning, and imagination (Descartes 1980/1641: 90)

> I believe that this power of imagining that is in me, insofar as it differs from the power of understanding, is not a necessary element of my essence, that is, of the essence of my mind; for although I might lack this power, nonetheless I would undoubtedly remain the same person I am now. Thus it seems that the power of imagining depends upon something different from me.

The second excerpt concerns the relation between the mind and the body (*ibid.*: 93):

> Although perhaps... I have a body that is very closely joined to me, nevertheless, because on the one hand I have a clear and distinct idea of myself – insofar as I

> am a thing that thinks and not an extended thing – and because on the other hand I have a distinct idea of a body – insofar as it is merely an extended thing, and not a thing that thinks – it is therefore certain that I am truly distinct from my body, and that I can exist without it.

2. The great debate of 1880: Sign versus speech

To see how Cartesian thought merges with signed languages we must journey to Milan, Italy, which in 1880 was the site of the infamous Milan Conference. The Milan Conference was, if not the first, certainly the most significant battle for deaf people's minds and souls. The battle lines had been drawn between those deaf educators who favored signing and those who favored speech, the "pure oral method." Deaf education in France and America had been, up until then, controlled by those who favored the use of sign language.

It was in this context that the Milan Conference was convened. The city of Milan was an oralist stronghold, and the conveners of the conference hoped to win the battle, and the war, on this ground. The arguments in support of speech and against sign powerfully influenced the world history of deaf education. They also reflected a centuries-long trend in how we view language and helped set the course for modern linguistic studies of signed languages, a course solidly based in Cartesian dualism.

The best way to summarize these views is to let the oral educators speak for themselves. I take their words from Harlan Lane's compelling history of the subject.. First let us set the stage with an overview of the oralist position by Marius Magnat, the director of an oral school in Geneva at the time (Lane 1984: 387-8):

> The advantages of articulation training [i.e., speech]... are that it restores the deaf to society, allows moral and intellectual development, and proves useful in employment. Moreover, it permits communication with the illiterate, facilitates the acquisition and use of ideas, is better for the lungs, has more precision than signs, makes the pupil the equal of his hearing counterpart, allows spontaneous, rapid, sure, and complete expression of thought, and humanizes the user. Manually taught children are defiant and corruptible. This arises from the disadvantages of sign language. It is doubtful that sign can engender thought. It is concrete. It is not truly connected with feeling and thought... It lacks precision... Sign cannot convey number, gender, person, time, nouns, verbs, adverbs, adjectives, he claims... It does not allow [the teacher] to raise the deaf-mute above his sensations... Since signs strike the senses materially they cannot elicit reasoning, reflection, generalization, and above all abstraction as powerfully as can speech.

We begin to get a hint of Cartesian dualism in this passage. Let us continue with the words of Giulio Tarra, the president of the conference. Tarra is my favorite character in this story, not because I agree with him – in fact, I profoundly disagree with him – but because he clarifies the battle lines so sharply.

> Gesture is not the true language of man which suits the dignity of his nature. Gesture, instead of addressing the mind, addresses the imagination and the senses. Moreover, it is not and never will be the language of society... Thus, for us it is an absolute necessity to prohibit that language and to replace it with living speech, the only instrument of human thought.... Oral speech is the sole power that can rekindle the light God breathed into man when, giving him a soul in a corporeal body, he gave him also a means of understanding, of conceiving, and of expressing himself.... While, on the one hand, mimic signs are not sufficient to express the fullness of thought, on the other they enhance and glorify fantasy and all the faculties of the sense of imagination.... The fantastic language of signs exalts the senses and foments the passions, whereas speech elevates the mind much more naturally, with calm and truth and avoids the danger of exaggerating the sentiment expressed and provoking harmful mental impressions. (Lane 1984: 391, 393-4)

The intertwining threads of Cartesian thought about spoken and signed language are summarized in Table 1 page 140.

For oralist educators, speech was associated with the mind, reason, concepts, and ideas; gesture and sign (they were regarded as the same) were associated with the body, imagination, passions, and the senses.

Spoken language	**Signed language**
Mind	Body
Language	Gesture
Speech	Sign
Acquisition of ideas	Concrete
Expression of thought; instrument of thought	Cannot engender thought
Restored to society: calm, prudence, truth (human-like)	Defiant, corruptible, undignified (animal-like)
Precision (grammar)	Lacks grammar (number, gender, nouns, verbs, etc.); mimic
Elicits and permits reasoning, reflection, abstraction, generalization, conceptualization; rationality	Associated with the senses (sensual), material, glorifies imagination and fantasy, foments passions, encourages harmful mental impressions
The soul; the spirit	The corporeal body; the flesh; the material world

The historical significance for signed language linguistics was tremendous, because it set the world view for the next 100 years. We were left with the following assumptions firmly entrenched in our understanding of language, speech, gesture, and sign:

- Speech is of the mind; signs are of the body.
- Language is equivalent to speech; gesture is not language.
- Signs are gesture and therefore are not language.

3. The three great bifurcations

The Cartesian tradition thus created three great bifurcations: mind versus body, language versus gesture, and language versus sign. The last bifurcation clearly has had the most effect on the research program of signed language linguistics. The first two have created an entire modern world view for how scientists understand language.

3.1. Mind versus body

In a way, it is not accurate to place the three bifurcations on equal footing: the mind versus body bifurcation is the grand bifurcation of them all, motivating and providing structure to the two lesser bifurcations of language versus gesture and language versus sign.

One way in which the mind/body bifurcation has influenced modern linguistics is the well-known distinction between competence (linguistic ability abstracted away from actual speakers and actual circumstances) and performance (linguistic ability awash in the messiness of flesh-and-blood people in real-world circumstances). A second way that this bifurcation is manifest is in the commonly accepted separation of form and meaning. The paradigm case for the expression of this bifurcation comes, not surprisingly, from Chomsky (1957: 93):

> A great deal of effort has been expended in attempting to answer the question: "How can you construct a grammar with no appeal to meaning?" The question itself, however, is wrongly put, since the implication that obviously one can construct a grammar *with* appeal to meaning is totally unsupported. One might with equal justification ask: "How can you construct a grammar with no knowledge of the hair color of the speaker?"

The bifurcation of form and meaning is also present in the design feature of language called *duality of patterning*, which captures the well-documented fact that the meaningful parts of language (morphemes, words) are made up of meaningless parts (phonemes). In sign linguistics, the bifurcation of form and meaning demands that we come to grips with iconicity, a point to which I will return.

3.2. Language versus gesture

The second bifurcation is that of language versus gesture. There is a long tradition in philosophy and linguistics which regards language and gesture as distinct modes of expression. Gesture is seen as primitive, crude, and imprecise; language is considered to be the pinnacle of civilization, the epitome of rational expression. As Farnell (1995: 34) points out, language and gesture were often seen to be in complementary distribution: "either a word or, in the absence of adequate vocabulary, a gesture." Of course, the lesson that we learn from the work of McNeill (1992) is that this is far too simple a characterization of language and gesture.

Another way in which the language versus gesture bifurcation is manifest is in the centuries-long debate about language origins. To take just one example, Condillac suggested that language began as actions, as a gesture language or *langage d'action* (the connection between these views on a "language of action" and views of sign languages as "languages of action" would be well worth exploring). Rousseau, Herder, Humboldt, and others caricatured and ridiculed this position, arguing instead that language could not have arisen from such natural, animalistic beginnings. Herder, for example, proposed that the fundamental linguistic act was naming; critically, this naming was based on an unemotional sense of curiosity, a desire for pure knowledge. Furthermore, Herder argued that the naming had to have been audible, unaccompanied by any visible movement. The reasoning behind this argument was that "when a man is under the influence of an emotion (such as fear of an enemy) and yet suppresses, from rational grounds, any movement which might reveal it, he is acting from reason, not from passion" (Wells 1987: 40). Language is reason – "without language man has no reason, and without reason no language" (Wells 1987: 40) – and the best evidence for reason is that we ignore our body, our senses, our feelings, and we exhibit a lack of movement. In the terminology of modern Cartesian linguistics, language is stimulus-free (Chomsky 1966).

This bifurcationist view led to the inescapable conclusion that language could not have arisen from gesture. Humboldt says (Wells 1987):

> Language must be regarded as built-in man; for as the work of his mind, in the clarity of consciousness, it is completely inexplicable. It is of no avail to allow for thousands and thousands of years for its invention. Language could not be invented if its archetype were not already present in the human mind.

If language could not have been invented or could not have evolved, where did it come from? Humboldt's answer (Wells 1987: 51-52) is remarkable because it predates the modern-day Cartesian linguistic position (Pinker 1994) that language is an instinct:

> If that to which there is really nothing analogous in the whole realm of the thinkable may be compared with anything else, then we can only recall the natural instinct of animals, and call language an intellectual instinct of the reason.

Finally, I'd be remiss if I did not cite Chomsky (1972: 70) once more, on the question of whether language can be derived from gesture:

> When we ask what human language is, we find no striking similarity to animal communication systems. There is nothing useful to be said about behavior or thought at the level of abstraction at which animal and human communication fall together. The examples of animal communication that have been examined to date do share many of the properties of human gestural systems, and it might be reasonable to explore the possibility of direct connection in this case. But human language, it appears, is based on entirely different principles. This, I think, is an important point, often overlooked by those who approach human language as a natural, biological phenomenon; in particular, it seems rather pointless, for these reasons, to speculate about the evolution of human language from simpler systems.

In a passage written at almost the same time, Stokoe (1974: 37) offers an alternative, non-Cartesian position. Stokoe had introduced the term **gSign**, the gestural manifestation of a sign-vehicle in a semiotic system, equivalent to **sSign**, the manifestation of a sign-vehicle in the spoken modality. With this foundation, Stokoe then asked a critical question: How do gSigns relate to language? Stokoe concluded that we often assume that "sSigns and language emerged fully formed, all at once, and indissolubly joined" (Stokoe 1974: 36). He continued:

> If one considers a natural human sign language from inside not outside, its gSigns denote the kinds of things that sSigns denote... Because the full language use of gSigns is not generally known, it has been supposed that there must be an unbridgeable gap between gSign as affect display and gSign as language element. Yet there may be a semiotic and evolutionary continuum as we shall see. The habit of thinking of animal gSigns as simple and human signs, both gestured and spoken, as complex is preposterous... The vertebrates' affect display gSign is immensely complex. Its reference is in fact to the whole ethology, and it is moreover complex in a semiotically exploitable way. Its vehicle, denotation, and denotatum are all rich material for evolutionary development. If it is foolhardy to maintain this kind of gSign evolved directly into language, it is foolish to dismiss it and seek elsewhere for the origins of more specialized gSigns and sSigns.

Consider the implications of these two passages. According to Chomsky, human language is based on entirely different principles than animal communication, with no possibility of an evolutionary continuum linking the two. But, he suggests, human gestural systems may be directly connected to animal communication systems, which thus logically implies that human gestural and human language systems are based on entirely different principles with no evolutionary link between them. For Chomsky there are thus two bifurcations: between animal communication and human language, and between human gesture and human language.

Stokoe's proposal was that no such bifurcations exists. If we search, Stokoe predicted, we will find an evolutionary continuity between animal communication and human language, and between human gesture and human language.

3.3. Language versus sign

The final and perhaps most imposing bifurcation for the sign linguist is language versus sign. The historical sediments surrounding deaf education and attitudes toward signed language, as well as a body of writings in linguistics prior to the 1960s which stated categorically that language was spoken and all other forms (written, signed) were secondary representations of speech, come together to impose a powerful mandate for every sign linguist: we all feel that, whatever else we do, we are also advocates for signed language. We feel the weight of centuries of misunderstanding and ignorance on our shoulders, demanding that we rescue signed languages from the shadows of false accusations that they are not true languages. This situation has led, I suggest, to a closet-full of "Great Fears" of the sign linguist. Among them are the fear of gesture, the fear of iconicity, and the fear of diachronic studies of signed languages.

3.4. The sign linguist's great fears

The first fear is of gesture. The second bifurcation tells us that language is not gesture. If language is not gesture, then signed language cannot be gesture. Signs are not gestures, sign linguists insist: they are words. This leaves open the question, of course, of what exactly words are, and, critically, whether words might themselves be gestures (Janney 1999), a question to which I will return. The second bifurcation also told us that language cannot be derived from gesture. It is therefore incumbent upon sign linguists to demonstrate that signs also cannot be derived from gesture. Thus, we see studies in which evidence is offered for a bifurcation in deaf children's language development between prelinguistic gestures and linguistic signs. Such an argument is made by Petitto (1987: 55). Petitto describes two models of language acquisition: an "interaction-based model" in which "language is seen as a part of the child's general cognitive capacity" and a so-called "child-based model" in which language "emerges from knowledge structures specific to language." She then makes predictions about the language acquisition process based on these two models (Petitto 1987: 55-56):

> The interaction-based model implies that the child's transition from prelinguistic communication to linguistic competence should be relatively smooth. That is, if linguistic structures are derived from prelinguistic forms, there should be no abrupt discontinuity in the use of these differing forms. On the other hand, if language is a distinct formal system reflecting a particular mental capacity not wholly built up from early communicative competence, one would predict a discontinuous transition from early prelinguistic to linguistic expression.

Petitto reports that her results support the second hypothesis: language acquisition is discontinuous with other forms of knowledge. Other researchers, however, come to different conclusions. McNeill, for example, on the basis of many years of psycholinguistic research on language and gesture, concludes that "gestures and speech should be viewed within a unified conceptual framework as aspects of a single underlying process" (McNeill 1992: 23). Blake (2000) reports a comprehensive longitudinal study of language and gesture development in children. Concerning Petitto's claims for the autonomy of language and gesture, Blake responds (109): "The seeming automaticity of the pairings of vocalizations and gestures, as well as the relationships found between gestural change and language outcome measures in our study, do not support a view that gestures and language develop autonomously (Petitto 1987)." Such a continuity view is also supported in the work of Virgina Volterra and her associates (Capirci, Caselli, Iverson, Pizzuto, & Volterra 1999).

The sign linguist's second great fear is of iconicity. The spectre of iconicity made its appearance in the first bifurcation: if true language depends upon the separation of form and meaning, then to the extent that a communication system is iconic, less arbitrary, it is less a true language. Whether understood in terms of Saussurean arbitrariness of the sign or duality of patterning, iconicity has been a cross to bear for sign linguists since we began telling the world that signed languages are not merely "mimic signs" but true human languages.

In our attempts to rid signed languages of this spectre, sign linguists have several weapons in our arsenal. First, we point out, iconicity appears to decrease over time: historical change in signed languages makes signs less iconic, more arbitrary (Frishberg 1975). Second, we argue that iconicity does not appear to afford much advantage for the child who is learning the language (Meier 1991). Third, the spectre-killing linguist points out that knowing what a sign means does not allow us to predict what the iconic sign might look like; conversely, seeing the sign does not allow us to predict its meaning. Although we can see an iconic relationship in signs after we know what they mean, it is not apparent beforehand. Fourth,we claim that iconicity is obliterated by grammar, the classic demonstration being that offered by Klima and Bellugi (1979), who claim that the modification of root signs by regular, morphological processes submerges their iconicity. As evidence, they offer the example of slow. The sign meaning 'slow' is made by slowly moving one hand along the top of the outstretched opposite hand (its palm facing downward) and forearm. A grammatical modification of this sign is possible, which changes the meaning to that of 'very slow.' This form is made using the same root sign slow, except that the movement includes a slight hold at the beginning followed by a rapid, tense movement. Klima and Bellugi point out that the sign meaning 'very slow' is thus made very fast: the grammar has submerged the iconicity.

Valli and Lucas (1995) also suggest that while iconicity may be present in the lexicon, it plays no role in explaining grammatical processes in ASL. Discussing morphologically related noun-verb pairs in ASL, for example, they state (Valli & Lucas 1995: 7):

> It is probably true that the form of the sign SIT is an iconic representation of human legs sitting...[However,] focusing on its iconicity will not provide much insight into the interesting relationship between sit and the noun CHAIR, and other noun-verb pairs.

What Valli and Lucas are suggesting here is that while the shape of the hand may iconically represent human legs dangling off a chair (see Figure 1 page 147), the relation between morphologically related nouns and verbs, such as CHAIR and SIT, is not iconic. Similarly, Valli and Lucas (1995) claim that verbal morphology is not iconic: "Nor will [iconicity] help explain how the movement of SIT can be modified to mean SIT FOR A LONG TIME (slow, circular movement) or SIT ABRUPTLY (short, sharp movement)."

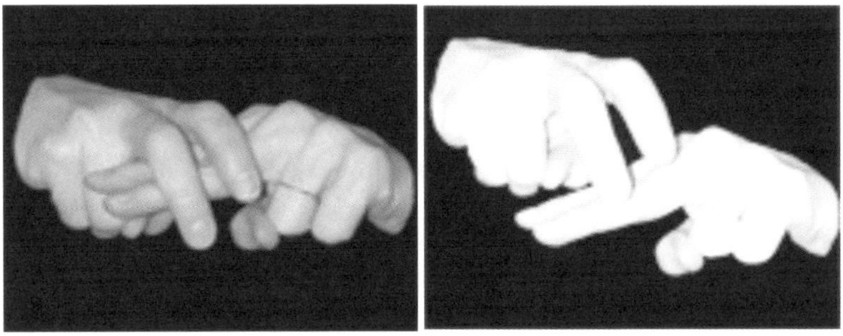

Figure 1: The ASL verb 'sit'

It is time we set aside our fears and start examining iconicity for clues that it might offer regarding the origin of semiosis and the nature of language. For example, we might ask: Where does iconicity erode over time – in the lexicon, in the grammar? What is the driving force behind this erosion? Is erosion the result of a linguistic process, a drive to become arbitrary (Singleton, Morford, & Goldin-Meadow 1993), or some more general non-linguistic process of habituation or ritualization (Haiman 1994). Do all linguistic units erode at the same rate, or is there differential resistance to erosion? Does iconicity ever emerge? If so, again we should ask where – in the lexicon, in the grammar? Finally, what is the nature of the iconic relationship – that is, what is the nature of meaning (certainly a non-trivial question) and (apparently more straightforward, though I believe equally non-trivial), what is the nature of the signed form?

Finally, I suggest that sign linguists have an unhealthy fear of diachronic studies of signed languages. Why should this be? Think about one type of diachronic study, etymology or the study of where words come from. It is perfectly acceptable for the spoken language linguist to ask, "Where did the word 'must' come from?" It is acceptable because no matter how far back we go, we only find more words. As Haiman (1998: 156) points out: "With insignificant exceptions like 'ouch' and 'boo hoo,' we cannot observe how words developed out of nonwords; however far back we go, it seems that all of our etymologies of words trace back to nothing but other older words."

For the sign linguist, though, this is tricky business. If we scrape too hard at the etymology of signs, we run the risk of scratching our knuckles. We shake our hand in a gesture of pain – and, to our amazement (or dismay), we discover a proto-sign.

I suspect there are two reasons for our fear of diachrony. First, asking why a sign means what it does conjures up images of hearing teachers, without a clue about what signed language really is, telling their students stories about why each sign means what it does. The stories that are told are often wrong, nothing more than quaint folk etymologies. The fact that these stories are usually wrong is probably not really what causes such a strong reaction among sign linguists. Rather, folk etymologies are seditious because they suggest that signs have a non-linguistic source: (linguistic) signs come from (non-linguistic) gestures. If folk etymology turns out to be even partially correct, we are left standing face-to-face with Tarra's pantomimic signs.

Linguists are not comfortable when external motivation, explanation outside of the limited scope of structural descriptions of language, is invoked. Sign linguists are even more uncomfortable with explanations which point outside of linguistic structure, to the structure of the world.

Not all linguists are resistant to allowing the structure of the world into the structure of language. Sign linguists would be well served by heeding the words of the Italian linguist Simone (1995: ix):

> [T]he anti-arbitrarist debate has re-ignited the discussion on the delicate question of naturalness in language... The less arbitrary we consider linguistic structures, the more 'natural' they reveal themselves – one would say... [T]his trend has had another important implication on the metatheoretical level: it has reminded that one has to doubt every kind of linguistics that does not take into account in a sufficiently complex way the problem of how the outside world (participants, settings, actions, etc.) is 'imported' into language.

The fear of diachrony in the short term, of the possible phylogensis of signs (which are, after all, the words of signed languages) from gestures, is nothing like the fear that is generated when we are asked to consider the ontogenetic origin of signs, the origin of semiosis. Here, at least, sign linguists are kept company by our spoken language colleagues. Even for spoken language linguists, pushing the envelope this far becomes frightening, so much so that one hundred years ago, while deaf educators were debating the nature and value of signs versus speech, the Linguistic Society of Paris declared that no discussion of the origin of language would be allowed. Exploring the origins of language and of semiosis is still seen by many language scholars as disreputable work, dabbling in unscientific speculation.

Of course, diachronic studies of spoken languages have taught us much. We find, for example, several processes which together have been termed *grammaticization* (Bybee, Perkins & Pagliuca 1994). While bifurcations and autonomous modules are part and parcel of the Cartesian linguistic approach, basic to an understanding of grammaticization is the notion of a cline. One cline of grammaticization is the continuum from content word to morpheme (Hopper & Traugott 1993: 7):

content item > grammatical word > clitic > inflectional affix

This cline appears to have been at work in the grammaticization of the ASL agentive affix. This suffix is now present in ASL as a downward movement of the outstretched hands, typically with the palms facing inwards towards each other, thumb side of each hand facing upward. Depending on the context, one or both hands may be used; in the sign meaning 'teacher' (TEACH+agentive suffix) both hands are used, while in the sign meaning 'student' (LEARN+agentive suffix) only one hand forms the suffix, which is also made with a greatly reduced downward movement. In films made at the turn of the twentieth century, these signs are made differently. The sign for 'teacher', for example, uses the same root sign (TEACH); the suffix, however, appears more like a full form: the same handshape is used, but here both hands touch the torso twice, once at the top of the chest, and then once again in the area of the stomach. In fact, this form is seen at the time, and presently, as a full lexical form meaning 'body'. Thus, at the turn of the century, 'teacher' was more like a compound or a clitic: 'teach-body'.

A few sign linguists are starting to conduct grammaticization studies of signed languages and, as we might expect, are coming face to face with the link between sign and gesture (Janzen 1998; Janzen & Shaffer, To appear; Shaffer 2000; Shaffer & Janzen 2000; Wilcox & Wilcox 1995; Wilcox 2000a, 2000b; Wilcox et al. 2000), as well as the relation between language and gesture (Liddell 1998; Liddell & Metzger 1998). A number of spoken language linguists have suggested that processes of historical change, including grammaticization, are structured along a metaphoricity cline (Heine, Claudi, & Hünnemeyer 1991; Sweetser 1990). Sign linguists are now reporting that this cline seems to be at work in ASL, in the historical evolution of lexical signs with concrete, physical senses into grammatical form. One example of this is the grammaticization of modal verbs in ASL (Wilcox & Wilcox 1995), where grammatical forms have been shown to have their source in lexical forms. For example, the ASL modal CAN 'ability' likely had as its lexical source the form STRONG 'strong, powerful'. Metaphor and iconicity also seem to unite with gesture in the expression of grammatical morphology in signed languages, as reported by Taub (2001), Wilcox (2001), and others.

We are clearly at the beginning of an era in such studies, but the results already suggest that the bifurcation of language and gesture is an unnecessary relic of the past.

3.5. The symbiotic solution to the third bifurcation

All of these fears were a result of the bifurcation of language and sign language. Sign linguists spend much of their time discrediting this bifurcation and indeed have been quite successful in doing so. However, much of modern sign linguistics continues to accept the mind versus body bifurcation. I suggest that this is because modern Cartesian linguistics also has accepted this bifurcation. In this way, Cartesian linguistics and sign linguistics have found themselves in a symbiotic relationship.

It works like this. Cartesian linguists welcome data from signed languages because they demonstrate that language is independent of form. Cross-linguistic studies of spoken languages demonstrate that the architecture of the model works independent of particular languages. A stronger case, however, would be to demonstrate that the model works across language modalities. This is precisely the evidence that signed languages provide.

For their part, sign linguists embrace Cartesian linguistics because it legitimizes signed languages. Cartesian linguistics assures sign linguists that the nineteenth-century oralists got it wrong: they mixed their mental apples and their corporeal oranges. It is not the case that speech is of the mind, while signs are of the body. Both speech and signs, according to the modern-day Cartesian linguistic account, are of the body. It is language, purified of its material form, treated as an abstract symbol system, that is created by and thus a reflection of the mind. Language is of the mind, whatever its modality; speech and signs are merely material vessels, corporeal bodies for language. For example, consider how a sign linguist working under Cartesian linguistic assumptions might conceptualize the study of signed language phonology (Brentari 1998: 2):

> We [sign phonologists] must try to imagine spoken languages stripped of their substantive phonetic link to the vocal apparatus and auditory system in order to consider the type of work that the units in question do for the grammar as a whole, and to consider their instantiations in a visual/gestural language.

In other words, the Cartesian method for discovering what signed and spoken languages share *as language* is to bleach language of all of its bodily substance until we arrive at the ultimate abstraction: disembodied language, pure structural relations. Like Descartes' disembodied mind, *language-as-mind* is fully purified of its spoken-signed body. The alternative approach, which I will explore below, proposes that an equally plausible way to proceed is to assume that language is not independent of modality; rather, gesture, sign, speech, and language are intrinsically bound in our evolutionary history to embodied perceptual, motor, and cognitive systems.

Following the implications even further, *language-as-mind-as-pure-reason* is seen by many linguists as distinct from all other body-based cognitive abilities. Thus, there is yet another bifurcation, the Cartesian linguistic expression of which is that language is an autonomous formal system (Chomsky 1966: 4-5):

> In short, man has a species-specific capacity, a unique type of intellectual organization which cannot be attributed to peripheral organs or related to general intelligence and which manifests itself in what we may refer to as the "creative aspect" of ordinary language – its property of being both unbounded in scope and stimulus-free.

4. The era of unification

There are approaches to understanding language that do not presuppose the duality of mind and body, but instead start with the position that language and the actions that express it are the products of an embodied mind. In this section I will briefly outline two necessary theoretical bridges that must be spanned if we are to unite the bifurcations discussed above. First, we must adopt a view of language that allows us to see all language as articulatory gesturing. Second, we require a linguistic framework that permits us to reunite the dichotomies cultivated under the ideology of Cartesian linguistics.

4.1. Speech as gesture: "Gesturizing the articulators"

At its most concrete level language, and in fact all communication, depends on signals which pass between participants in the communication act. For spoken languages these signals are acoustic patterns; for signed languages they are optical arrays. Whatever the form, acoustic or optical, of this proximal signal, the distal source is articulatory gesturing produced by moving parts of the communicator's body – the tongue, glottis, and vocal folds for speaking, or the hands, face, and body for signing. It is this movement with the capacity for conveying meaning that I call gesture.

I define gesture, after Studdert-Kennedy (1987), as a functional unit, *an equivalence class of coordinated movements that achieve some end.* Gesture is a fundamental unit of organization in an organism's motoric interactions with the physical world. Given the nature of our brain's evolution, gesture is also implicated in perception. As Churchland (1986: 473) notes, "evolution being what it is, pattern recognition is there to subserve motor coordination... if we ignore motor control as the context within which we try to understand pattern recognition, we run the risk of generating biologically irrelevant solutions." Gesture is thus an important unit for unifying action and perception. By grounding disparate signals in the movements made by a physical body, this notion of gesture offers a biologically relevant alternative to the Cartesian linguists' proclivity to abstract away from the body.

Of course, in defining gesture in this way, I realize that I am juxtaposing two senses of the word: the more commonsense use in which gesture refers to bodily actions that are expressive or meaningful, and a more technical sense, as used in the phonetic and movement sciences, of articulatory gesture as a dynamic, coordinative structure without symbolic meaning (Browman & Goldstein 1989; Fowler 1986).

Many researchers would claim that these are two distinct types of gestures which are unrelated to each other. They prefer, shall we say, a minor bifurcation of gesture-as-symbolic versus gesture-as-articulation. Clearly, however, gestures of the first type are composed of gestures of the second type. This is true across commonsense gestures, spoken words, and the signed words of signed languages. A "thumbs up" gesture is composed of a coordinated assembly of non-symbolic gestures (closing the fingers, extending the thumb, raising the arm, etc.). Words are likewise assemblies of non-symbolic gestures into symbolic, gestural complexes. Thus, under this gestural view a spoken word, a sign of a signed language (that is, a signed word), and a communicative gesture are seen as remarkably similar. Each is a coordinated assembly of non-symbolic gestures into a larger symbolic unit. Describing spoken words, Kelso (1986: 31) points out that "words are not simply strings of individual gestures, produced one after the other; rather, each is a particular pattern of gestures, orchestrated appropriately in time and space." The same description works equally well for signs and for communicative gestures.

Furthermore, I would go beyond noting that gestures of the first type are constitutive of gestures of the second type and suggest that they are phylogenetically and ontogenetically related. Thus, this theoretical perspective on gesture is essential for understanding the evolution of neural mechanisms which form the basis for perceptual categorization, memory, and language (Edelman 1987; Kimura 1993).

4.2. Cognitive linguistics: "Conceptualizing the articulators"

There is a linguistic framework, called cognitive linguistics, which challenges all of the essential assumptions of Cartesian linguistics. Two versions of this framework are pertinent here, the first being developed by Ronald Langacker (Langacker 1987a; Langacker 1991b) called cognitive grammar, and the second being developed by George Lakoff and several of his colleagues (Lakoff 1987; Lakoff & Johnson 1999 (Lakoff 1987; Lakoff & Johnson 1999), which emphasizes the metaphorical structure of language and thought. I will discuss only the first.

Cognitive grammar expressly rejects many of the underpinnings of contemporary linguistic theory, among them that (Langacker 1991b: 1):

- language is a self-contained, autonomous system, independent from general cognitive processing
- grammar is an independent aspect of linguistic structure distinct from both lexicon and semantics
- meaning, to the extent that it is necessary at all to linguistic (i.e., grammatical) analysis, is properly described by some formal logic based on truth conditions.

Cognitive grammar proposes instead that:

- language is neither self-contained nor describable without essential reference to cognitive processing;
- grammar is inherently symbolic; lexicon, morphology, and syntax form a continuum of symbolic units (that is, pairings of form and meaning):
- meaning is equated with conceptualization, encompassing novel conceptions as well as fixed concepts; sensory, kinesthetic, and emotive experience; and imagery, or the ability to construe a situation in alternate ways.

The second point is quite significant: within the framework of cognitive grammar, grammar and meaning are not bifurcated. Cognitive grammar posits only three types of linguistic structures: phonological structure, semantic structure, and symbolic structures (the symbolic pairing of phonological and semantic structures). Grammar resides in the symbolic relationship between semantic and phonological structure. Grammatical structure is inherently symbolic; all grammatical constructs have conceptual import (Langacker 1987a, 1991a).

Most relevant for the present discussion is how cognitive grammar describes the conceptual foundation of grammatical structures. As an extended example, consider how a cognitive linguist would ground the conceptual basis of two basic grammatical categories, nouns and verbs, in our bodily experience of the world. Langacker (1991b: 13-14) offers what he calls the billiard ball model:

> We think of our world as populated by discrete physical objects. These objects are capable of moving about through space and making contact with one another. Motion is driven by energy, which some objects draw from internal resources and others receive from the exterior. When motion results in forceful physical contact, energy is transmitted from the mover to the impacted object, which may thereby be set in motion to participate in further interactions.

Physical objects and energetic interactions stand in conceptual opposition to one another. To demonstrate this, Langacker analyzes the billiard ball model into four components: space, time, material substance, and energy.

The essence of space and time is *extensionality*; together they provide a multidimensional setting within which the other two components are manifested, Moreover, we think of material substance as being manifested primarily in space... whereas energy is only observable through change and thus requires time for its manifestation. I will therefore refer to space as the *domain of instantiation* for material substance, and time for change and energy (Langacker 1991b: 14).

Physical objects are composed of material substance and are instantiated in space. They are discrete and have limited spatial expanse. Objects are also autonomous: their existence does not rely intrinsically on another object or on participation in an interaction. Interactions, on the other hand, are quite different from objects on these dimensions.

An interaction does not reside in physical substance, but rather in the transfer of energy and the change thereby induced. Time and not space is thus an interaction's domain of instantiation, and the domain in which we think of it as being located. Also reversing what we observed for objects, an archetypal interaction is discrete, compact and continuous along the temporal axis, but spatially expansive: at the very least, its spatial extension includes the locations of its various participants and the trajectories they follow through its duration. Finally, an interaction does not exist independently of its participants. Though we can perfectly well conceptualize an object separately from any interaction involving it, the conception of an interaction inherently presupposes some references – however vague or schematic – to the entities through which it is manifested (Langacker 1991b: 14).

To summarize: "Physical objects are prototypical for nouns, and overt physical actions for verbs" (Langacker 1987b: 54).

Langacker's description of the conceptual underpinnings of grammar in physical objects and their interactions provides an integrated framework for understanding how language and cognition might be derived from systems based on perception and movement of the human organism. It also provides the framework for deriving semantic roles (and eventually grammatical classes) from the structure of events (Langacker 1991: 284-5):

> I do not believe that semantic roles are first and foremost linguistic constructs, but rather prelinguistic conceptions grounded in everyday experience... In order to call attention to their primal status and nonlinguistic origin, I refer to these as *role archetypes*. These archetypes reflect our experience as mobile and sentient creatures and as manipulators of physical objects. The archetype *agent* is a person who volitionally initiates physical activity resulting, through physical contact, in the transfer of energy to an external object. Its polar opposite is an archetypal *patient*, an inanimate object that absorbs the energy transmitted via externally initiated physical contact and thereby undergoes an internal change of state.

Cognitive grammar thus provides a framework for understanding how our *conception* of the world is grounded in our *perception* of the world. By grounding grammar in embodied conceptualization, cognitive grammar provides the theoretical link between our perception of objects moving through space and time, and our conceptual linguistic categories. For theories of language and the origins of semiosis, cognitive grammar bridges the great divide of mind-body dualism. For signed languages, it allows us to establish a critical link between form and meaning: because the sign articulators are visible, language users can exploit the semiotic capacity of hands as objects moving in space to represent space and time. The articulators of signed languages are able to iconically represent the conceptual content of language.

4.3. Iconicity: "Is a fist a fist or a phoneme?"

The significance of cognitive grammar for a unified view of language, speech, sign, and gesture is thus twofold. First, it enables sign linguists to embrace an approach which expressly challenges the basic assumptions of Cartesian linguistics. Second, cognitive grammar provides a model for conceptualizing the articulators. Thus, it allows us to ask and begin to answer the question of the relation between meaning and form for signed languages. The key point is that for signed languages, the articulators – hands, bodies, and faces – are both the *means of expression* and an *object of conception*. A fist is both a fist and a phoneme. And more. A fist can be conceptualized as a compact object; as a compact object, it invites conceptualization as a potent force, an agent. Further, a fist can act, it can move. And in its verb-like movement, the agent can act on another object, perhaps another hand. This second hand will likely be affected by the forceful action of the fist, becoming a patient of the action.

What does this buy us? Note that these same conceptualizing abilities are brought to play in determining the semantic structure of linguistic units; in the framework of cognitive grammar, meaning is equated with conceptualization. Iconicity, under this view, is much more than a relation between a sign's form and its real-world referent. Icons are a special type of symbolic structure marked by a diagrammatic isomorphism across their phonological and semantic structures.

Let us now reanalyze the previous examples of the putative submersion of iconicity by grammar. First, consider the case of ASL VERY-SLOW. The form VERY-SLOW is multi-morphemic, consisting of a root form, the stative slow, and a bound, grammatical form expressing the intensifier translated here as 'very'. While the composite form does not iconically reflect the meaning of the lexical root (the form 'slow'), it does iconically represent the grammatical morpheme indicating intensity. Intensity can be understood metaphorically in terms of the build up and sudden release of pressure. A prototypical, real world example of intensification is a closed container that has been thrown into a fire. Heat from the fire causes pressure inside the container to build up, eventually causing the container suddenly and explosively to burst open. In the ASL grammatical form meaning 'very' this build up of intensity is iconically signaled by a build up of muscular energy in the initial hold of the sign's movement. Then, this metaphoric pressure is released, resulting in a sharp, energetic movement. Thus, the grammar of ASL has not submerged iconicity; rather, iconicity has shifted from the lexical form to the grammatical marker of intensity.

What about Valli and Lucas' claim that iconicity will not explain the relation between noun-verb pairs in ASL such as CHAIR and SIT, or between different aspectual forms of verbs? Klima and Bellugi (1979: 295-96) elaborate on the formal characteristics of nouns and verbs:

> Both continuous and hold manner occur in the verb signs (a continuous sweep as opposed to a noticeable stop at the end of the movement); the related noun forms show a consistently restricted pattern: they are the same as the verb forms except that they have reduplicated movement and a restrained manner (that is, the muscles are tightened in performing the movement). As a result of the restrained manner the nouns are typically made with smaller movements than their related verbs.

I suggest that noun and verb forms in those signed language which have noun-verb morphology are iconic in two ways. First, as Valli and Lucas noted, both forms are often iconic of their lexical content: both 'chair' and 'sit' iconically represent legs. More importantly, and totally unrecognized by Valli and Lucas, these forms iconically represent their grammatical category: noun forms iconically represent nouns, and verb forms iconically represent verbs. Noun forms are articulated in a restricted region of space, making them conceptually things[1] at both their phonological and semantic poles. Verb forms make salient in articulation their movement through space, making them processes at both their phonological and semantic poles.

Further evidence for this iconic mapping of verb forms comes from the systematic way in which the verb forms are grammatically marked to reflect verb aspect. Comrie (1976: 3) defines aspect as "different ways of viewing the internal temporal constituency of a situation." Aspect refers to situation-internal temporal features such as the inception, duration, or completion of an event (Langacker 1972). Clearly the forms that Lucas and Valli describe – SIT FOR A LONG TIME (slow, circular movement) and SIT ABRUPTLY (short, sharp movement) – are examples of verb aspect.

Equally clearly, aspectual marking on ASL verbs is iconic; changes in the temporal profile of the verb (the semantic pole) are represented by modifying the temporal profile of the movement parameter of the sign. This need not be so; we could logically envision a signed language in which verb aspect is marked by changing the location parameter: SIT FOR A LONG TIME might be made by producing the sign in front of the forehead, while SIT ABRUPTLY might be produced in front of the chin, and so on. In fact, of those signed languages which use morphology (as opposed, for example, to lexical or periphrastic means) to mark verb aspect, none do it this way. All rely on modifications to the temporal profile of the sign's movement to represent the semantic distinctions of aspect.

All of this leads me to propose a radical iconicity hypothesis for signed languages. I suggest that isomorphism across phonological and semantic structures is the preferred situation for signed language, both in the lexicon – fully instantiated symbolic structures – and in the grammar – highly schematic symbolic structures (Wilcox & Wilcox 1995; Wilcox 2002). Iconicity is a universal in signed language lexicon and grammar. This also suggests a partial answer to the question posed previously concerning differential resistance to erosion: of the two types of symbolic structures, lexical and grammatical, grammatical structures seem to be the most resistant to erosion of their iconicity.

5. Holding language constant

More than forty years ago, William C. Stokoe launched the modern field of signed language linguistics with his pioneering analysis of ASL. It is easy to lose sight of the significance Stokoe's most basic insight about signed languages (Stokoe 1960: 10): "All too few... are willing to face the fact that a symbol system by means of which persons carry on all the activities of their ordinary lives is, and ought to be treated as, a language." Certainly Stokoe was reacting to the centuries of misconceptions about signed languages that resulting from blind acceptance of Cartesian bifurcations. But even more importantly, Stokoe was proposing a strategic move, a paradigm shift, that was simple yet profound: hold signed language constant. Stokoe proposed that we embark on a scientific study of signed languages in which we examine the data from signed language on their own terms, free from assumptions based on centuries of systematically biased studies – that is, studies in which spoken languages comprised the only data. Only after we have made progress in understanding not just how signed languages are similar to spoken language, but also how they differ, do we return to the larger question of what signed languages can tell us about the origin of semiosis.

I like to compare Stokoe's proposal to Einstein's insight about holding constant the speed of light. Once we assume that light travels at a constant rate independent of observers, prior understandings and assumptions about the physical world are called into question, often in the most remarkable, counter-intuitive ways: we learn that time slows down for moving observers, that mass increases as objects approach the speed of light, and so forth.

Just as relativity brought about a new stage in our understanding of the physical world, I believe that treating language relatively, by not forcing signed language data into a predetermined mold formed by the study of data derived only from spoken languages, will lead to a new stage in the scientific study of signed languages and reveal new truths about the nature of human language. In his posthumous book *Language in hand* Stokoe (2001) calls this the second stage of signed language research:

> [That second stage is] recognizing that the difference between signing and speaking is highly important... When the materials of languages are as different as sounds and visible movements, and when the channels for receiving them are as different as hearing and seeing, the differences cry out to be noted, and they have something to tell us. After all, sameness tells us very little; it is differences that make a difference.

6. Grasping language: What can sign languages tell us about the origin of signs?

The description of signed language presented here has relied on a model of language which departs significantly from Cartesian linguistic theory. Rather than viewing language as pure structure, cognitive grammar assumes that language, not just lexicon but also grammar, is inherently symbolic, "providing for the structuring and conventional symbolization of conceptual content" (Langacker 1991a: 1). Moreover, rather than assuming that language is a self-contained system which functions autonomously from general cognitive processing, cognitive grammar assumes that "language is neither self-contained nor describable without essential reference to cognitive processing" (Langacker 1991a: 1). These cognitive processes are held to be of the type described by Varela and his colleagues (Varela, Thompson, & Rosch 1991) as "embodied cognition." According to Mark Johnson (Johnson 1987), embodied cognition may be characterized by image schemata: "An image schema is a recurring, dynamic pattern of perceptual interactions and motor programs that gives coherence and structure to our experience." Human cognition is formed by these image schema, the fruit of our bodily experience with the world consisting of "human bodily movement, manipulation of objects, and perceptual interactions" (p. xix).

From this perspective the factors that are critical to the origin of semiosis are embodied cognition based on visual perception and motor action, primarily manipulative actions of the hands. The view that emerges is one in which the moving hand and perceiving eye are bound together in the emergence of human semiotic ability. The remaining question is, what was it in our evolutionary history that brought together hands and eyes, motor action and visual perception, with language?

Recent research by Rizzolatti and his colleagues (Arbib & Rizzolatti 1996; Rizzolatti & Arbib 1998) suggests an answer. Rizzolatti reports on the function of so-called "mirror neurons" in Broca's area of primates and humans which mediate visual perception and recognition of manual motor actions such as grasping, holding, and tearing. Rizzolatti and Arbib (1998: 190) suggest that the "precursor of Broca's area was endowed before speech appearance with a mechanism for recognizing actions made by others." They conclude from this that "language in humans... evolved from a basic mechanism originally not related to communication: the capacity to recognize actions" (Rizzolatti & Arbib 1998: 193).

It may seem odd to suggest that language evolved from non-language, and even odder still to suppose that language evolved from non-communication, but I believe that is precisely the explanation we should be seeking if we are to understand the origins of semiosis. In making this proposal, I take my lead from the physical anthropologist Matt Cartmill, who writes (1990: 188):

> To understand the origin of anything, we must have an overarching body of theory that governs both the thing itself and its precursors. Without such a body of theory, we have no way of linking the precursor to its successors, and we are left with an ineffable mystery, like the one that Chomsky and Lenneberg have always insisted must lie at the origin of syntax.

I believe that the framework that I have been advocating here allows us to develop such an overarching body of theory. It also allows us to reunite gesture and language.

As powerful as Stokoe's work has proven to be since he first wrote *Sign Language Structure*, his goal of finding the deep connections between language and gesture has yet to be fully realized. For the past forty years, sign linguists have firmly denied that signed languages have anything to do with gesture.

Admittedly, this is tricky business. How do we acknowledge that signed languages are not simply gestures, and yet embrace and explore the deep links between language, whether spoken or signed, and gesture? Though Stokoe (1960: 2) set the agenda early on in *Sign Language Structure* to explore gesture as "the metalinguistic communicative phenomena out of which the primary communicative patterns of the deaf are built," sign linguists have been quite hesitant to follow this line of research. We are still mired in past histories, it seems, so burdened with proclaiming that signed languages are languages and not gestures that we are unable to take the next step, to explore the ways in which signed languages are related to gestures.

Perhaps it is not so surprising that linguists find it difficult to search for precursors of language in non-language since. But to be fair, understanding how things that appear different can be related is difficult for most people, as Cartmill again reminds us (1998: 78):

> [Y]ou might think that by now everyone would have gotten used to the idea that we are blood kin to all other organisms, and closer kin to great apes than to spi-

> ders. On the face of it, the idea makes a certain amount of plain common sense. We all know that we share more features with apes than we do with spiders or snails or cypress trees. The theory of evolution simply reads those shared features as family resemblances. It doesn't deny that people are unique in important ways. Our kinship with apes doesn't mean we're only apes under the skin, any more than the kinship of cats with dogs means that your cat is repressing a secret urge to bark and bury bones.

Likewise, recognizing that signed languages are kin to gestures does not mean that signed languages are only gestures under the skin. It simply means that we must recognize that the remarkable family resemblances between signs and gestures, and the tight integration of speech and gesture, imply a common semiotic ancestor.

Perhaps the antidote for the out-of-body delirium that Cartesian linguistics has induced is to set aside for a time all theoretical and disciplinary barriers between our understanding of human expression. I suggest that sign language studies can be good medicine. As Stokoe (1986: 171) saw clearly, "study of the language of deaf people helps to get around hypothetical constructions that block the view."

By studying signed languages perhaps we can also begin to see past the barriers that separate not just body and mind, language and gesture, sign and speech, but which also isolate language from the myriad other ways that humans use their bodies to make meaning. I propose we begin our task of deconstruction by asking artists, dancers, or musicians about the relation of form to meaning. Consider art. Rudolf Arnheim (1974: 460) understood better than many the intimate link that exists between form and meaning:

> [T]he visual form of a work of art is neither arbitrary not a mere play of shapes and colors. It is indispensable as a precise interpreter of the idea the work is meant to express. Similarly, the subject matter is neither arbitrary nor unimportant. It is exactly correlated with the formal pattern to supply a concrete embodiment of an abstract theme. The kind of connoisseur who looks only for the pattern does as little justice to the work as the kind of layman who looks only for the subject matter.

Cartesian linguistics has left a legacy which makes it exceedingly difficult to reunite language and other semiotic abilities. Just as there are no phylogenetic precursors to syntax, language is ontogentically isolated from other forms of expression such as dance, music, and art. This legacy has been particularly detrimental to the scientific study of signed languages. I would suggest that when we adopt a view of language such as that offered by cognitive grammar, and when we examine signed languages on their own terms, we may arrive at a view of the origins of semiosis that is compatible with what we might learn by studying any other form of expression. Arnheim asked, "If vision is an active grasp, what does it take hold of?" (1974: 43). My tentative answer is: It takes hold of language.

Notes

[1] In cognitive grammar, thing is a technical term for a region in some domain of conceptual space. Nouns are symbolic structures whose semantic pole profiles a thing. Process is a technical term meaning a relation having a positive temporal profile. A verb in cognitive grammar is a symbolic structure whose semantic pole profiles a process.

References

ARBIB, M.A. & G.RIZZOLATTI
1996 "Neural expectations: A possible evolutionary path from manual skills to language", *Communication & Cognition*, 29 (3-4): 393-424.

ARNHEIM, R.
1974 *Art and Visual Perception: A Psychology of the Creative Eye* (The new version ed.), Berkeley, CA: University of California Press.

BLAKE, J.
2000 *Routes to Child Language: Evolutionary and Developmental Precursors*. Cambridge/New York: Cambridge UP.

BRENTARI, D.
1998 *A Prosodic Model of Sign Language Phonology*, Cambridge, MA: MIT Press.

BROWMAN, C. & L. GOLDSTEIN
1989 "Articulatory gestures a phonological units", *Phonology*, 6: 201-251.

BYBEE, J., PERKINS, R. & W. PAGLIUCA
1994 *The Evolution of Grammar: Tense, Aspect, and Modality in the Languages of the World*. Chicago: University of Chicago Press.

CAPIRCI, O., CASELLI, M.C., IVERSON, J.M., PIZZUTO, E. & V. VOLTERRA
1999 *Gesture and the Nature of Language in Infancy: The Role of Gesture as a Transitional Device Enroute to Two-Word Speech*, Paper presented at the William C. Stokoe and the Study of Language, Washington, DC.

CARTMILL, M.
1990 "Human uniqueness and theoretical content in paleoanthropology", *International Journal of Primatology*, 11(3): 173-192.

CARTMILL, M.
1998 "Oppressed by evolution", *Discover*, 19 (3): 78-83.

CHOMSKY, N.
1957 *Syntactic Structures*, The Hague: Mouton.
1966 *Cartesian Linguistics*, NY: Harper & Row.
1972 *Language and Mind*, NY: Harcourt Brace Jovanovich.

CHURCHLAND, P.
1986 *Neurophilosophy*, Cambridge, MA: MIT Press.

COMRIE, B.
1976 *Aspect: An Introduction to the Study of Verbal Aspect and Related Problems*, Cambridge: Cambridge UP.

DESCARTES, R.
1980/1641 *Discourse on Method and Meditations on First Philosophy* (trans. D.A. Cress), Indianapolis: Hackett Publishing Co.

EDELMAN, G.M.
1987 *Neural Darwinism: The Theory of Neuronal Group Selection*, New York: Basic Books.

FARNELL, B.
1995 *Do you See what I mean: Plains Indian Sign Talk and the Embodiment of Action*, Austin: University of Texas Press.

FOWLER, C.A.
1986 "An event approach to the study of speech perception from a direct-realist perspective", *Journal of Phonetics*, 14, 3-28.

FRISHBERG, N.
1975 "Arbitrariness and iconicity: Historical change in American Sign Language", *Language*, 51: 676-710.

HAIMAN, J.
1994 "Ritualization and the development of language", in W. Pagliuca (ed.), *Perspectives on Grammaticalization*, Amsterdam: John Benjamins: XX-XX

HAIMAN, J.
1998 *Talk is Cheap: Sarcasm, Alienation, and the Evolution Of Language*, Oxford: Oxford UP.

HEINE, B., CLAUDI, U. & F. HÜNNEMEYER
1991 *Grammaticalization: A Conceptual Framework*, Chicago: University of Chicago Press.

HOPPER, P. & E.TRAUGOTT
1993 *Grammaticalization*. New York, NY: Cambridge University Press.

JANNEY, R.W.
1999 "Words as gestures", *Journal of Pragmatics*, 31(7), 953-972.

JANZEN, T.
1998 *Topicality in ASL: Information Ordering, Constituent Structure, and the Function of Topic Marking*, unpublished doctoral dissertation, University of New Mexico, Albuquerque, NM.

JANZEN, T. & B.SHAFFER

To appear "Gesture as the substrate in the process of ASL grammaticization", in R. Meier, D. Quinto, & K. Cormier (eds.), *Modality and Structure in Signed and Spoken Languages*, Cambridge: Cambridge UP.

JOHNSON, M.

1987 *The Body in the Mind: The Bodily Basis of Meaning, Imagination, and Reason*, Chicago, IL: University of Chicago Press.

KELSO, J.A.M., SALTZMAN, E.L. & B. TULLER

1986 "The dynamical perspective on speech production: Data and theory". *Journal of Phonetics*, 14, 29-59.

KIMURA, D.

1993 *Neuromotor Mechanisms in Human Communication*, Oxford: Oxford UP.

KLIMA, E. & U. BELLUGI

1979 *The Signs of Language*, Cambridge, MA: Harvard UP.

LAKOFF, G.

1987 *Women, Fire, and Dangerous Things: What Categories Reveal about the Mind*, Chicago, IL: University of Chicago Press.

LAKOFF, G. & M. JOHNSON

1999 *Philosophy in the Flesh: The Embodied Mind and its Challenge to Western Thought*, New York, NY: Basic Books.

LANE, H.

1984 *When the Mind Hears: A History of the Deaf*, New York, NY: Random House.

LANGACKER, R.W.

1972 *Fundamentals of Linguistic Analysis*, New York: Harcourt Brace Jovanovich, Inc.

1987a *Foundations of Cognitive Grammar* (vol. 1: *Theoretical Foundations*), Stanford: Stanford UP.

1987b "Nouns and verbs", *Language*, 63 (1): 53-94.

1991a Concept, Image, and Symbol: the Cognitive Basis of Grammar, Berlin: Mouton de Gruyter.

1991b *Foundations of Cognitive Grammar*, vol. II: *Descriptive Application*, Stanford: Stanford UP.

LIDDELL, S.K.

1998 "Grounded blends, gestures, and conceptual shifts", *Cognitive Linguistics*, 9 (3): 283-314.

LIDDELL, S.K. & M.METZGER

1998 "Gesture in sign language discourse", *Journal of Pragmatics*, 30 (6): 657-697.

MCNEILL, D.

1992 *Hand and Mind: What Gestures Reveal about Thought*, Chicago: University of Chicago Press.

MEIER, R.
1991 "Language acquisition by deaf children", *American Scientist*, 79: 60-70.

PETITTO, L.A.
1987 "On the autonomy of language and gesture: Evidence from the acquisition of personal pronouns in American Sign Language", *Cognition*, 27: 1-52.

PINKER, S.
1994 *The Language Instinct*, NY: Morrow.

RIZZOLATTI, G. & M.A. ARBIB
1998 "Language within our grasp", *Trends in Neurosciences*, 21 (5): 188-194.

SHAFFER, B.
2000 A syntactic, pragmatic analysis of the expression of necessity and possibility in American Sign Language, Unpublished Dissertation, University of New Mexico, Albuquerque, New Mexico.

SHAFFER, B. & T. JANZEN
2000 *Gesture, Lexical Words, and Grammar: Grammaticization Processes in ASL*, Paper presented at the 26th Annual Meeting of the Berkeley Linguistics Society, Berkeley, CA.

SIMONE, R.
1995 "Under the sign of Cratylus", in R. Simone (ed.), *Iconicity in Language*, Amsterdam: John Benjamins: vii-xi

SINGLETON, J. L., MORFORD, J.P. & S. GOLDIN-MEADOW
1993 "Once is not enough: Standards of well-formedness in manual communication created over three different timespans", *Language*, 69 (4): 683-715.

STOKOE, W.C.
1960 *Sign Language Structure* (reprint 1978 ed.), Silver Spring, MD: Linstok Press.

STOKOE, W.C.
1974 "Motor signs as the first form of language", in R.W.Wescott, G.W. Hewes & W.C. Stokoe (eds.), *Language Origins*, Silver Spring, MD: Linkstok Press.
1986 "Where should we look for language?", *Sign Language Studies*, 51: 171-181.
2001 *Language in Hand*, Washington, DC: Gallaudet UP.

STUDDERT-KENNEDY, M.
1987 *The Phoneme as a Perceptuomotor Structure*, in D. A. Allport (ed.), *Language Perception and Production: Relationships between Listening, Speaking, Reading, and Writing*, London: Academic Press.

SWEETSER, E.E.
1990 *From Etymology to Pragmatics: Metaphorical and Cultural Aspects of Semantic Structure*, Cambridge: Cambridge UP.

TAUB, S.
2001 *Language in the Body: Iconicity and Conceptual Metaphor in American Sign Language*, Cambridge: Cambridge UP.

VALLI, C. & C. LUCAS
1995 *Linguistics of American Sign Language: An Introduction* (2nd ed.), Washington, DC: Gallaudet UP.

VARELA, F.J., THOMPSON, E. & E. ROSCH
1991 *The Embodied Mind: Cognitive Science and Human Experience*, Cambridge, MA: MIT Press.

WELLS, G.A.
1987 *The Origin of Language: Aspects of the Discussion from Condillac to Wundt*, La Salle, IL: Open Court.

WILCOX, P. & S. WILCOX
1995 "The gestural expression of modality in American Sign Language", in J. Bybee & S. Fleischman (eds.), *Modality in Grammar and Discourse*, Amsterdam: John Benjamins.

WILCOX, P.P.
2001 *Metaphors in American Sign Language*, Washington, DC: Gallaudet UP.

WILCOX, S.
2000a *Gesture, Icon, and Symbol: The Expression of Modality in Signed Languages*, Paper presented at the Berkeley Linguistics Society, Berkeley, Calif.
2000b *What Can Signed Languages Tell Us about the Origins of Semiosis*, Paper presented at the Origins of Semiosis, University of San Marino, San Marino, Italy.
2001 "The iconic mapping of space and time in signed languages", in L. Albertazzi (ed.), *Unfolding Perceptual Continua*, Amsterdam: John Benjamins.

WILCOX, S., SHAFFER, B., JARQUE, M.J., VALENTI, J.M.S.I., PIZZUTO, E. & P. ROSSINI
2000 *The Emergence of Grammar from Word and Gesture: A Cross-Linguistic Study of Modal Verbs in Three Signed Languages*, Paper presented at the 7th International Conference on Theoretical Issues in Sign Language Research, Amsterdam.

Alex Martin

THE NEURAL BASIS OF SEMANTIC KNOWLEDGE

1. Introduction

Semantic knowledge is a type of long-term memory, commonly referred to as semantic memory, consisting of concepts, facts, ideas, and beliefs (e.g., Tulving 1983). Semantic memory is thus distinct from *episodic* or *autobiographical* memories which are unique to an individual and tied to a specific time and place. For example, answering the question: "What does the word *breakfast* mean?" requires semantic memory. In contrast, answering the question "What did you have for breakfast yesterday?" requires episodic memory, to retrieve information about events in our personal past, as well as semantic memory, to understand the question. Semantic memory therefore includes the information stored in our brains that represents the meaning of words and objects.

Understanding the nature of meaning, however, has proven to be a fairly intractable problem; especially regarding the meaning of words. One important reason why this is so is that words have multiple meanings. The specific meaning of a word is determined by context, and comprehension is possible because we have contextual representations.[1] Cognitive neuroscientists have begun to get traction on the problem of meaning in the brain by limiting inquiry to concrete objects as represented by pictures, and by their names.

Consider, for example, the most common meaning of two concrete objects; a camel and a wrench. Camel is defined as "either of two species of large, domesticated ruminants (genus camelus) with a humped back, long neck, and large cushioned feet", the object wrench is defined as "any number of tools used for holding and turning nuts, bolts, pipes, etc." (*Webster's New World Dictionary*, Third college Edition, 1988). Two things are noteworthy about these definitions. First, they are largely about features; camels are large and have a humped back, wrenches hold and turn things. Second, different types of features are emphasized for different types of objects. The definition of the camel consists of information about its visual appearance, whereas the definition of the wrench emphasizes how it is used.

Differences in the type of features that define different objects has played, and continues to play, a central role in models of how semantic knowledge is organized in the human brain.

Another point about these brief definitions is that they include only part, and perhaps only a small part, of the information we may possess about these objects. For example, we may know that camels are found primarily in Asia and Africa, that they are known as the "ships of the desert", and that the word camel can refer to a color as well as a brand of cigarettes. Similarly, we also know that camels are larger than a bread box and weigh less than a 747 jumbo jet. Although this information is also part of semantic memory, little is known about the brain bases of these associative and inferential processes. Neuroscientists are, however, beginning to gain insights into the functional neuroanatomy associated with identifying objects and retrieving information about specific object features and attributes.

2. Semantic representations

A central question for investigators interested in the functional neuroanatomy of semantic memory has been to determine how information about object concepts is represented in the brain. A particularly influential idea guiding much of this work is that the features and attributes that define an object are stored in the perceptual and motor systems active when we first learned about that object. For example, information about the visual form of an object, its typical color, its unique pattern of motion, would be stored in or near regions of the visual system that mediate perception of form, color, and motion. Similarly, knowledge about the sequences of motor movements associated with the use of an object would be stored in or near the motor systems active when that object was used. This idea has a long history in behavioral neurology. Indeed, many neurologists at the turn of the century assumed the concept of an object was composed of the information about that object learned through direct sensory experience and stored in or near sensory and motor cortices (e.g., Lissauer 1988, 1890).

3. Semantic deficits result from damage to the left temporal lobe

The modern era of study on the organization of semantic knowledge in the human brain began with Elizabeth Warrington's seminal paper "The selective impairment of semantic memory" (Warrington 1975). Warrington reported three patients with progressive dementing disorders that provided neurological evidence for a semantic memory system. There were three main components to the disorder. First, it was selective. The disorder could not be accounted for by general intellectual impairment, sensory or perceptual problems, or an expressive language disorder. Second, the disorder was global, in the sense that it was neither material- nor modality-specific. Object knowledge was impaired regardless of whether objects were represented by pictures or their written or spoken names. Third, the disorder was graded. Knowledge of specific object attributes (e.g., does a camel have two, four, or six legs?) was more impaired than knowledge of superordinate category information (i.e., is a camel a mammal, bird, or insect?).

Following Warrington's report, similar patterns of semantic memory dysfunction have been reported in patients with brain damage resulting from a wide range of etiologies. These have included patients with progressive dementias such as Alzheimer's disease and semantic dementia, herpes encephalitis, and closed head injury.[2] Consistent with the properties established by Warrington, these patients typically had marked difficulty producing object names under a variety of circumstances, including naming pictures of objects, naming from the written descriptions of objects, and generating lists of objects that belong to a specific category (e.g., animals, fruits and vegetables, furniture, etc.). In addition, the deficits were primarily associated with damage to the left temporal lobe, suggesting that information about object concepts may be stored, at least in part, in this region of the brain.

4. Brain damage can lead to category-specific semantic deficits

Other patients have been described with relatively selective deficits recognizing, naming, and retrieving information about different object categories. The categories that have attracted the most attention are animals and tools. This is because of a large and growing number of reports of patients with greater difficulty naming and retrieving information about animals (and often other living things) than about tools (and often other man-made objects). Reports of the opposite pattern of dissociation (greater for tools than animals) are less frequent. However, enough carefully studied cases have been reported to provide convincing evidence that these categories can be doubly dissociated as a result of brain damage. The impairment in these patients is not limited to visual recognition. Deficits occur when knowledge is probed visually and verbally, and therefore, assumed to reflect damage to the semantic system or systems.[3]

While it is now generally accepted that these disorders are genuine, their explanation, on both the cognitive and neural levels, remains controversial. Two general types of explanations have been proposed. The most common explanation focuses on the disruption of stored information about object features. Specially, it has been proposed that knowledge about animals and tools can be selectively disrupted because these categories are dependent on information about different types of features stored in different regions of the brain. As exemplified by the definitions provided previously, animals are defined primarily by what they look like. Functional attributes play a much smaller role in their definition. In contrast, functional information, specifically, how an object is used, is critical for defining tools. As a result, damage to areas where object form information is stored leads to deficits for categories that are overly-dependent on visual form information, whereas damage to regions where object use information is stored leads to deficits for categories overly-dependent on functional information. The finding that patients with category-specific deficits for animals also have difficulties with other visual-form based-categories, such as precious stones, provides additional support for this view.[4]

This general framework for explaining category-specific disorders was first proposed by Warrington and colleagues in the mid to late 1980's.[5] Influential extensions and reformulation of this general idea have been provided by a number of investigators including Farah and McClelland (1991), Damasio (1990), Caramazza et al. (1990), and Humphreys and Riddoch (1987).

The second type of explanation focuses on broader semantic distinctions (e. g., animate versus inanimate objects), rather than on features and attributes, as the key to understanding category-specific deficits. A variant of this argument has recently been proposed by Caramazza and Shelton (1998) to counter a number of difficulties with feature-based formulations. Specifically, these investigators note that a central prediction of at least some of feature-based models is that patients with a category-specific deficits for animals should have more difficulty answering questions that probe knowledge about visual information about animals (does an elephant have a long tail?), than about functional information (is a elephant found in the jungle?). As Caramazza and Shelton (1998) show, at least some patients with an animal-specific knowledge disorder (and, according to their argument, all genuine cases) have equivalent difficulty with both visual and functional questions about animals. As a result of these and other findings, Caramazza and Shelton argue that category-specific disorders can not be explained by feature-based models. Instead, they propose that such disorders reflect evolutionary adaptations for animate objects, foods, and perhaps by default, tools and other man-made objects (the "domain-specific hypothesis"; Caramazza and Shelton 1998).

5. Functional brain imaging reveals that semantic knowledge about objects is distributed in different regions of the brain

Functional brain imaging allows investigators to identify the neural systems active when normal individuals perform different types of tasks. These studies have confirmed findings with brain damaged subjects, and have begun to extend our knowledge of the neural basis of semantic memory. Although functional brain imaging is a relatively new tool, the current evidence suggests that information about different object features are stored in different regions of the cerebral cortex. One body of evidence in support of this claim comes from experiments using word generation tasks. Subjects are presented with the name of an object, or a picture of an object, and required to generate a word denoting a specific feature or attribute associated with that object. In one study, positron emission tomography (PET), was used to investigate differences in patterns of brain activity when subjects generated the name of an action typically associated with an object (e.g., saying the word "pull" in response to a static, achromatic line-drawing of a child's wagon), relative to generating an associated color word (e.g., saying "red" in response to the wagon) (Martin et al. 1995). Relative to generating a color word, action word generation activated a posterior region of the left temporal lobe, called the middle temporal gyrus. This location was of particular interest because it was just anterior to sites known to be active during motion perception (area MT). In contrast, relative to generating action words, color word generation activated a region on the ventral, or under side of the temporal lobe, called the fusiform gyrus. This location was of particular interest because it was just anterior to sites known to be active during color perception. Finally, the same pattern of results were found when subjects were presented with the written names of objects, rather than an object picture (Figure 1, p. 180).[6]

These findings, and findings from other studies using a wide range of semantic processing tasks, provide support for two important ideas about the neural representation of semantic knowledge. First, there is a single semantic system in the brain, rather than separate semantic systems for different modalities of input (visual, auditory) or types of material (pictures of objects, words) (e. g., Vandeberghe, et al. 1996). This system includes multiple brain regions, especially in the temporal and frontal lobes of the left hemisphere.[7] Second, information about object features and attributes are not stored in a single location, but rather are stored as a distributed network of discrete cortical areas. Moreover, the locations of the sites appear to follow a specific plan that parallels the organization of sensory systems, and, as will be reviewed below, motor systems, as well.

6. Ventral occipitotemporal cortex and the representation of object form

Another body of evidence that object concepts may be represented by distributed feature networks comes from studies contrasting patterns of neural activity associated with naming, and performing other types of tasks with objects from different categories. A feature common to all concrete objects is that they have physical shape or form. Evidence is accumulating that suggests that many object categories elicit distinct patterns of neural activity in regions involved in object form processing (ventral occipital and temporal cortex). Moreover, the locations of these category-related activations appear to be consistent across individual subjects and processing tasks (e.g., naming object pictures, matching pictures, reading object names). This seems to be especially so for objects defined primarily by visual form-related features such as animals, faces, and landmarks.

Early reports using PET found that naming (Martin et al. 1996), and matching (Perani et al. 1995), pictures of animals resulted in greater activation of the left occipital cortex than performing these same tasks with pictures of tools. Because occipital cortex is primarily involved in the early stages of visual processing, it was suggested that this activity reflected top-down activation from more anterior sites in the occipitotemporal object processing stream (Martin et al. 1996). This may occur whenever detailed information about visual features or form is needed to identify an object. Specifically, naming objects that differ from other members of the same category by relatively subtle differences in visual form (four-legged animals) may require access to stored information about visual detail. Retrieving this information, in turn, may require participation of early visual processing areas in occipital cortex. A subsequent report showing that unilateral occipital lesions could result in greater difficulty naming and retrieving information about animals than tools provided converging evidence for this view (Tranel et al. 1997).

However, most patients with semantic deficits for animals have had lesions confined to the temporal lobes.[8] Functional brain imaging of normal individuals has now provided evidence for category-related activations in the ventral region of the temporal lobes. This has been accomplished by using functional magnetic resonance imaging (fMRI), which provides better spatial resolution than was possible using PET.

A number of investigators have found that distinct regions of ventral temporal cortex show differential responses to different object categories. In one study, viewing, naming, and matching pictures of animals, as well as answering written questions about animals, were found to activate the lateral region of the fusiform gyrus, relative to performing these tasks with pictures and names of tools. In contrast, the medial fusiform was more active for tools than animals. A similar, but not identical pattern of activation was found for viewing faces (lateral fusiform) relative to viewing houses (medial fusiform) (Chao et al. 1999). Other investigators have also reported face-related activity in the lateral region of the fusiform gyrus, and house-related activity in more medial regions of the ventral temporal lobe, including the fusiform, lingual, and parahippocampal gyri (Figure 2, p. 182).[9]

These findings suggest that different object categories elicit activity in different regions of ventral temporal cortex, as defined by the location of their peak activation. Moreover, the topological arrangement of these peaks was consistent across subjects and tasks. Importantly, however, the activity associated with each object category was not limited to a specific region of ventral occipitotemporal cortex, but rather was distributed over much of the region (Chao et al. 1999).

Additional evidence for the distributed nature of object representations in ventral temporal cortex comes from single cell recordings from intracranial depth electrodes implanted in epileptic patients (Kreiman et al. 2000a). Recordings from the regions of the medial temporal cortex (entorhinal cortex, hippocampus, and amygdala), which receive major inputs from the ventral temporal regions described above, identified neurons that showed highly selective responses to different object categories including animals, faces, and houses. Moreover, the responses of the neurons were category-specific rather than stimulus-specific. That is, animal-responsive cells responded to all pictures of animals, rather than to one picture or a select few.

Studies reporting similar patterns of neural activity when subjects view and imagine objects provide further support that object information is stored in these regions of cortex. For example, regions active during face perception are also active when subjects imagine famous individuals (O'Craven & Kanwisher 2000). Similar findings have been reported for viewing and imagining known landmarks (O'Craven & Kanwisher 2000), houses, and even chairs (Ishai et al. 2001). In addition, the majority of category-selective neurons recorded from human temporal cortex also responded selectively when the patients were asked to imagine these objects (Kreiman et al. 2000b).

Taken together, the data suggest that ventral occipitotemporal cortex may be best viewed, not as a mosaic of discrete category-specific areas, but rather as a lumpy feature-space, representing stored information about features of object form shared by members of a category. How this feature space is organized, and why its topological arrangement is so consistent from one subject to another, are critical questions for future investigations.

7. Lateral temporal cortex and the representation of object motion

Information about how objects move through space, and patterns of motor movements associated with their use, are other features that could aid object identification. This would be especially true for categories of man-made objects like tools that have a more variable mapping between their name and their visual form than a category like four-legged animals. Thus access to these additional features may be required to identify them as unique entities. Here again, evidence is accumulating that naming and identifying objects with motion-related attributes activate areas close to regions that mediate perception of object motion (posterior region of the lateral temporal lobe) with different patterns of activity associated with biological and man-made objects.

A number of laboratories using a variety of paradigms with pictures and words have reported that tools elicit greater activity in the posterior, left middle temporal gyrus than animals and other object categories.[10] Moreover, the active region was just anterior to area MT and overlapped with the region active in the verb generation studies discussed above. Damage to this region has been reported to selectively impair tool recognition and naming (Tranel et al. 1997). In contrast, naming animals and viewing faces elicits greater activity in the superior temporal sulcus (STS) (Figure 2, p. 182). This region is of particular interest because of its association with the perception of biological motion in monkeys as well as humans.[11] As suggested for ventral temporal cortex, neurons in the lateral temporal cortex may also be tuned to features that objects within a category share. The nature of these features is unknown; however, based on its anatomical proximity to visual motion processing areas, this region may be tuned to features of motion associated with different objects. In support of this conjecture, increased activity in posterior, lateral temporal cortex has been found when subjects viewed static pictures of objects that imply motion (Kourtzi & Kanwisher 2000; Senior et al. 2000) and when subjects focused attention on the direction of eye gaze (Hoffman & Haxby 2000). Investigation of the differences in the properties of motion associated with biological and man-made objects may provide clues to the organization of this region.

8. Ventral premotor cortex and the representation of use-associated motor movements

If activations associated with different object categories reflect stored information about object properties, then one would expect tools to elicit activity in motor-related regions. Several laboratories have reported this association. Specifically, greater activation of left ventral premotor cortex has been found for naming tools relative to naming animals, viewing pictures of tools relative to viewing pictures of animals, faces, and houses, and generating action words to tools (Figure 2, p. 182). Mental imagery (e.g., imagining manipulating objects with the right hand) has also resulted in ventral premotor activation (Figure 2, p. 182).[12]

Electrophysiological studies have identified cells in monkey ventral premotor cortex that responded not only when objects are grasped, but also when the animals viewed objects they have had experience manipulating (Jeannerod et al. 1995). The ventral premotor activation noted in the human neuroimaging studies may reflect a similar process. These findings are consistent with reports of patients with greater difficulty naming tools than animals following damage to left lateral frontal cortex,[13] and suggest that left ventral premotor cortex may be necessary for naming and retrieving information about tools.

9. Conclusions and future directions

Evidence from functional brain imaging studies provide considerable support for feature-based models of semantic representation. However, some of the findings could be interpreted as evidence for the "domain-specific" hypothesis, as well. For example, the clustering of activations associated with animals and faces, on the one hand, and tools and houses, on the other hand, may be viewed as consistent with this interpretation. Other evidence suggests, however, that all non-biological object representations do not cluster together. For example, it has been reported that activity associated with a category of objects of no evolutionary significance (chairs) was located lateral to the face-responsive region (in the inferior temporal gyrus), rather than medially where tools and houses elicit their strongest activity (Ishai et al. 1999). Both functional brain imaging and patient studies suggest that object knowledge is represented in distributed cortical networks. There does not seem to be single regions that map on to whole object categories. Nevertheless, there may be a broader organization of these networks that reflects evolutionarily adapted, domain-specific knowledge systems for biological and non-biological kinds. This possibility remains to be explored.

Although progress is being made in understanding the neural substrate of some aspects of meaning, many important questions and issues remain. For example, semantic representations are pre-lexical. Yet, to be of service they must be intimately linked to the lexicon.

Little is known about how the lexicon is organized in the brain and how lexical and semantic networks interact (Damasio et al. 1996).

Another important issue concerns the neural basis of retrieval from semantic memory. Semantic knowledge, like all stored information, is not useful unless it can be efficiently retrieved. Studies of patients with focal lesions have shown that the left lateral prefrontal cortex is critically involved in word retrieval, even in the absence of a frank aphasia (e. g., Baldo and Shimamura 1998). Functional brain imaging studies have confirmed this association (Figure 2). Moreover, recent evidence suggests that different regions of left inferior prefrontal cortex may mediate selection among competing alternatives in semantic memory, whereas other regions may be involved in retrieving, manipulating, and maintaining semantic information in working memory.[14] Much additional work will be needed to describe the role that different regions of prefrontal cortex play in semantic processing.

Another critical question will be to determine how semantic object representations are modified by experience. Some of the findings discussed here suggest that the topological arrangement among object categories in the cortex is relatively fixed. Other evidence suggests a much more flexible organization in which the development of expertise with an object category involves a particular portion of the fusiform gyrus (Gauthier et al. 1999). Longitudinal studies tracking changes in the brain associated with learning about completely novel objects should help to clarify this issue.

There is also little known about where object information unrelated to sensory or motor properties is stored (e.g., that camels live in Asia and Africa). Similarly, little is known about the representation of abstract concepts (e. g., honor, liberty, and justice), metaphors, and the like.

Finally, questions concerning the neural systems involved in object category formation have been nearly totally neglected. E. E. Smith and colleagues have shown that exemplar-based and rule-based categorization activate different neural structures (Smith et al. 1999). This finding suggests that categorization processes may be a fruitful area for future investigation. The advent of techniques to converge fMRI data with technologies such as magnetoencephalography (MEG) that provide temporal information on the order of milliseconds, should provide a wealth of new information on the neural basis of semantic knowledge.

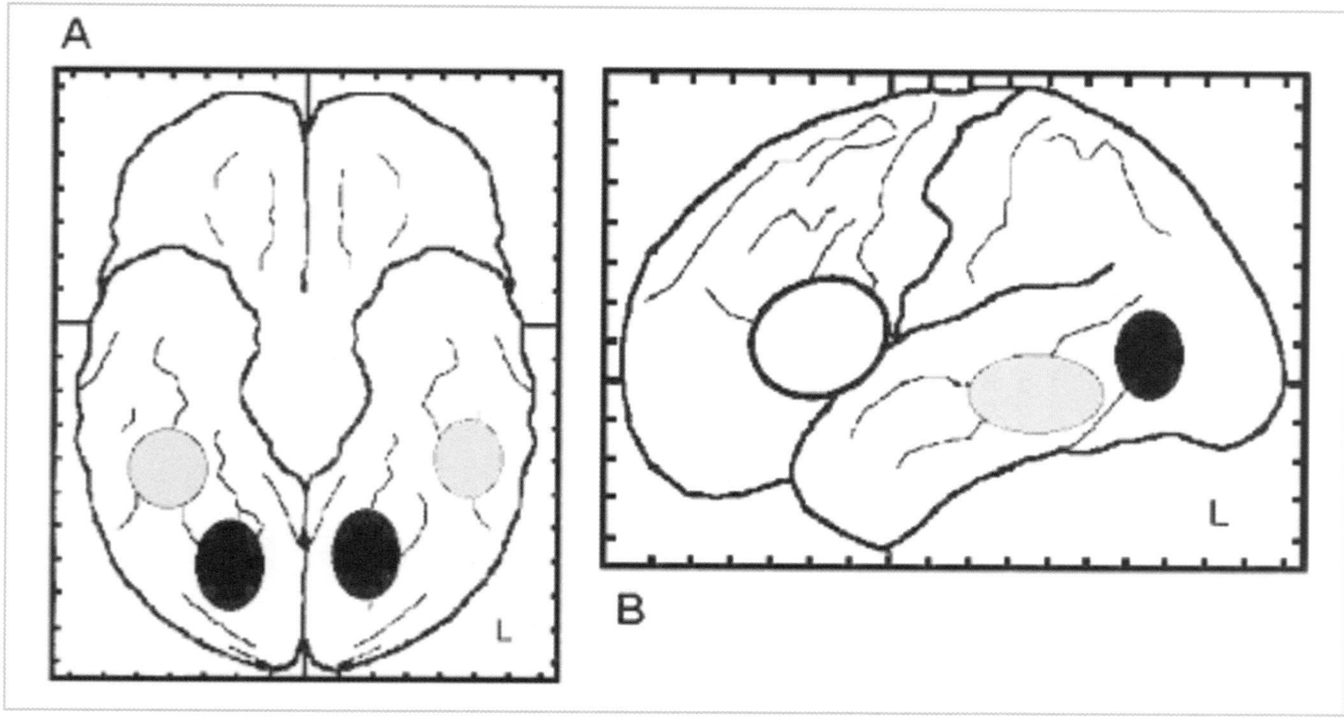

Figure 1. Brain regions active during retrieval of color and action knowledge

Figure 1

Brain regions active during retrieval of color and action knowledge: A Ventral view of the human brain showing approximate locations of regions in occipital cortex active during color perception (black ovals), and color word generation in response to object pictures and object names (gray ovals). Gray region is based on four brain imaging studies. This region is also active when subjects generate color imagery in response to verbal commands, and in subjects with auditory word - color synethesia when spontaneously experiencing color imagery in response to hearing words (for review see Martin 2001). B Lateral view of the left hemisphere showing location of the region active during motion perception (area MT; black oval). Also shown is the region of the middle temporal gyrus active when subjects generated action words to object pictures, and object names (gray oval). Location of this region is based on over 20 studies encompassing nine native languages ranging from English to Mandarin Chinese (for review see Martin 2001). The white oval indicates the approximate location of the region of inferior prefrontal cortex implicated in selecting, retrieving, and maintaining lexical and phonological information (for review see Martin and Chao 2001).

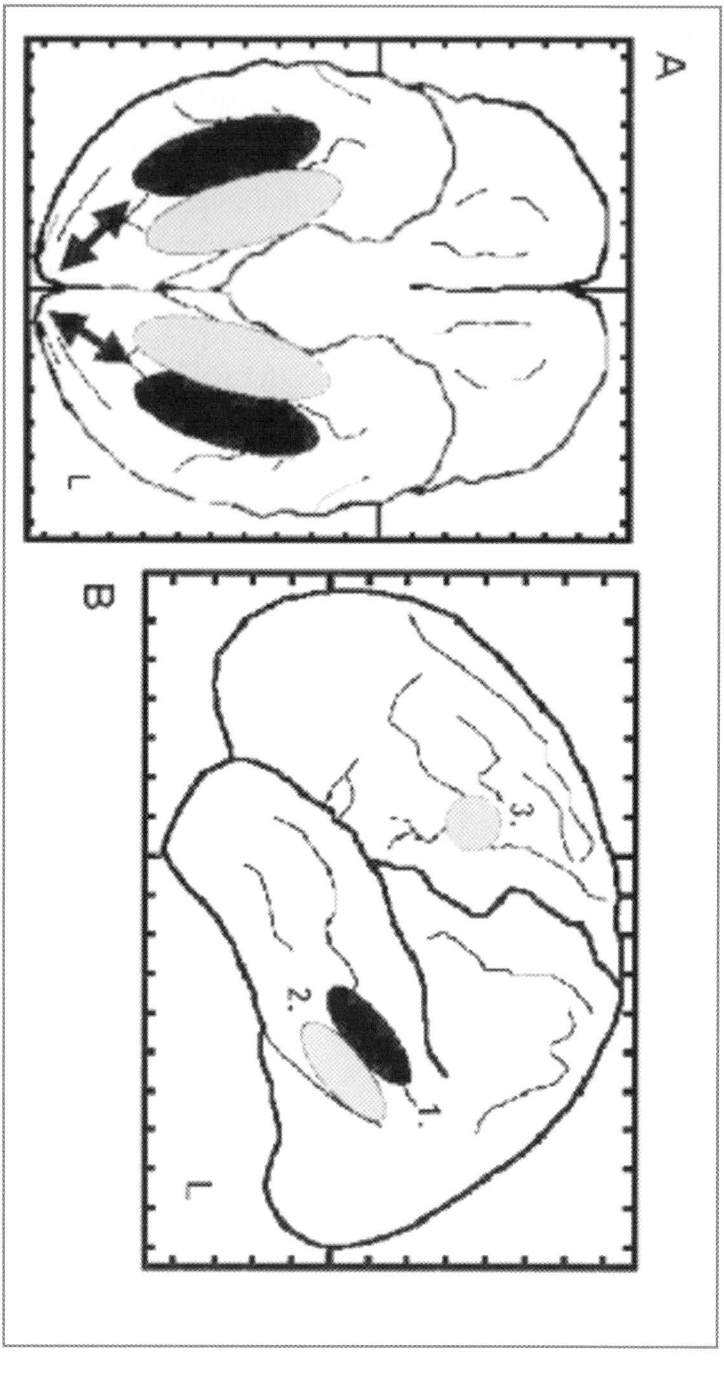

Figure 2. Brain regions showing object category-related patterns of activation

Figure 2

Brain regions showing object category-related patterns of activation. Approximate location of regions in the ventral temporal cortex (A), and lateral cortex (B), active during viewing, naming, and retrieving information about animals (black ovals) and tools (gray ovals). These categories, as well as other object categories like human faces and houses, produce complex, overlapping, but consistent, patterns of activity; especially in ventral temporal cortex. Because of their anatomical proximity to visual object form (and form-related features like color), motion, and motor processing areas, it has been suggested that information about how an object appears, moves, and is used, is stored in these regions (see text for details). These regions interact with lower-level visual processing areas in occipital cortex (double arrows); especially when discriminating among items of similar appearance (e. g., four-legged animals, faces). 1. Superior temporal sulcus (STS). 2. Middle temporal gyrus. 3. Premotor cortex.

Notes

[1] See Miller 1999 for a discussion of lexical semantics and context.
[2] For review see Patterson and Hodges 1995.
[3] For review see Forde & Humphreys 1999.
[4] See Warrington & Shallice 1984.
[5] See Warrington and Shallice 1984.
[6] For review see Martin 2001.
[7] For review see Price et al., 1999 and Martin 2001.
[8] For review see Gainotti et al. 1995.
[9] For review see Kanwisher et al. 2001 and Martin 2001.
[10] For review see Martin 2001.
[11] For review see Allison et al. 2001.
[12] For review see Martin 2001.
[13] For review see Gainotti et al. 1995.
[14] For review see Martin and Chao 2001.

References

ALLISON, T., PUCE, A. & G. MCCARTHY
2000 "Social perception and visual cues: Role of the STS", *Trends in Cognitive Science*, 4: 267-278.

BALDO, J.V. & A.P. SHIMAMURA
1998 "Letter and category fluency in patients with frontal lobe lesions", *Neuropsychology*, 12: 259-267.

CARAMAZZA, A. & J.R. SHELTON
1998 "Domain-specific knowledge systems in the brain the animate-inanimate distinction", *J. Cognitive Neuroscience*, 10: 1-34.

CARAMAZZA, A., HILLIS, A.E., RAPP, B.C. & C. ROMANI
1990 "The multiple semantics hypothesis: multiple confusions?", *Cognitive Neuropsychology*, 7: 161-189.

CHAO, L.L., HAXBY, J.V. & A. MARTIN
1999 "Attribute-based neural substrates in temporal cortex for perceiving and knowing about objects", *Nature Neuroscience*, 2: 913-919.

DAMASIO, A.R.
1990 "Category-related recognition deficits as a clue to the neural substrates of knowledge", *Trends in Neuroscience*, 13: 95-98.

DAMASIO, H., GRABOWSKI, T.J., TRANEL, D., HICHWA, R.D. & A.R. DAMASIO
1996 "A neural basis for lexical retrieval", *Nature*, 380: 499-505.

FARAH, M.J. & J.L. MCCLELLAND
1991 "A computational model of semantic memory impairment: Modality specificity and emergent category specificity", *Journal of Experimental Psychology: General*, 120: 1991.

FORDE, E.M.E. & G.W. HUMPHREYS
1999 "Category-specific recognition impairments: a review of important case studies and influential theories", *Aphasiology*, 13: 169-193.

GAINOTTI, G., SILVERI, M.C., DANIELE, A. & L. GIUSTOLISI
1995 "Neuroanatomical correlates of category-specific semantic disorders: a critical survey", *Memory*, 3: 247-264.

GAUTHIER, I., TARR, M.J., ANDERSON, A.W., SKUDLARSKI, P. & J.C. GORE
1999 "Activation of the middle fusiform 'face area' increases with expertise in recognizing novel objects", *Nature Neuroscience,* 2: 568-573.

HOFFMAN, E.A. & J.V. HAXBY
2000 "Distinct representations of eye gaze and identity in the distributed human neural system for face perception", *Nature Neuroscience*, 3: 80-84.

HUMPHREYS, G.W. & M.J. RIDDOCH
1987 "On telling your fruit from your vegetables: A consideration of category-specific deficits after brain damage", *Trends in Neurosciences*, 10: 145-148.

ISHAI, A., UNGERLEIDER, L.G. & J.V. HAXBY
2001 "Distributed neural systems for the generation of visual images", *Neuron,* in press.

ISHAI, A., UNGERLEIDER, L.G., MARTIN, A., SCHOUTEN, J.L. & J.V. HAXBY
1999 "Distributed representation of objects in the ventral visual pathway", *Proceedings of the National Academy of Sciences*, USA., 96: 9379-9384.

JEANNEROD, M., ARBIB, M.A., RIZZOLATTI, G. & H. SAKATA
1995 "Grasping objects: the cortical mechanisms of visuomotor transformation", *Trends in Neurosciences*, 18: 314-320.

KANWISHER, N., DOWNING, P., EPSTEIN, R. & Z. KOURTZI
2001 "Functional neuroimaging of visual recognition", in R. Cabeza & A. Kingstone (eds.), *Handbook of Functional Neuroimaging of Cognition*, Cambridge, MA: MIT Press.

KOURTZI, Z. & N. KANWISHER
2000 "Activation in human MT/MST by static images with implied motion", *J. Cognitive Neuroscience*, 12: 48-55.

KREIMAN, G., KOCH, C. & I. FRIED
2000a "Category-specific visual responses of single neurons in the human medial temporal lobe", *Nature Neuroscience*, 3: 946-953.
2000b "Imagery neurons in the human brain", *Nature*, 408: 357-361.

LISSAUER, H.
1988 (1890) "A case of visual agnosia with a contribution to theory", *Cognitive Neuropsychology,* 5: 157-192.

MARTIN, A.
2001 "Functional neuroimaging of semantic memory", in R. Cabeza & A. Kingstone (eds.), *Handbook of Functional Neuroimaging of Cognition*, Cambridge, MA: MIT Press.

MARTIN, A. & L.L. CHAO
2001 "Semantic memory and the brain: Structure and processes", *Current Opinion in Neurobiology*. in press.

MARTIN, A., HAXBY, J.V., LALONDE, F.M., WIGGS, C.L. & L.G. UNGERLEIDER
1995 "Discrete cortical regions associated with knowledge of color and knowledge of action", *Science* 270: 102-105.

MARTIN, A., WIGGS, C.L., UNGERLEIDER, L.G. & J.V. HAXBY
1996 "Neural correlates of category-specific knowledge", *Nature*, 379: 649-652.

MILLER, G.A.
1999 "On knowing a word", *Annual Review of Psychology*, 50: 1-19.

O'CRAVEN, K.M. & N. KANWISHER
2000 "Mental imagery of faces and places activates corresponding stimulus-specific brain regions", *J. Cognitive Neuroscience*, 6: 1013-1023.

PATTERSON, K. & J.R. HODGES
1995 "Disorders of semantic memory", in A.D. Baddeley, B.A. Wilson & F.N. Watts (eds.), *Handbook of Memory Disorders*, New York, NY: John Wiley and Sons.

PERANI, D., CAPPA, S.F., BETTINARDI, V., BRESSI, S., GORNO-TEMPINI, M., MATARRESE, M. & F. FAZIO
1995 "Different neural systems for the recognition of animals and man-made tools", *Neuroreport*, 6: 1637-1641.

PRICE, C.J., INDEFREY, P. & M. VAN TURENNOUT
1999 "The neural architecture underlying the processing of written and spoken word forms", in C.M. Brown & P. Hagoort (eds.), *Neurocognition of Language Processing*, New York: Oxford UP.

SENIOR, C., BARNES, J., GIAMPIETRO, V., SIMMONS, A., BULLMORE, E.T., BRAMMER, M. & A.S. DAVID
2000 "The functional neuro-anatomy of implicit motion perception of 'representational momentum'", *Curr. Biol.*, 10: 16-22.

SMITH, E.E., PATALANO, A.L. & J. JONIDES
1999 "Alternative strategies of categorization", *Cognition*, 65: 167-196.

TRANEL, D., DAMASIO, H. & A.R. DAMASIO
1997 "A neural basis for the retrieval of conceptual knowledge", *Neuropsychologia*, 35: 1319-1327.

TULVING, E.
1983 *Elements of Episodic Memory*, New York: Oxford UP.

VANDENBERGHE, R., PRICE, C., WISE, R., JOSEPHS, O. & R.S.FRACKOWIAK
1996 "Functional anatomy of a common semantic system for words and pictures", *Nature*, 383: 254-256.

WARRINGTON, E.K.
1975 "The selective impairment of semantic memory", *Quarterly Journal of Experimental Psychology*, 27: 635-657.

WARRINGTON, E.K. & T. SHALLICE
1984 "Category specific semantic impairments", *Brain*, 107: 829-854.

Webster's New World Dictionary, Third College Edition, 1988 New York: Simon & Schuster, Inc.

Philip Lieberman

SUBCORTICAL BRAIN CIRCUITS, SPEECH, AND THE EVOLUTION OF SEMEOSIS

The Greek philosophers of the classical period were very clever people who formulated theories concerning the nature of the physical universe and the human mind. Although many of their theories have been supplanted, their views concerning the mind-brain persist in the "modular" theories proposed by present-day philosophers and linguists (Fodor 1983; Chomsky 1986; Pinker 1997). These theories take as a given, the premise that the brain is organized into "organs" or "modules" that correspond, more or less, to the three senses and various aspects of human behavior for which we have words, e.g., language, thought, syntax, attention, manual motor control, emotion, etc. Extreme modular theories claim that innate specialized organs exist that are dedicated to a specific task. In attempting to account for uniqueness of human language the Chomskian school of linguistics, for example, claims that human syntactic ability derives from a genetically transmitted syntax organ of the human brain (Chomsky 1986). The Chomskian syntax organ like other hypothetical modules is "encapsulated," and is functionally, perhaps morphologically, independent of neural modules that regulate other aspects of cognition, emotion, and motor activity. It supposedly instantiates the "Universal Grammar", that exists in all human brains and specifies the morphologic and syntactic structure of all human languages. Culture and learning supposedly play little part in determining syntax or word structure.

These claims are accepted by most linguists, many behavioral scientists, and some neuroscientists, who believe that neural "organs" that each supposedly regulate different aspects of human behavior exist in specific localized parts of the human brain. This belief accounts for recent brain imaging studies that supposedly isolate distinct neural "centers" of emotion, fear, speech, syntax, esthetics and so on. Comparison of these claims refutes the theory since different studies often state with certainty that the same part of the brain controls a different aspect of behavior. These imaging studies bear a striking resemblance to the claims of early 19th century phrenology which claimed that particular bumps on a person's skull were the "sites" of avarice, mathematics, music, language, and so on.

1. Some aspects of evolutionary biology

Since hypothetical modular brain organs are supposedly independent entities that regulate one and only one aspect of human behavior, it becomes difficult to account for their evolution. Animals clearly do not possess human language or human cognitive ability, necessary elements of semeosis. Many scholars therefore wonder how the neural capacities for the "new" behaviors that characterize human beings such as language or abstract thought could have evolved? As Charles Darwin (1859) noted, the evolutionary mechanism that accounts for new distinct qualitative qualities that differentiate species involves a process by which an organ might be modified for some other and quite distinct purpose... The illustration of the swim bladder in fishes is a good one, because it shows us clearly the highly important fact that an organ originally constructed for one purpose, namely flotation, may be converted into one for a wholly different purpose, namely respiration (1859, 1964: 190).

In short, evolution is opportunistic. Organs that were adapted through gradual Natural Selection to carry out a particular operation, take on a new role in response to an environment change. Natural selection then can shape the organ, enhancing its new role, but the modified organ continues to play a part in its "old" behavior if the environment so dictates. As we shall see, the parts of the human brain that apparently were modified to make human language and thought possible, continue to support phylogentically earlier, "primitive," functions. And this inherently integrates the study of semeosis with the study of such seemingly unrelated behaviors as walking, manual motor control, the physiology of speech production, syntax, emotion, mood, as well as abstract cognition.

It is germane to explain the concepts "primitive" and "derived" signify in their evolutionary context. The evolutionary history of a species, its relationship to other species, and its species-specific behavioral attributes are evident when we take stock of its "primitive" and "derived" properties. Primitive features are those qualities and characteristics that derive from ancestral species. Primitive features are shared with the related species that can be traced back to the same ancestral species. Derived properties are new features that differentiate a species from related species. For example, we share three primitive characteristics with frogs: feet that have five toes, mouths that have tongues, and brains that are lateralized to control vocalization. In both frogs and human beings, the dominant hemisphere of their lateralized brains play a major role in regulating vocal signals. Hence, these primitive features can not be the basis of the observed qualities that differentiate the behavior of human beings and frogs. In contrast, one of the derived features of modern human beings is our "flat" face . Our mouths are positioned in line with our foreheads. This aspect of human facial anatomy differentiates us from closely related species, such as the extinct Neanderthals. The "primitive" Neanderthal face has a mouth that projects forwards (D.E. Lieberman 1990), similar to the faces of chimpanzees, gorillas, dogs, and most mammals. The derived flat human face supports the unique, derived, human supralaryngeal vocal tract, the airway above our larynx which can produce sounds that enhance the reliability of vocal speech (Lieberman and Crelin 1971; Lieberman 1984, 2000).

The common ancestor of hominoids, human beings and apes, lived some 5 million years ago. No fossil remains of the common hominoid ancestor have yet been found – the date has been established by means of genetic analysis of the DNA of human and apes. Living apes share many of the primitive characteristics of some of the earliest 4 million-year old "hominid" fossils that have been found. These hominid fossils are in the general line of human descent since their bones show that they possessed one of the derived properties that differentiate human beings from apes, upright bipedal locomotion – walking. And as we shall also see, another prerequisite for walking is a brain that can learn and control the precise sequence of motor acts necessary for upright bipedal locomotion. The neural mechanism regulating walking crucially includes the subcortical basal ganglia – which also are essential neural elements of the brain mechanisms that regulate the derived human behaviors that separate us from apes – thinking and language, as well as emotion. I shall argue here that the evolutionary process that yielded human semeosis – an interplay and integration of language, thought, and emotional constructs – can be traced back to the earliest stages of hominid evolution. The evolution of walking in early hominids and the subsequent evolution of the neural mechanisms that yield articulate human speech. The primitive attributes of human language that are evident in living apes, namely a limited store of words and simple syntax, are not the properties that account for the uniqueness of semeosis. In other words, the Chomskian claim that syntax is the defining characteristic of human language is not justified. Vocal speech is the derived property that sets us aside from apes; The evolution of the neural mechanisms that confer speech is one of the keys to the evolution of human language, thought, emotion – i. e., semeosis.

2. Primitive characteristics of human language

Human language and the communication systems of living apes share many primitive characteristics. Although we cannot assume that living apes retain all of the characteristics of the extinct five-million-year old common ancestor of humans and apes, examination of the fossil record of hominid evolution shows that living apes retain many of the skeletal characteristics of early hominids. Therefore, it is probable that any aspect of linguistic ability that contemporary day apes and humans share is a primitive component of human language that also was present in early hominids. Several independent studies that used sign language and manual devices as phonetic modalities have shown that apes have limited lexical and syntactic abilities. The distinction between the lexical ability of humans and apes is quantitative rather than qualitative. Apes can produce about 150 words using manual sign language (Gardner and Gardner 1984) or computer keyboards (Savage-Rumbaugh and Rumbaugh 1993), roughly equivalent to the abilities of children between ages two and two and one half years. Human vocabularies typically are at least 100 times greater.

The distinction between human and ape syntactic ability is likewise quantitative and may reflect the limits of neural working memory. Only humans have the ability to comprehend sentences that have moderately complex syntax, such as English sentences containing relative clauses like, "The boy who fell down won the prize." Studies of the communications of pygmy chimpanzees (Savage-Rumbaugh and Rumbaugh 1993) show that they have limited syntactic ability. Apes can follow instructions conveyed by the word order of English in spoken commands such as, "Put the leaf on the paper," versus "Put the paper on the leaf." Pygmy chimpanzees also can "recover" the deleted "you" of the command – an ability that some linguists have claimed is the "litmus test" for syntactic ability (Calvin and Bickerton 2000). Nor are these abilities the special property of pygmy chimpanzees; reanalyses of the sign language communications of common chimpanzees reveals similar syntactic ability expressed in the complex morphology of American Sign Language (Gardner and Gardner 1994).

3. The derived characteristic of human language – speech

The derived, unique aspect of human language has been apparent for thousands of years. Animals can not talk. This obvious fact is noted in creation myths that state that speech is the gift of the gods or a particular god to humans. In folk tales, books, and dramas, animals "become" human when they talk. Speech clearly is the derived property that differentiates human linguistic ability from that of apes. All natural human languages use speech sounds that have no inherent meaning to convey referential information. As has been frequently observed, the "phonetic" elements of human speech are combined to specify words formed into sentences that convey and shape human thought. Human beings do communicate their emotional state vocally. However, they can also produce voluntary vocal signals, speech, that transmits referential information that is not tied to an emotional state or a particular, stereotyped situation. Although a person may smack his or her lips when presented with food or utter an involuntary cry in response to a particular situation, speech communication is not "bound" to particular events or emotions.

Although apes lack the vocal anatomy that would allow them to produce the full range of human speech sounds, they can produce many of the signals that have phonetic value in human speech. Acoustic analyses of chimpanzee calls show that they make use of phonetic contrasts that play a linguistic role in human speech (Lieberman, 1968). For example, chimpanzees vocalize while they protrude and round their lips; this changes the filtering characteristics of their supralaryngeal airways (the air passages above the larynx) and produces falling formant frequency transitions that are similar to those that specify "labial" sounds like [b] and [w] in English. (Formant frequencies are the frequencies at which maximum acoustic energy can pass through the supralaryngeal airway.) Different formant frequency patterns yield different speech sounds. The vowels of English, for example, are differentiated by their different formant frequency patterns. Chimpanzees have speech producing anatomy that, in principle, could produce vowels similar to the human vowels [I], [U], [ae], (the vowels of the English words “bit,” “but,” “bat,” etc. (Lieberman et al. 1972). Chimpanzees also have functional larynges and most of their calls are phonated. Therefore, chimpanzees have vocal anatomy that could produce the labial stop consonants [b] and [p] which are differentiated by means of the voice-onset-timing distinction discussed below. In other words, would permit them to produce the formant frequency patterns and temporal features that specify different vowels and bilabial consonants of human speech (Lieberman, 1968). Chimpanzees have the vocal anatomy that would let them say words like “bit,” “bat,” “pat” and so on.

However, although many chimpanzees have been raised from infancy in proximity to humans speaking to them and to other humans and have been actively tutored (Gardner et. al., 1989), no chimpanzee has ever produced voluntary speech-like vocalizations to communicate simple words such as “ma,” “bad,” “bat,” etc, that their vocal apparatus could produce. Though the stereotyped vocalizations of chimpanzees incorporate elements that could be reordered to approximate many human words, they are not able to “free” these elements from fixed linkages to particular affective states or situations. The most that non-human primates can do is to change the rate at which they produce some stereotyped utterance. As many observers of chimpanzees and other non-human primates note, primate calls are part of a stereotyped response pattern that signals a particular affectual or emotional state (Goodall 1986). Operant conditioning of non-human primates that changes their affectual state would also modify their calls. As the primates’ affective state changes, so would their stereotyped calls, yet the calls would still be involuntary, stereotyped calls.

4. How brains appear to work – neural circuits

Some prefatory remarks on neurophysiology are useful before discussing the possible evolution of the human brain’s capacity for speech. It is evident that complex behaviors including language are regulated by “distributed” neural circuits that integrate activity in many parts of the brain (Mesulam 1990). The brain is not an amorphous mass; different parts of the brain perform particular operations. However, these localized operations are not coordinate with observed complex behaviors such as picking up a pencil, talking, or recalling the meaning of a word. Distributed neural circuits link the operations that occur in different parts of the brain to yield the neural substrate that regulates a complex behavior. Information is transferred in these neural circuits by means of populations (large groups) of neurons in each particular neural structure that project to neuronal populations in other parts of the brain, that in turn, project to other neuronal populations in other parts of the brain (Mesulam 1990). A particular structure, such as the putamen (part of subcortical basal ganglia), is typically involved in different aspects of behavior. The distributed neural circuits of the brain are formed by linking segregated neuronal populations linked to different parts of the cortex (Alexander et al. 1986; Cummings 1993; Marsden and Obeso 1994). In short, neural pathways (circuits) connect different parts of the brain – the total ensemble is the mechanisms that regulates some aspect of behavior. The putamen, for example, controls sequencing in motor control in a motor circuit that connects it to premotor cortex and motor cortex (Cummings 1993; Marsden and Obeso 1994). The putamen, working with other basal ganglia structures, can interrupt a motor act when appropriate sensory information indicates that changing from one course of action to another is appropriate. The putamen, acting in "cognitive" circuits to prefrontal cortex, likewise, can interrupt a particular sequence of cognitive operations when a sentence is being comprehended when appropriate; for example, interrupting a cognitive sequence that expects to find a verb following the word "boy" in the sentence, "The boy who sat down fell."

I have proposed that the human brain has a specialized functional language system (FLS) adapted for the production and perception of spoken language (Lieberman 1998; 2000), keeping in mind that the FLS can be redirected to regulate manual sign language. The structure of the FLS can be understood by considering the two aspects of the neurophysiological organization of the brain noted above: (a) particular neuroanatomical structures are implicated in different aspects of behavior through (b) circuits connecting these neuroanatomical structures that carry out particular activities that enhance biological fitness. Converging evidence from many independent studies shows that the FLS involves the subcortical basal ganglia structures of the human brain as well as Broca's and Wernicke's areas, the areas of neocortex traditionally associated with human language (Lieberman 2000). In fact, it can be safely said that the Broca's-Wernicke's area theory first proposed by Lichtheim in 1885 is wrong.

The primary evidence for Broca's and Wernicke's areas being the "seats" of human linguistic ability was derived from studies of the linguistic deficits, "aphasia," that supposedly occurred after these cortical areas were damaged. However, contemporary neuroanatomical studies clearly show that permanent aphasia does not occur in the absence of subcortical damage; victims of strokes and other trauma that results in purely cortical damage recover, usually after a period of months (Stuss and Benson, 1986; Elman et al., 1997). In contrast, subcortical brain damage can result in permanent linguistic deficits. This is not surprising because many independent studies show that subcortical neural circuits involving basal ganglia support at least six different functional circuits in human beings (Alexander et al. 1986; Cummings 1993). Populations of neurons in the basal ganglia that project to prefrontal cortex form parts of neural circuits implicated in cognition and the comprehension of syntax. Other subcortical-to-cortical circuits regulate walking, other circuits regulate manual and speech motor control, still others affect and emotion. In other words, different aspects of behavior appear to be regulated by neuronal basal ganglia circuits that project to different parts of the brain. The basal ganglia components of these circuits appear to be responsible for both motor and cognitive flexibility – switching from one course of action to another. (Marsden and Obeso 1994). When basal ganglia are destroyed or degraded "perserveration" – the ability to sequence motor patterns, to adapt to new circumstances or learn to form new patterns of behavior, to plan ahead – the "abstract" capacity noted by Kurt Goldstein (1948) deteriorates.

5. Some of the evidence for subcortical neural circuits

Meaning derives from language and thought expressed by means of movement and speech. Subcortical neural circuits regulate these aspects of behavior and are responsible for our ability to change behavior and thought patterns. A brief review of some of the studies discussed in detail elsewhere (Lieberman 2000) will illustrate the basal ganglia function and possible evolution of the cortico-striatal circuits of *Homo sapiens*.

5.1. Innate syntax of rat grooming

Rats execute an innate series of movements that constitute "grooming" sequences. The "syntax" of the grooming sequence is regulated by the rat brain's basal ganglia, damage to other parts of the its does not affect the grooming sequence. In contrast, damage to the rat's basal ganglia disrupts the sequences that normally occur, but does not disrupt the individual gestures that constitute a grooming sequence. Aldridge and his colleagues (1993) confirmed the role of the basal ganglia in rodent grooming by using microelectrodes to monitor the firing patterns of rat basal ganglia neurons. The onset and offset times of more than 6,000 events were recorded and entered into a computer which correlated frame-by-frame photographic analyses of the grooming sequences with the neurons' firing patterns. Aldridge et al. (1993) concluded that, Hierarchal modulation of sequential elements by the neostratum [basal ganglia] may operate in essentially similar ways for grooming actions and thoughts, but upon very different classes of elements in the two cases... very different behavioral or mental operations might be sequenced by essentially similar neural processes. (Aldridge et al. 1993: 393).

5.2. Learned motor syntax in primates

The basal ganglia of primates are implicated in acquiring and regulating sequential learned motor responses. Neurophysiological studies of monkeys show that basal ganglia circuits regulating learned behavior can be formed through associative learning. Kimura et al. (1993) studied the responses of neurons within the basal ganglia as monkeys learned a Pavlovian task in which the monkeys had to associate an arbitrary sound with getting food. The monkeys heard a sound that signalled the availability of food. At the start of the conditioning process 10-20% of the neurons monitored showed small responses to the sound. After three weeks of conditioning, 60-70 percent responded to the sound. The neurotransmiter dopamine is essential for proper basal ganglia functioning Injection of a dopamine antagonist which inhibits basal ganglia functioning reduced response to 10 percent and the monkeys were unable to perform the task.

5.3. Human manual motor control

Circuits involving the Basal ganglia and areas of the cortex carry out similar motor-control functions in human beings. Cunnington et al. (1995) demonstrated their role in human subjects executing sequential, self-paced, manual, motor-control tasks. The experiment monitored the activity of the supplementary motor area of the cortex to which these circuits project by means electrodes placed on the surface of a subject's head, similar to those commonly used to record electrical brain activity for clinical purposes. The procedure is noninvasive. These electrodes recorded movement-related potentials (MRPs) in both normal subjects and subjects suffering from Parkinson's Disease which degrades basal ganglia activity. The subjects executed both voluntary internally-generated and voluntary externally-cued manual sequential activity by pushing buttons with their index fingers. MRPs are signals that reflect the planning and execution of these movements. Cunnington and his colleagues conclude that the basal ganglia provide an internal cue to terminate supplementary motor area activity following movement, and to activate the preparatory phase for the next submovement, thereby switching between components of a motor sequence (Cunnington et al. 1995: 948).

5.4. Manual movements and thinking in human subjects

In a careful and comprehensive review Marsden and Obeso (1994) surveyed the data of hundreds of instances in which surgical lesions in basal ganglia were made in human subjects to relieve some of the effects of Parkinson's Disease. The observed results lead Marsden and Obeso to conclude that, the role of the basal ganglia in controlling movement must give insight into their other functions, particularly if thought is mental movement without motion. Perhaps the basal ganglia are an elaborate machine, within the overall frontal lobe distributed system, that allow routine thought and action, but which responds to new circumstances to allow a change in direction of ideas and movement. Loss of basal ganglia contribution, such as in Parkinson's disease, thus would lead to inflexibility of mental and motor response (Marsden and Obeso 1994: 893).

5.5. Speech and syntax

Direct evidence for the role of basal ganglia in human language were found by Lieberman et al. (1992). The pattern of speech production deficits and syntax comprehension deficits in Parkinson's Disease (PD) subjects was similar in nature to that noted for Broca's aphasia. Parkinson's Disease affects the basal ganglia mostly sparing the cortex. PD is an "experiment in nature" that isolates basal ganglia activity. The results are significant since, as noted earlier, permanent aphasia does not occur absent subcortical damage.

Acoustic analysis of the speech of 40 PD subjects showed a breakdown in 9 subjects' ability to control the production of stop-consonant vowel sequences. The acoustic parameter that differentiates the syllable "ba" from "pa" is "Voice-onset-time" (VOT), the time interval between the instant at which a person's lips open and the start of phonation generated by the larynx. Phonation results when the larynx produces periodic "puffs of air;" the rate at which these occur is perceived as the "pitch" of a person's voice. VOT differentiates the stop consonants in syllables such as "ta," "da," "ga," "ka." The supralaryngeal airway is obstructed at the start of these syllables. The sequence in which the supralaryngeal airway is opened relative to the start of phonation results in short VOTs for "ba, da, ga" and long VOTs for "pa, ta, ka."

Broca's aphasics and some PD subjects lose the ability to control the VOT sequence. The problem does not simply involve timing since Broca's (Blumstein et al., 1980) and PD subjects are able to control the distinctions in vowel length that signal the same consonants when the occur after a vowel. The PD subjects in this experiment, like Broca's aphasics, also had difficulty comprehending sentences that had relatively complex syntax or that were long. The number of VOT sequencing errors and number of syntax errors was highly correlated for these subjects. Syntax comprehension errors have been noted in a number of independent studies (cf. Lieberman 2000).

5.6. Cognitive effects of basal ganglia dysfunction

A battery of cognitive tests was also administered in the study reported by Lieberman and his colleagues (1992). Moderately impaired PD subjects made significantly more errors than mildly impaired PD subjects on the Odd-Man-Out test (Flowers and Robinson 1985) – a sorting test that measures the ability to derive an abstract criterion necessary to solve a problem and then shift to a new criterion. The Odd-Man-out test can be regarded as a probe of both visual and verbal working memory since it involves sorting both geometrical figures that differ in size and shape, and upper and lower case letters of the alphabet that appear to be represented and phonetically rehearsed in verbal working memory (Baddeley 1986). Working memory can be regarded as a sort of neural space in which calculations are carried out on perceived information (Baddeley 1986; Martin et al. 1995). One of the mechanisms whereby words are maintained in verbal working memory is phonetic rehearsal, a sort of "silent-speech" in which the brain mechanisms that regulate overt speech internally model the words that a person has heard or read (Baddeley 1986; Awh et al. 1996). Therefore, it is not surprising to find impaired verbal working memory in PD and aphasia patients who have damage to the neural bases of speech production. The moderately impaired PD subjects also made significantly more errors than mildly impaired PD subjects on other tests involving working memory.

The data of Lange *et al.* (1992) demonstrate beyond reasonable doubt that basal ganglia dysfunction, in itself, produces cognitive deficits similar in nature to those associated with frontal lobe dysfunction. This again confirms the cognitive role of basal ganglia circuits that project to areas of prefrontal cortex (Cummings 1993). The error rates and "thinking times" (the time necessary to plan the task's solution) of PD subjects were compared when they were unmedicated and medicated on the Tower of London test which tests planning usually associated with frontal lobe function. Patients who suffer focal frontal lobe damage have difficulty with this test. In this test the PD subjects saw a computer-generated "target" picture of three colored balls inside two hoops. The third hoop was empty. The subject's task was to move the balls in the two hoops of a second computer-generated image presented below the target image to match the target configuration. Error rates and thinking times were significantly higher and longer when the subjects were not medicated. Thinking times were calculated by subtracting the increases in the time required by PD subjects to move their fingers on the computer screen. A subtractive procedure allowed the investigators to factor out the motor movement delays due to PD.

5.7. Focal damage to basal ganglia

Further evidence for basal ganglia activity regulating sequencing in speech production, syntax, and cognition was noted by Pickett et al. (1998) in a woman who had suffered brain damage restricted to profound bilateral damage to the putamen and some damage to the anterior caudate nucleus (two basal ganglia structures). The subject had difficulty sequencing the articulatory gestures that generate speech. Acoustic analyses showed that her speech was degraded due to inappropriate sequencing of various articulatory movements, resulting in inappropriate nasalization, malformed consonants, and peculiar VOTs. The subject also was unable to properly sequence the chest muscles that regulate lung air pressure during speech. She had a 14 percent error rate when she was required to comprehend distinctions in meaning conveyed by syntax in spoken English sentences. Her sentence comprehension errors appeared to reflect an inability to shift syntactic frameworks. She, for example, had problems in syntactic-semantic processing of sentences containing embedded clauses, where it is necessary to switch to the analysis of new material at a clause boundaries. Cognitive sequencing deficits also occurred; she had a 70 percent error rate on the Odd-Man-Out test (Flowers and Robertson 1985 see above). She was unable to shift cognitive strategies when she was asked to shift from sorting by shape to size or from size to shape. In contrast, performance was within normal ranges in tests of lexical access and long-term memory.

Other studies of motor control, cognitive, and linguistic deficits deriving from damage or degraded activity in basal ganglia to cortical circuits are noted in Lieberman (2000). These include cognitive and speech deficits arising from oxygen deficits in mountain climbers ascending Mount Everest, neurologically intact aged people, and speakers of languages other than English.

5.8. The evolution of semeosis

Can animals dance?

I should like to propose that data of the studies noted above (and in detail in Lieberman (2000) bears the mark of evolution. These studies show that the neural circuits of the human brain that allow us to freely sequence the articulatory maneuvers underlying speech and other forms of movement also are implicated in our ability to comprehend complex syntax and to form novel thoughts. This capacity is evident in living humans, but what selective pressure or behavior might account for the start of the evolutionary process that yielded this derived human quality? The answer may rest in the adaptive value of walking – upright bipedal locomotion, one of the first derived hominid characteristics.

Sometime between 5 and 4 million years ago, early hominids began to walk. The late acquisition of walking by primates is consistent with its being a learned rather than an innately specified characteristic in living human beings. Although the neural capacity for walking is an innate human capacity, the details are learned. Human infants start out with a quadripedal "walking reflex" and gradually learn to walk with proper heel strike (Thelen 1984). If you wish to view a demonstration of an innate walking reflex look at a horse, not a human. It is clear that proper basal ganglia function is crucial to walking; the primary deficit of Parkinson's Disease which derives from impaired basal ganglia function, is impaired walking and upright balance.

As all biologists know, "Nothing in biology makes sense except in the light of evolution". The recent knowledge of the present structure and physiology of the human brain reveals the role of basal ganglia to cortical circuits in the sequential control of motor commands and cognitive acts. The initial selective force shaping enhanced human basal ganglia function in switching rapidly between the different learned motor sequences necessary to walk – may have been the early derived hominid characteristic, walking upright. And humans can in dance construct sequences wherein the motor control maneuvers that follow a predictable sequence while walking, are modified to conform to novel abstract principles. And humans construct thoughts yielding novel insights. In other words, the neural basis for human invention, artistic sensibility and semeosis may derive from the evolution of basal ganglia activity, initially directed towards enhancing the acquisition of walking in small-brained hominids some 4 to 5 million years ago, then directed to talking and thinking. All of these aspects of human behavior as well as emotion and affect are in present day human beings regulated by our cortico-striatal neural circuits involving subcortical basal ganglia.

Darwinian evolution did not yield a modular human brain resembling the departmental structure of a late 20th century university. As Charles Darwin noted 150 years ago, evolution takes surprising turns. Semeosis involves the integrated activity of a brain that is not rigidly compartmentalized. In short, we walk, we dance, and therefore we think.

References

ALDRIDGE, J.W., BERRIDGE, K.C., HERMAN, M. & L. ZIMMER
1993 "Neuronal coding of serial order: Syntax of grooming in the neostratum", *Psychological Science,* 4: 391-393.

ALEXANDER, G.E., DELONG, M.R. & P.L. STRICK
1986 "Parallel organization of segregated circuits linking basal ganglia and cortex", *Annual Review of Neuroscience*, 9:357-381.

AWH, E., JONIDES, J., SMITH, R.E., SCHUMACHER, E.H., KOEPPE, R.A. & S. KATZ
1996 "Dissociation of storage and rehearsal in working memory: Evidence from Positron Emission Tomography", *Psychological Science*, 25-31.

BADDELEY, A.D.
1986 *Working memory*, Oxford: Clarendon Press.

BLUMSTEIN, S.E., COOPER, W., GOODGLASS, H., STATLENDER, H. & J. GOTTLEIB
1980 "Production deficits in aphasia: A voice-onset time analysis", *Brain and Language*, 9: 153-170.

CALVIN, W.H. & D. BICKERTON
2000 *Lingua ex machina: Reconciling Darwin and Chomsky with the human brain*, Cambridge, MA: MIT Press.

CHOMSKY, N.
1986 *Knowledge of language: Its nature, origin and use*, New York: Prager.

CUMMINGS, J.L.
1993 "Frontal-subcortical circuts and human behavior", *Archives of Neurology*, 50: 873-880.

CUNNINGTON, R., IANSEK, R., BRADSHAW, J.L. & J.G. PHILIPS
1995 "Movement-related potentials in Parkinson's disease: Presence and predictability of temporal and spatial cues", 118: 935-950.

DARWIN, C.
1859 *On the origin of species*, Facsimile ed. 1964, Cambridge, MA: Harvard University Press.

ELMAN, J., BATES, E., JOHNSON, M., KARMILOFF-SMITH, A., PARISI, D. & K. PLUNKETT
1997 *Rethinking innateness: A connectionist perspective on development*, Cambridge MA: MIT Press/Bradford Book

FLOWERS, K.A. & C. ROBERTSON
1985 "The effects of Parkinson's disease on the ability to maintain a mental set", *Journal of Neurology, Neurosurgery, and Psychiatry*, 48: 517-529.

FODOR, J.
1983 *Modularity of Mind*, Cambridge, MA: MIT Press.

GARDNER, R.A. & B.T. GARDNER
1984 "A vocabulary test for chimpanzees (Pan troglodyte)", *Journal of Comparative Psychology*, 4: 381-404.

GARDNER, R.A., GARDNER, B.T. & T.E. VAN CANTFORT.
1989 *Teaching Sign Language to Chimpanzees*, Albany: State University of New York Press.

GARDNER, B.T. & R.A. GARDNER
1994 "Development of phrases in the utterances of children and cross-fostered chimpanzees", in R.A. Gardner, B.T. Gardner, B. Chiarelli, R. Plooj (eds.), *The Etholoical Roots of Culture*, Kluwer Academic Publishers.

GOLDSTEIN, K.
1948 *Language and Language Disturbances*, New York: Grune & Stratton.

GOODALL, J.
1986 *The Chimpanzees of Gombe: Patterns of Behavior*, Cambridge, MA: Harvard UP.

KIMURA, M., AOSAKI, T. & A. GRAYBIE
1993 "Role of basal ganglia in the acquisition and initiation of learned movement", in N. Mano, I. Hamada and M. R. DeLong (eds), *Role of the Cerrebellum and Basal Ganglia in Voluntary Movements*, Amsterdam: Elsevier: 83-87.

LANGE, K.W., ROBBINS, T.W., MARSDEN, C.D., JAMES, M., OWEN, A.M. & G.M. PAUL
1992 "L-Dopa withdrawal in Parkinson's disease selectively impairs cognitive performance in tests sensitive to frontal lobe dysfunction", *Psychopharmacology*, 107: 394-404.

LICHTHEIM, L.
1885 "On aphasia", *Brain*, 7:433-484.

LIEBERMAN, D.E.
1998 "Sphenoid shortening and the evolution of modern human cranial shape", *Nature*, 393:158-162.

LIEBERMAN, P.
1968 "Primate vocalizations and human linguistic ability", *Journal of the Acoustical Society of America*, 44:1157-1164.
1984 *The Biology and Evolution of Language*, Cambridge, MA: Harvard UP.
1998 *Eve Spoke; Human Language and Human Evolution*, New York: W. W. Norton. London: Picador, Macmillan.
2000 *Human Language and Our Reptilian Brain: The Subcortical Bases of Speech, Syntax, and Thought*, Cambridge, MA: Harvard UP (Perspecitves in Cognitive Neuroscience).

LIEBERMAN, P. & E.S. CRELIN
1971 "On the speech of Neanderthal man", *Linguistic Inquiry*, 2:203-222.

LIEBERMAN, P., CRELIN, E.S. & D.H. KLATT
1972 "Phonetic ability and related anatomy of the newborn, adult human, Neanderthal man, and the chimpanzee", *American Anthropologist*, 74:287-307.

LIEBERMAN, P., KAKO, E.T., FRIEDMAN, J., TAJCHMAN, G., FELDMAN, L.S. & E.B. JIMINEZ
1992 "Speech production, syntax comprehension, and cognitive deficits in Parkinson's disease", *Brain and Language*, 43:169-189.

MARSDEN, C.D. & J.A. OBESO
1994 "The functions of the basal ganglia and the paradox of sterotaxic surgery in Parkinson's disease", *Brain*, 117: 877-897.

MARTIN, A., WIGGS, C.L., UNGERLEIDER, L.G. & J.V. HAXBY
1995 "Neural correlates of category-specific knowledge", *Nature*, 379:649-652.

MESULAM, M.M.
1990 "Large-scale neurocognitive networks and distributed processing for attention, language, and memory", *Annals of Neurology*, 28:597-613.

PICKETT, E., KUNIHOLM, R., PROTOPAPAS, A., FRIEDMAN, J. & P. LIEBERMAN
1998 "Selective speech motor, syntax and cognitive deficits associated with bilateral damage to the head of the caudate nucleus and the putamen. A single case study", *Neuropsychologia*, 36:173-188.

PINKER, S.
1994 *The Language Instinct; How the mind creates language*, New York:William Morrow.
1997 *How the mind works*, W. W. Norton: New York.

SAVAGE-RUMBAUGH, E.S. & D. RUMBAUGH
1993 "The emergence of language", in K.R. Gibson and T. Ingold (eds.), *Tools, language and cognition in human evolution*, Cambridge: Cambridge UP.

STUSS, D.T. & D.F. BENSON
1986 *The Frontal Lobes*, New York: Raven.

THELEN, E.
1984 "Learning to walk: Ecological demands and phylogenetic constraints", in Lipsitt, L. (ed), *Advances in Infancy Research*, 3: 213-250, Norwood NJ: Ablex.